IN SEARCH OF THE CONSTITUTION:

Reflections on State and Society in Britain

IN SEARCH OF THE CONSTITUTION:

Reflections on State and Society in Britain

BY

NEVIL JOHNSON

Nuffield College, Oxford

PERGAMON PRESS

Oxford · New York · Toronto · Sydney
Paris · Frankfurt

U. K.	Pergamon Press Ltd., Headington Hill Hall, Oxford OX3 0BW, England
U. S. A.	Pergamon Press Inc., Maxwell House, Fairview Park, Elmsford, New York 10523, U.S.A.
C A N A D A	Pergamon of Canada Ltd., 75 The East Mall, Toronto, Ontario, Canada
A U S T R A L I A	Pergamon Press (Aust.) Pty. Ltd., 19a Boundary Street, Rushcutters Bay, N.S.W. 2011, Australia
F R A N C E	Pergamon Press SARL, 24 rue des Ecoles, 75240 Paris, Cedex 05, France
WEST GERMANY	Pergamon Press GmbH, 6242 Kronberg-Taunus, Pferdstrasse 1, Frankfurt-am-Main, West Germany

First edition 1977

Library of Congress Cataloging in Publication Data

Johnson, Nevil.
In search of the constitution.

1. Great Britain – Politics and government – 1964 –
I. Title.
HN234 1977.J64 1977   320.9'41'0857   76-43316
ISBN 0-08-021379-0

Printed in Great Britain by A. Wheaton & Co., Exeter

Contents

Foreword

The reflections contained in this book were written in 1975, and chiefly during the first part of that year. They were prompted by growing anxiety about the political future of Britain, not merely in respect of the capacity of the country's political institutions to facilitate an effective handling of day-to-day problems, but also in respect of the terms on which political life is being conducted. It seemed to me — and still does — that it is unconvincing to explain the course of decline on which the country has been set for some considerable time simply by reference to internal social and economic conditions, or to changes in its position in the world. Such explanations may suffice on some occasions and for some problems. But if a nation reveals persistent failure to find a way forward through the tangle of practical problems which it must face, and especially one like Britain which can look back on a remarkable record of political achievement, then that is reason enough for suspecting that it has run into a political impasse. And to say that is to go beyond matters affecting the quality of political leadership, important though that may be. It is to suggest that the rules governing political life may have lost some of their vitality, and that in consequence political authority is weakened and effective political co-operation jeopardised. It is roughly a diagnosis of this kind which leads me to the conclusion that some of the underlying problems have become constitutional in nature. But "constitutional" is not to be taken in a narrow and technical sense; I use this term to refer broadly to the conditions on which political authority in its various manifestations is constituted and exercised.

In the conduct of political affairs there must always be some gap between constitutional principles or theory, and political practice: what is can never coincide exactly with what ought to be. But dangers arise, and particularly in a society claiming to respect certain principles of free government, when the gap becomes very wide, and when such constitutional doctrine as there is no longer seems to explain very much of what happens. This has occurred in Britain and some of the consequences appear to me to be disturbing. It becomes more and more difficult to set limits to the powers of government; there is growing uncertainty about the terms on which public bodies are expected to act; the authority of those in political life is weakened; and it becomes steadily harder to justify political action by reference to constitutional norms. Indeed, there has over a fairly long period been a retreat from constitutional ways of thinking in Britain. We run the risk of finding ourselves with no plausible justifications for the manner in which political life is conducted: that is the price which must ultimately be paid for the atrophy of constitutional habits and for the neglect of principles in the understanding of the political order.

However, these essays make no claim to look at constitutional problems systematically, nor even impartially. As I have just explained, I have a thesis to propound and have, therefore, written chiefly about those aspects of the British political and social condition which bear most closely on my principal argument. Thus, the first two chapters sketch out a historical evolution in the society and its economy which seems to me to be a necessary foundation for what is then said about the political and constitutional nature of the problem. Then follows the larger part of the study in which the emphasis is on trying to delineate the principles now underlying particular institutions and practices, political habits and modes of behaviour. The conclusion emerges that some degree of constitutional reconstruction is required, and it is to prescription – along with discussion of what consequences certain kinds of change might have – that the final two chapters are devoted.

It is necessary to make reference to a matter of style. Originally these reflections were set down in the form of letters addressed to a continental European friend. This permitted a freedom of style and expression which can rarely be achieved in a more conventional academic mould. But later, when I came to prepare the work for publication, I became conscious that there was some artificiality in presenting it as "Letters". For the addressee was not so much my long-suffering continental friend who actually received the letters as people in Britain who might share my concern for the state of its political institutions. So, finally, I decided that the work should be revised and presented in the form of twelve loosely connected chapters. But for the polemical flavour which has survived this change of presentation I make no apology: the issues at stake are serious ones and I am presenting a plea that they should be considered in a particular way which, if accepted, would have practical consequences. For this reason alone there would be a certain falsity in any claim to academic detachment.

I wish to thank some of my colleagues in Oxford for helpful advice and criticism, notably Professor S. E. Finer, Mr. Geoffrey Marshall and Mr. Alan Fox, as well as Mr. Michael Lee of Birkbeck College, London. I am deeply grateful to my secretary, Mrs. Lyn Yates, and to Mrs. Audrey Roberts, for their indispensable work on the typescript. And, finally, I must acknowledge with gratitude the sympathetic encouragement and perceptive comments of my friend Wilhelm Hennis, Professor of Political Science in the University of Freiburg-im-Breisgau, to whom these reflections were first addressed.

NEVIL JOHNSON

Oxford
January 1976

CHAPTER 1

The Domestic Economy and the Providential Power of Government

Much has been written about what is now called on all sides "the British crisis". There was a time when it could be shrugged off as the expression of a national propensity to grumble introspectively about the alleged defects of political and social life, and by so doing to conceal an inner confidence in a capacity to solve problems in accustomed ways. But this is no longer possible: the malaise is deeply felt throughout the country, bringing in its train that loss of a sense of shared purposes and cohesion which has nearly always marked societies in decline.

In this condition it is inevitable that many are anxious for the future as well as being perplexed by the nature of the problem. And of course, no judgement can be made on the future and the possibilities it may hold unless an effort is first made to examine honestly the character of this crisis and how Britain has slipped into it. The aim here is to make an attempt at this by considering in some detail why it is that the authority of one of the world's reputedly most stable political orders has weakened so much that it is apparently no longer capable of resolving many of the problems of the society.

In order to prepare for what follows, it is reasonable to indicate right at the beginning the plan of attack. It has been often argued that the British problem is economic and social, but not at all political. My contention is, however, that the root of the trouble is now political: we have an old and tired political order under which it has proved increasingly difficult to solve serious economic and social problems. Perhaps the disease need not have progressed this far: perhaps at some point in time in the past a stroke of luck in the management of the economy might have opened the way to a new and more hopeful context in which to handle the conflicts of interest which inevitably exist. But the fact is that poor economic performance has persisted, and there are too many social tensions which

1

we have not succeeded in removing. The explanation of this is to be found in a progressive failure of political will and method. Our institutions and the rules on which they rest, as well as our rulers, have revealed a diminishing capacity to identify the issues which are vital, to devise and pursue consistently appropriate policies for handling them, and to sustain consent. More generally, the perception of the authority vested in our political institutions has weakened, and with that the recognition of their claim to express a public interest.

If one is suggesting that the basic difficulties are of a political nature, then clearly it follows that one has to look carefully at the political procedures and methods of the society, and at the institutions in which these are embodied. This is what I hope to do: to examine the parliamentary system and the role of Parliament, the character and powers of the central government, the consequences of political and administrative centralisation, the pressures for a new diffusion of authority, the question of the citizens' rights in our political order, and the character of the parties and ruling élites. But I do not intend to concentrate on describing these institutions and arrangements and how they have been used in recent history. My concern will rather be with trying to determine the principles on which they now apparently rest. This is why these reflections claim to be concerned rather more with "the British Constitution" than with "British Politics": they seek to reappraise the terms on which many of our political institutions are said to rest, and thereby to make a contribution to the characterisation of the political order. And as will be seen, there are grounds for believing that many of the traditional accounts of the principles upon which British political life is supposedly based nowadays obscure more than they illuminate. To that extent we are uncertain about what is the constitution of our political order, what is the character of the State.

Yet before it is possible to come to explicitly political questions, it is necessary to consider some aspects of the condition of society which have conspired to weaken political methods and institutions. The underlying social disease can be best characterised as the pursuit of illusions. In particular we have fallen victim to a grave misunderstanding of the significance of effective economic performance and of the conditions under which this might be achieved, and we have remained blind to the probable consequences of the haphazard pursuit of certain egalitarian postulates in the provision of social welfare. This chapter will be concerned with illusion in relation to the economy and with one of the major political results of this. In order to pursue this theme it is necessary both to say something about the history of a long-standing misjudgement of the importance of producing more resources, and about the doctrinal foundation of post-war British economic management. It is this second point which leads straightaway to an important political consequence, the acceptance of an exaggerated view of the role of government in the steering of the economy, and *pari passu* a declining sense of the importance of private decision and responsibility, both as conditions of economic progress and as elements in the maintenance of a liberal political order.

Hardly anyone doubts that many of the weaknesses of contemporary Britain have their origin in an ailing economy and in the social difficulties which are bound to be associated with a failure of the economy to provide enough resources to meet those expectations of private consumption and public benefits which have become widely accepted in the society. And, of course, expectations have grown as fast here as elsewhere. The problem is that in Britain we have had relatively less and less resources with which to satisfy them.

More important than any specific event was the gradual retreat into a realm of economic myths which took place during and after the Second World War. It is doubtful whether it can be shown precisely when this retreat occurred. Certainly it was not like a general's decision to pull back his troops. It was more like a sliding accumulation of failures to recognise the realities of the situation. This failure is vividly underlined by a reference in Margaret Gowing's recent study of the post-1945 British development of atomic energy (itself a sad record of economic unrealism). Right at the beginning of the story she records some words of Keynes, put down in a paper submitted to the War Cabinet on the day Japan surrendered. Without immediate help from the United States, Britain was, so Keynes wrote, "virtually bankrupt and the economic basis for the hopes of the public non-existent".[1] This was indeed an accurate summary of the situation! This country, endowed with material and human resources vastly less than those possessed by the two world powers, had

[1] M. Gowing, *Independence and Deterrence, Britain and Atomic Energy 1945–52*, vol. I, p. 3.

impoverished itself in an effort which also, as one can see in retrospect, appears to have drained it of much of its creative energy. In sober practical terms the British people ought in 1945 to have been confronted with the reality of their economic situation. Essentially this was that their prospects were in the medium and longer terms no better than those of their neighbours who had been more visibly devastated and weakened by war. Instead, as if in a great spasm of emotional relief, Britain began to move into the realm of illusion.

The primary economic illusion consisted essentially in a refusal to accept the implications of the words of Keynes just quoted. Common sense required that it should have been understood that the first priority was to renew the capital equipment of the economy and by effective social co-operation and appropriate political decisions to make this process a practical possibility. But this was never clearly understood even in the years straight after the war. And, in so far as it was understood, it was never put across in a way which would have established a keen awareness of the problem in the minds of the people. The reasons for this are rather interesting — and take us beyond economics. It was not that the Labour Government of 1945–51 had no grasp of the economic weakness of the country and of the urgent need to get on with the reconstruction of much of the industrial structure. To be fair to that Government, it did its best to achieve an orderly transition from war to peace and did not hesitate to preach the need for hard work, wage restraint, more investment, forward planning, priority to exports and so on. Indeed, it showed more courage and honesty than most of its successors. But the trouble was that the real economic challenge could have been faced only at the cost of raising and answering the one question which in 1945 and ever since most strands of opinion in the country have always sought to evade: What is to be the motivation for economic activity and by what mechanism is that motivation to be made effective? And, of course, this in turn becomes a question about the kind of society we want to see and the political order appropriate to achieving it.

It is reasonable to hold that there are for complex societies only two viable answers to this dual question. One sees motivation in the economy essentially in terms of individual and private advantages, and so the operating mechanism must be that of the market, even though it may be qualified in practice by various social welfare considerations. The other sees the motivation somehow or other in terms of serving the public good, and as an inescapable consequence is compelled to see the mechanism for making this effective in terms of public, which means governmental, direction.

There was a time when this would have seemed obvious to any student of political economy. Ironically, the growth of economics as a discipline in Britain has been accompanied by a steady decline in the perception of this question. Of course, the contention is not that in the real world these motivations and mechanisms always manifest themselves with such clarity and sharpness. The choice is not between a pure competitive market economy dedicated only to private benefit and a pure command economy resting on politically determined welfare postulates. The market principle has to be qualified in many ways, and, *mutatis mutandis*, the same goes for the collectivist command principle. Nevertheless, there is a real choice here and, depending on which decision is made, a society must expect to move in directions broadly prescribed by that choice. And the choice is one with political consequences, too. Part of the problem was that the 1945 Labour Government *could not* make such an explicit choice, whilst its Conservative successors were too lazy and foolish even to see the need for it.

Having committed itself to the first and basic illusion that there was no need for overriding priority to be given to economic reconstruction, this country then refused to see the need for having any principles with which to shape such policies as were applied to the post-war adjustment to a peace-time economy. In other words there was no facing up to the choice between an economy founded on market principles and one based on the primacy of public welfare criteria and, *a fortiori*, on an extension of public power. Yet this may put the matter too sharply. Perhaps in reality we drifted into a decision against the market. There was an ambivalence and ambiguity about the policies of the post-1945 Labour Government which has characterised the approach of all subsequent governments. Attlee's Administration faced both ways. It carried out a far-reaching programme of public ownership, it liked to assert the social responsibility of industry and it attempted to maintain and develop a pattern of administrative controls which in theory at least gave the central government a capability for "economic planning". But at the same time it avoided the extension of public ownership beyond the public utility sector (though it later expressed the intention of departing from this position), emphasised the crucial role of private manufacturing industry in maintaining the external trading position of this country, and in the end gave up whatever hopes it might have had of imposing anything recognisable as a pattern of planning schemes on private business. In this way we achieved something usually described as "the mixed economy".

Whatever this phrase may mean — and thirty years on it is still hawked around by politicians and pundits of all kinds — it certainly signified a deal of intellectual confusion. The problem is that it focused attention on ownership, suggesting that a mixed economy was simply one in which there were public and private sectors (an idea which even at the end of the last century would have caused little stir in many continental countries). But, of course, the precise mixture of ownership between public authorities and private individuals or organisations is not all that crucial, though the liberal is entitled to believe that there are good reasons for trying to restrain the relative growth of the public domain. The point is rather that "mixed economy" is a vacuous expression if it is considered to refer *merely* to ownership issues. What matters are the principles on which the mixed economy operates, and here one gets back to the basic options of which I have already spoken. The choice of principles lay between the individual benefit motive and its concomitant mechanism, the market, and the public welfare motive and its concomitant mechanism, the determination by a public authority of the terms on which productive resources are used. Fundamentally, the decisions taken by the Attlee Government (1945—51) in its handling of economic questions expressed a political preference for the second option. True, the preference was often veiled and muted, but it was there and as far as can be judged, approved by many of the British people. What is more — and this is of crucial significance — this preference appears to have been shared by the war-time coalition, achieving its classic formulation in the 1944 commitment to full employment as well as in the acceptance by all parties of a major extension of social security benefits.[2]

---

[2] The most notable papers leading to these commitments were those on *Employment Policy*, Cmd. 6527, 1944, through which Keynesian doctrine received full official approval, and the *Beveridge Report on Social Insurance and the Allied Services*, Cmd. 6404, 1942. The latter opens with a strong statement of principle on the Victorian virtues of self-help and reliance, an aspect later to be forgotten.

This is one reason why the transition to Conservative political control in 1951, leading to thirteen years of Conservative dominance, made surprisingly little difference as far as the basic options were concerned. For the sake of consolidating their hold on power the Conservatives were not anxious to challenge in any fundamental way the economic and social measures of the early post-war years. Though ostensibly favouring reliance on the market, they did not succeed in giving any intellectual coherence to this view and, indeed, hardly tried to do so. Instead they were far too much preoccupied with rather irrelevant arguments about the balance of ownership between public and private sectors. Moreover, circumstances favoured governments after 1951: world trade began to expand, commodity prices fell, and for a while the British national product expanded modestly but sufficiently fast to allow a steady improvement in living standards. Much of this was achieved at the expense of investment and structural adaptation, but that was to be a problem for the future. For a decade or so there seemed to be a progressive consensus about how to manage the economy.

But let me come back to the questions of motivation and principle. A vital element in the post-war definition of a welfare economy was its ability to sustain full employment. This was slowly to have dramatic consequences. Until very recently few dreamt of questioning this orthodoxy or of recognising that there might be other sensible objects of economic policy to be balanced against the pursuit of full employment *per se*. Sadly enough there is little reason to believe that some of those who thirty or more years ago advocated and defined this commitment realised quite how serious were its implications for the national understanding of the economic issues facing the country. Keynes and Beveridge, key figures in this movement of opinion, seem to have had a certain blindness to the connections in a free society between the principles governing economic activity and the terms on which great social ends may be pursued. Both appear to have overestimated the extent to which governments can commit a society to certain desirable social aims without running the risk that dedication to these may have very negative effects on motivation in the economy and on the way in which it operates. This is not to argue that either Beveridge or Keynes (and certainly not Keynes) was naive in his understanding of economic conditions: both, for example, accepted definitions of "full employment" as equivalent to toleration of margins of unemployment which nowadays hardly any politician cares to defend; both had some perception of the dangers of inflation inherent in the monopoly power of trade unions. But both were naive in failing to recognise that if the major welfare objective they advocated − the maintenance of full employment − was to be pursued in isolation and for its own sake, then this was likely to distort economic policy-making and breed confusion about the principles on which economic activity was to be based and the terms in which it could be justified to the society. This point becomes clear through a comparison with post-1945 German neo-liberal economists who saw more clearly the interconnections between principles governing economic activity and the creation of conditions favourable to the satisfaction of social welfare claims than did the fathers of British post-war economic orthodoxy. And, of course, this means that they grasped more firmly the obvious fact that the successful pursuit of social ends depends heavily on the capacity of the economy to produce resources (or at any rate it does this side of Utopia).

Instead, what happened here was that much of public opinion came in a shallow way to accept the welfare motivation as morally superior to the pursuit of particular economic interests. Inevitably this meant that an understanding of the market mechanism, and of its political and social justification, atrophied. Gradually people came to accept the beneficence and the necessity of a high degree of centralised decision-making in the management of the economy. The ground was prepared for that slide into a veiled command economy which has now been achieved with its attendant political dangers. We thought that the need to make a choice between principles of operation could be avoided after 1945, but that was an illusion. The options are still basically the same, the difference being that thirty years of relative economic decline[3] have made it all the more difficult to face up to the consequences of taking that option which, as so much of the evidence shows, has generally been associated both with prosperity and the survival of a politically free society.

The theoretical basis for the post-war orthodoxy concerning the

---

[3] There are many sources from which evidence about the relative performance of the British economy can be derived, notably the regular surveys published by OECD. Many of the arguments about why there has been a low rate of economic growth in Britain are summarised in "Economic growth", by E. F. Denison, in *Britain's Economic Prospects*, Brookings Institution, 1968.

economic role of government is to be found in Keynesian economics. To simplify greatly, it was the idea of achieving full employment, stable prices and rising output through macro-economic adjustment by means of manipulation of public expenditure levels and taxation which came to constitute the core of the Keynesian heritage. This particular element in Keynes' work — though it was by no means his major theoretical contribution to economics — had at least two serious dangers implicit in it. One was that to some extent it was backward-looking, expressing a reaction to the problems of mass unemployment of the thirties. Thus it tended to distract attention from the problems inherent in a full-employment situation in which powerful unions and large enterprises were increasingly dominant. The second was that it took for granted the principles according to which a competitive market economy might be maintained, simply assuming that a single-minded concentration on macro-economic guidance through the manipulation of abstract quantities by government action would have no effect on many of the assumptions about economic behaviour in a market situation, which were to be found both in Keynes' own writings and in those of his classical predecessors.

This leg of the Keynesian orthodoxy was accepted well before the Second World War ended, and became virtually unassailable after 1945. For thirty years or so it has been the unchallenged conventional wisdom that the central government must have enough power "to manage the economy". From the adjurations of Sir Stafford Cripps between 1947 and 1950, to the exhortations of Edward Heath after 1970, from the benign assertions of the Plowden Report on the Control of Public Expenditure[4] to the platitudes of the Kilbrandon Commission on the Constitution[5] on the need to maintain the economic unity of the United Kingdom, from the advice of Keynes to the pleas of his latter-day disciples in the Cambridge Faculty of Economics, the same theme can be detected: the economic health of the country depends *in the first place* on the actions of government.

Without doubt the available evidence suggests that this great faith in government has been misplaced. Indeed, it is a reasonable conclusion that the effects of the primacy attaching to a government's ability to steer the

---

[4] *The Control of Public Expenditure*, Cmnd. 1432, 1961.
[5] *Commission on the Constitution 1969—73*, Cmnd. 5460.

economy through demand management of the now conventional kind have been pervasive and disastrous. Inevitably the postulates of the doctrine have required that an increasing proportion of what is managed, i.e. national resources, should be disposed of by government.[6] There has been a degree of febrile instability in economic policy-making which is without rival elsewhere, at any rate in western Europe. Public expenditure programmes have been constantly adjusted to suit short-term political claims. Innumerable measures of intervention by government to stimulate economic activity directly or indirectly have been devised, tried and cast aside. A taxation system has been built up, unstable, complex, oppressive and subversive of economic enterprise. We have tolerated a centralisation of power which has steadily stifled the political energies of the country and now threatens to be destructive of political rights too. In sum, the harsh reality is that neither the successive groups of politicians who have held office since 1945, nor the Treasury, nor the many other administrative agencies involved over the years in British economic management have been able to impose a decisive check on the forces of decline. The best that can be said of their combined efforts is that they have imposed upon this decline a more orderly and measured pace than it might otherwise have shown, though sometimes their rotation in office has been too fast even to permit that.

Of course some would regard such criticisms as too harsh and even unjust. Surely some good must have come from the devotion and application of so many able and public-spirited people to the tasks of central economic management? But I fear the answer is "No" and for two simple and clear reasons. One is that we vastly overestimate the level of efficiency which a centrally managed economy can achieve compared with

---

[6] The proportion of GDP disposed of in one way or another by the public sector varies according to the basis of calculation, including the manner in which transfer payments are handled. It can, however, be safely assumed that well over half of the GDP now falls into the public expenditure net. Moreover, there has been in the past decade a steady rise in public employment and a decline in private investment, thus accelerating the rise in the ratio of non-marketed to marketed outputs. This aspect has been dealt with by R. Bacon and W. Eltis in several articles, including a series in *The Sunday Times*, 2–16 November 1975. In western Europe only Sweden shows a similarly high level of public sector claims on resources, though its productive base is relatively stronger than that of the United Kingdom.

one which is required broadly to work within the conditions defined by market principles and methods. And this overestimation has been particularly naive within the context of a political system in which the responsiveness of politicians to every breath of public criticism is taken to be a sign of virtue. The other reason is closely linked with this point. It is that the attempt to provide economic management by central government has always been marked by a generous dose of make-believe or bluff. Our central institutions of government, despite a vast increase in their formal powers, have not really been able to exercise the kind of powers which are logically entailed by the claims made on their behalf. Social forces and interests as well as inherited political habits have held them back. Even if one disapproves of it and condemns it as inefficient, the method of centralised economic management by command has a certain intellectual coherence and perhaps offers prospect of some progress, though the political cost will be high. In contrast, centralised management without adequate powers is fraudulent and rather pointless. Yet this is essentially what successive administrations have been forced to sustain.

My reason for going back to the economic foundations of the present political malaise lies, of course, in the belief that the economic system and the political system have, in certain respects, to be congruent. Much of the economic doctrine accepted over thirty years ago had a profound impact on political assumptions and expectations, and on the tasks imposed on the political system. To put the matter starkly, the failure to recognise the importance of producing more resources more effectively, and the refusal to opt for a market solution to the basic economic question, nourished the belief that in fact the economy could be safely managed only by government, and indeed that the health of the economy depends more on the actions of government than on the behaviour of those actually engaged in economic activity. The Keynesian argument for macro-economic demand management was vitiated by its political naivety in relation to its probable consequences for the role of government and, *a fortiori*, for the political constitution of the country. But it had the equally harmful effect of subverting the possibility of a principled and realistic discussion of the nature of a market economy and of the conditions required for its maintenance. Thereby it frustrated any coherent statement of the responsibility of government for the regulative principles within which economic activity should take place, and substituted for that a purely expedient view of the economic role of government as an unending exercise in political manipulation. Inevitably this has resulted in an inexorable increase in the powers of government over the economy and over much else besides. Relentlessly this process has imposed on the political and administrative institutions a burden which they are inherently incapable of bearing. Yet despite repeated failures and disillusionment, despite the political dangers presented by this trend of events, the voices raised in protest are still muted and scattered. Why is this so?

The explanation is basically political. It is to be found in the failure to discern clearly enough and soon enough the tendency inherent in the collectivist solution to the economic question. Keynes and his epigoni have stood in a tradition which optimistically believed that there is a real choice to be made between liberal or democratic collectivism and totalitarian collectivism. It was held that the attenuation of the market economy in favour of decision-making by public authorities could take place with advantage to all and at no significant political cost. It was not understood that liberal collectivism is likely to be unstable, and in certain conditions (many of which have prevailed in Britain) is certain to be unstable. As a result it always runs the risk of sliding towards a centralisation of power which points towards the totalitarian condition. But then we face a further question. Given the undoubted fact of powerful liberal traditions in politics why have these dangers been taken so lightly?

The answer is a simple one. It is a peculiar misfortune of the British that the continuity of their institutional development has hidden from them the dangers of tyranny. They pride themselves on traditions of limited government which have blunted their sense of the fallibility of all government and prevented them from recognising the peculiar dangers inherent in accepting an indefinite expansion of public powers in the pursuit of economic and social welfare. Perhaps, too, they remain blind to a certain absolutism implicit in the Benthamite and utilitarian tradition which has, after all, profoundly influenced modern British political and social development. Be that as it may, to an extraordinary degree the British now exemplify de Tocqueville's grim judgement of the likely effects of an uncritical acceptance of the idea of bringing about by public action equality of social benefit in a society pervaded by what are taken to be democratic sentiments: "The notion they all form of government is that of a sole, simple, providential and creative power. All secondary opinions in politics are unsettled, this one remains fixed, invariable and consistent".[7]

It is a sad irony that it was the very strength of the political order which favoured the absorption of doctrines which have brought us to this depressing conclusion. It was widely believed thirty years ago that the key to orderly and progressive economic growth had been found. But this was an illusion fraught with great dangers for the management of political life. The underlying doctrine looked backward at least as much as forwards, and as time passed it became less and less relevant to the needs of the society. Moreover, even as Britain moved in this direction after 1945, the political and moral foundation for such an evolution had largely been removed in many other countries by the solvent of war and destruction. To most of our neighbours the benevolence of government seemed improbable, the wisdom of government questionable, and its capacity to determine what is good for the people wholly suspect. Thus our rivals and competitors escaped the deadening influence of a body of ideas peculiarly liable to over-simplification. For no matter how sophisticated some of the economic reasoning associated with the Keynesian orthodoxy, the doctrine rested on a shallow understanding of the interdependence of politics and economics as well as on a rarified view of the real world of productive activity. Its ultimate effect has been to erode, through the sheer weight of the role attributed to government, that sense of dispersed responsibility for economic decisions and of the importance of a stable regulative framework for economic activity which are the *sine qua non* of any genuine market economy. The justification for the practice of Keynesian economic management came to be expressed primarily in terms of the social welfare function of full employment: the theory became an appendage to a bundle of abstract social aims. Needless to say, any economic theory which mistakes its purposes so completely is in danger of tipping over into illusion, and that is what happened long ago. There was a steady but inexorable retreat into a dream world of effortlessly produced cakes and ale. And it is because reality eventually begins to break through even into that dream world, that the political order is now exposed to strains which it is ill-equipped to bear.

[7] A. de Tocqueville, *Democracy in America*, OUP, 1959, p. 553.

CHAPTER 2

Equality and Welfare in the Static State

So far I have been concerned with probing some of the errors in the appreciation of economic needs and in economic doctrine which have contributed to the present situation of Britain and with identifying in broad terms their political consequences. But may be the consequences of these mistakes would have been less severe, and there might have been more prospect of counteracting the illusions to which they gave rise, had there not been certain judgements of social values and policy at work which reinforced and complemented the misunderstanding of economic reality. Underlying this was something yet more serious, the psychological aversion to any kind of change which required an explicit revision of principles. Pushed far enough, such aversion expresses the retreat into a morality which simply denies the necessities of the world. However, at this stage it is necessary to turn to some aspects of social values and policy, leaving until later the general question of attitudes towards change.

The matters to be raised here concern the pursuit of what will be called distributive social equality and the priority accorded to what is commonly described as "the Welfare State". Equality has been for many years now a persistent theme in social analysis of all kinds in Britain and has its roots in a different ordering of values from that which has predominated elsewhere, e.g. in the continental European tradition of social inquiry. The contrast can be seen when the work of Max Weber is compared with that of R. H. Tawney.[1] The former drew from his study of capitalism and the Protestant ethic precious few conclusions about the virtues of equality: that was not what he thought to be important. But the latter extracted

[1] Much of the confusion about the terms on which a market operated is revealed in Tawney's belief that the function of industry is service. It is not: its function is to satisfy expressed needs, and a market represents a particular set of terms on which this can be achieved. Service in this context is merely a sympathetic fallacy which has, however, been productive of much mischief. See R. H. Tawney, *The Acquisitive Society*, 1921.

14

from his meditations on the relationships between religion and the growth of capitalist economies support for some harshly critical judgements of the "acquisitive" society in respect of its inequality. Such views helped to make a whole generation believe that the achievement of equality in the distribution of social goods was impossible within such a society. There developed a lop-sided understanding of equality, along with a blindness to the fact that the "acquisitive" society might in some respects be a necessary condition of creating the very resources which were to be more widely distributed. By the end of the Second World War, therefore, the country settled into a new orthodoxy, according to which the preoccupation with equality in distributive terms began to set the framework for political argument. Nevertheless, a generation ago the idea of social equality was still expressed chiefly in terms of equalising social chances and of improving the condition of the poorer sections of the community. Equalisation as continuous redistributive social engineering had not yet taken root. The emphasis on distributive equality did, however, portend a declining perception of equality of civil and political rights. Indeed, we have now become oddly complacent and indifferent about rights in these senses: we hardly seem to care about the evidence of inequality of treatment before our courts and quasi-courts, we are not worried by flagrant inequalities in the operation of our electoral law, and we apparently care nothing about the discretionary arbitrariness attaching to the actions of so many of those in public office.

The concern with a particular aspect of equality, its social dimension, to the exclusion of other and more fundamental senses of the idea, owes much to our social history as well as to political factors which appeared to confer some security on equality in respect of civil and political rights. It was the very sharpness of social cleavages resting on great differences in the ownership of wealth, and the manner in which these were expressed, which earlier this century and before fed a sense of injustice which persists, even though the reality which nourished it has been substantially modified. In particular economic differences reinforced cultural differences which have proved extremely resistant to change. Looking at the matter politically, despite major social differences there seems to have been a widespread belief, shared apparently by dukes and dustmen, that an Englishman's rights were quite safe and as good as anybody else's into the bargain. Our sense of political and civil rights rested chiefly on a robust individualism, first expressed in the common law, later in Lockean contract theory and finally in Victorian *laissez-faire* economics, which simply assumed that public powers were bad, that the more they were reduced the better, and that so long as they were kept down, any Englishman worth his salt could and would claim such rights as were part of his heritage. The protection of liberty lay in the negative state.

It was this climate of opinion which persuaded so many that equality of civil rights was no problem: everything in that department was secure and always would be. Meanwhile the cause to be fought for was a more equal distribution of material resources. As always war was an engine of change, and 1939–45 initiated major changes. We began to move towards a much more equal distribution of incomes, though, of course, marked inequalities in the ownership of resources still persisted.[2] But since consciousness of social status differences cannot easily be legislated out of men's minds that has remained a problem, though of diminishing intensity for many. However, there have been many Rip Van Winkles who would have none of this. For them the world had not changed, and the more equality was achieved in the distribution of material goods with a concomitant widening of social opportunities, the more vigorously they protested that nothing had been gained. Gradually, in the years between 1955 and 1965, the notion of equality gave way to a doctrine of egalitarianism. Equality of social opportunities was dismissed as a fraud productive of inequality. Setting everybody at the same point in the scale of social benefits became the aim.

That this view has gained widespread support as the natural framework for political argument owes much to the part played by the Labour Party in modern British politics and to the peculiarities of its own internal structure. The party was committed in its early years to a composite programme of social reform which could satisfy the aspirations of different elements in it, though each could interpret the long-term aims

---

[2] A standing Royal Commission on the Distribution of Income and Wealth was set up in 1974, issuing its first report in July 1975, Cmnd. 6171. This underlines the extreme difficulty of establishing reliable criteria for the definition and measurement of these matters, but the preliminary findings confirm a marked trend towards income equalisation and to a lesser extent towards a diminution in the concentration of wealth at the top of the scale. See also A. B. Atkinson, *Unequal Shares*, Pelican Books, 1972.

differently. The virtual completion of the Labour Party's post-war programme of "gas-and-water socialism" and welfare statism (much of which would hardly have shocked Bismarck) left something of a moral vacuum. This was gradually to be filled by a reinvigorated commitment to the values of distributive social equality. By some this was still interpreted with humanity and a respect for human diversity. But during the fifties most of the older generation of Labour leaders disappeared, and a few years later the balance and forces of opinion in the party shifted substantially in favour of those who, on grounds of interest or ideology, were preoccupied with the search for substantive equality. It was then that the cause of equality quickly acquired a kind of sectarian hardness. It was preached (and practised) during the sixties in more bigoted ways, the obsession with its pursuit became slightly neurotic. Yet this happened precisely when some people at least began to realise that in the post-war years the country had been in an economic situation which rendered a more rapid creation of wealth the indispensable condition of any genuine progress towards greater equality of social chances. In other words the new egalitarianism was from the outset another example of the pursuit of an illusion: the aspirations which fired it were destined to turn to dust and ashes.

It is a sad but obvious fact that the dedication of the progressive Left in politics to egalitarianism destroyed any prospect of this truth being understood, particularly as the years between 1952 and 1958 had constituted a misleading interlude in which for a short time there was the appearance of adequate economic growth. But once this fleeting period of hope had passed, the pursuit of egalitarian social policies demonstrated its devastating effects. It is hardly an exaggeration to assert that from then on to the present day every measure of economic policy which attempted to take a serious view of the need to produce more real wealth more quickly has been soured or frustrated by the interposition of the egalitarian argument. For since all effective measures directed to the increase of wealth must by definition have the consequence that some people will benefit more than others (even if only as a result of their own exertions), the same objection can always be raised by the egalitarian: how can policies be tolerated which might bring about what he and his brethren regard as an unfair distribution of benefits? That such arguments have often been motivated by envy and built on ignorance has mattered little: a degree of egalitarianism has insinuated itself into the moral platitudes of the age.

The pursuit of egalitarian aims certainly has its morally offensive side. But it is its practical absurdity which has been most important in relation to the economic errors which have already been discussed. For the egalitarian commitment encouraged and indeed deepened the primary illusion in respect of the economic condition. Not only did we fail to see the need for a more rapid rate of economic growth, we came to believe that it was laudable and rational to devote more energy to arguing about distribution than to devising means of producing more efficiently what there was for distribution. We have become like people fighting over the distribution of the eggs whilst forgetting to feed the hens which have yet to lay them. In contrast with the experience of so many other countries, there has in Britain been hardly any popular awareness of the simple fact that a more productive economy would have eased the problem of distribution: more people could have benefited by their own exertions and more resources would have been available for such redistribution as might be undertaken by public action.[3]

Not surprisingly, in view of this failure of understanding, there has been a steady fall in the national dividend up for distribution, both relative to expectations and to the achievements of other comparable societies. This in turn has added an increasingly unpleasant dimension of greed and covetousness to the arguments about distribution. Furthermore, the continuing faith in government as the engine of economic management has meant that the pressures on the political system arising from this situation have become heavier and more insistent. In this way social values have worked through economic illusion to present a challenge to the political order.

This criticism of the stultifying effects of egalitarian thinking does not mean, of course, that there are no problems in the British social structure. Indeed, I have already suggested the contrary. Certainly a social structure has survived in which the perception of class and status differences is still unusually widespread. This in turn has fed the preoccupation with equal

[3] The point is expressed with matter-of-fact clarity by one of the founders of the social market economy in Western Germany in an essay first written in 1947: "Only when a yield has been obtained is there any point in having thoughts about its distribution", A. Müller-Armack, "Die Anfange der Sozialen Marktwirtschaft", in *Die Zweite Republik*, edited by R. Löwenthal and H. P. Schwarz, 1974.

distribution, irrational though this reaction may often have been. But class differentiation is not a vested interest only of those at the top end of the scale. Unfortunately there are innumerable vested interests at *all* levels of social organisation which prefer to maintain these differences or some version of them. Indeed, this is one reason why most of the policies advocated by the egalitarian zealots are unlikely to have more than a marginal effect on the social rigidities to which they object. It may, for example, give some moral satisfaction to the middle-class progressive to witness the introduction of comprehensive schooling and "no selection". Unfortunately this panacea almost certainly leaves working-class self-isolation untouched, and barely affects the survival of a fiercely separatist working-class hostility to educational self-improvement.[4] In fact, as we know well enough, historical experience suggests that except in periods of genuine revolution significant social restructuring is far more likely to take place in a society subject to rapid economic growth and a high rate of technological change than as a result of any deliberate measures of social equalisation. In a rapidly changing economic context social relationships become more fluid – hardly a surprising conclusion. Britain has, however, had nothing like a consistently high rate of economic growth since 1945; her record of technological achievement is patchy, and the dominant reaction to most forms of change requiring new forms of organised social co-operation has been negative and defensive. Nobody need be in the least astonished if, in these conditions, many of the social relationships and attitudes of the past survive, proving themselves resistant even to the policies of the most egalitarian-minded social engineers. Here may well lie much of the explanation for the fiercely selfish pursuit of group interests which now has such serious effects. Their intensity reflects both the slow pace of natural social change and the fears which are inspired by politically motivated equalisation programmes.

It is now necessary to pass from the problem of equality and its re-interpretation to another aspect of the social situation, the priority attached to those welfare policies which, taken together, are often dubbed "the Welfare State".

---

[4] This is not to overlook powerful traditions of "working-class self-improvement" nor to underestimate what was achieved in this way. But there is hardly any doubt that these traditions are now in decay along with some of the organisations which carried them forward.

Let us remember at the outset two characteristics of the British view of welfare policies which distinguish this country from many others. First, social welfare policy has its origins in the desire to help the poor, followed by a growing conviction that the State should assume this obligation. It is a tribute to the strength of these roots as well as to the influence of egalitarianism that much of social policy is *still* discussed in these terms: it is assumed that pensions, housing subsidies, health services, even much of education, are somehow or other provided primarily for "the less-well off", "the disadvantaged", "the socially weak", "the underprivileged", "working people" or even "ordinary people". We never seem to have freed ourselves from the influence of those Victorian philanthropists who had to feel that "they were doing good" to the lower orders. As a result of this we have little idea of social services simply as the means of meeting a wide range of claims which, according to circumstance and need, are available to all within the limits of resources available. Secondly, we have the odd habit of conferring upon many of our welfare policies the status of holy cows, even though their form and content may stem from the needs and beliefs of a vanished age and the benefits they provide may be wholly unrelated to contemporary social needs. Moreover, there have always been plenty of self-appointed guardians of this or that aspect of welfare policy, tiresome latter-day saints who can be relied on to uphold past precedent and to frustrate change. The consequence of this complacent view of what has been built up in the past is that we have been reluctant to reappraise priorities in social policy and suspicious of any change of methods.

Housing policy provides a vivid example of this. The notion that subsidised or "social" housing should be provided by local authorities, that is to say by public decision and action, has its roots in the last century, "housing for the working classes" as it was actually called in the statutes until 1949. Despite the fact that the segregation of a large part of the community into council estates is a vital support of social division, that there is ample evidence that subsidies via local authorities have been grossly mal-distributed, and that there are serious political objections to the continuiing growth of local authority power and patronage in the housing sector, we adhere stubbornly to the idea that the bulk of housing made available as a social service must be in the hands of local authorities. The Labour party accepts this as an article of faith as well as a calculation of self-interest, whilst the other parties have generally lacked the courage to challenge the policy in any fundamental way. (The Conservatives had a stab at so doing in 1972, but that was soon reversed.)[5]

Another example of the tendency to sanctify what has been achieved is provided by the National Health Service. The original motivation lying behind the establishment of a centrally controlled and financed service was undoubtedly praiseworthy — the desire to make medical services available to all regardless of ability to pay. Unfortunately the determination to adhere rigidly to this pattern has had very mixed results. As medical services have developed technically and become more costly in equipment and personnel, so the dependence on a central allocation of funds has weighed restrictively on what can be achieved. A preference for economies of scale has favoured the creation of ever larger units of service, remote from the users and requiring cumbersome and often slow administrative procedures. The principle of free access with its accompanying reliance on financing out of taxation has obscured the cost of the services provided, both to the users and to the providers. There remains little room for the expression of private preferences in the choice of medical services, few incentives to economy in use other than administrative controls, and no means of encouraging a flow of private resources into the service. Needless to say, there is little if any competition in the provision of medical services, a situation which does not always benefit the user. All this is not to condemn the service out of hand, but rather to underline the fact that there has been too much rigidity in relation to the problems of adapting its structure and methods to a changing social and economic context. And the case is politically relevant because it provides so many examples of the strains imposed on government by the assumption of direct responsibility for such a major social service.

However, there is no need to offer a lengthy commentary on specific areas of social policy. My argument is that the prejudice in favour of state-provided welfare services — a public monopoly in the welfare business, justified by pleas on behalf of "the poor" — has worked against the achievement of a better understanding of social needs and economic possibilities. It has into the bargain depressed the quality of many social services as can be illustrated in several ways. Had our social insurance

[5]Chiefly under the Housing Finance Act 1972, subsequently repealed on the return of a Labour government in 1974.

policies relied more on employer financing, then maybe a more prudent approach to the wasteful use of labour would have been encouraged; if public support for housing had been channelled through a far wider range of agencies and owners, may be the rate of provision of new housing would have been higher and the quality less uniformly mediocre; if the National Health Service had been less sacrosanct, perhaps methods might have been found long ago for diversifying the provision of health care with a consequent raising of standards and a relative reduction in the burden on public resources. After all, there is plenty of experience elsewhere of alternative policies which might have stimulated a much more efficient use of resources and at the same time an enhanced production of new resources. The crucial point is simply that social policy has in many fields been flat and dreary, more or less designed to depress improvement in quantity and quality. The traditional methods have encouraged the belief that the State alone can and will provide, that the butter must be spread thinly and equally, and that no good can come of prompting initiatives which might escape the control of those who "manage the economy" and act as guardians of the social conscience.

Thus there has been a remarkable correspondence between the bias of post-1945 welfare statism and the dominant beliefs about the economy and economic policy. In both sectors there was a rejection of serious change: in the economy because we eventually persuaded ourselves that none was needed, and in social welfare policy because most people believed that by 1950 or thereabouts all the foundations had been well and truly laid. In both sectors there was a failure to discern that the flow and availability of resources was a crucial problem, and that if resources were to decline relative to expectations and perceived needs, then one enters a vicious circle from which there may be no escape. And, finally, there was in both sectors a willingness to accept without question the assumption that the central political authority knows best. Welfare policy just as much as economic policy conspired to increase faith in the "providential power" of government.

I must now try to summarise this economic and social introduction to the political analysis of our decline. The initial thesis is that this country has been the victim of serious and pervasive economic illusions. These have interacted with certain social values and social welfare policies in such a manner as finally to persuade successive governments of both parties to tolerate a steadily growing mortgage on the future in order to facilitate rising consumption standards and increasing public benefits in the present. More and more the political economy of the country has been adapted to the principles which governed the domestic economy of that sweet and feckless woman, Madame Ranevskaya, in Chekhov's *The Cherry Orchard*. Surrounded by old retainers and importunate hangers-on she maintained a state far beyond what her income would support, struggling against change and the threat to the cherry orchard. Yet in the end it had to be chopped down and Madame Ranevskaya made way for that vulgar but successful capitalist, Lopakhin. However, in the life of societies, it is rarely practicable to sell the assets to a new management: we cannot follow the advice of a professor of economics and ask the Hong Kong Government to take over (efficacious though that course might be).[6] What has to be done is to work against the illusions, to try to take a few steps towards replacing them by an understanding of the realities of the situation, and to provide a coherent statement of some of the options which face us and of their probable consequences. And to do this is to keep alive the hope that political choice can become a reality.

The clichés of modern social science are against such an effort. They tell us that the really profound "causes" of particular situations and events are socio-economic forces embedded in the texture of social life. Such an outlook easily leads to the conclusion that not much can be done about the present British crisis. Even if it were to be agreed that its treatment might require political changes, it would be suggested that these could have no real effect on the underlying social and economic determinants.

This quietist view – one which, let it be said, passes for progressive in the best circles – is both conservative and pessimistic. It accepts a downward drift no matter what may be the risks of shipwreck on the way. But more seriously it is a view which is mistrustful of man's claim to political self-determination. There is certainly an interdependence between a society and its political order, and between its economic system and its political methods. Similarly, social conditions impose many constraints on the adaptation of political rules as well as on the pursuit of substantive ends in political life. But social circumstances do not determine political

---

[6]Harry G. Johnson, facetiously no doubt, in *Crisis '75 . . . ?*, p. 118, published by the Institute of Economic Affairs, 1975.

choice nor can they extinguish the claim to freedom and rationality which is implied in the choice of political procedures and the pursuit of particular political relationships. Indeed, it is precisely in conditions of social weakness and confusion that the challenge of political reconstruction is most clearly presented, for it is then that it becomes possible to see that the constraints in society can be overcome only by a re-thinking of the ground rules of political co-operation and association.

Yet at the same time it is important to avoid illusions about the difficulties and dangers of trying to induce deliberate and genuine political change in a society. Political change is not to be equated with the conventional kind of measures which politicians and their officials produce in a never-ending stream in contemporary Britain. This kind of "reform" is febrile and often pointless, a disease of societies foolish enough to treat management consultants as latter-day witch doctors. No: genuine political change must mean deliberate attempts to re-fashion the rules of the political order and to adopt new methods of political co-operation which in turn will compel those subject to them to see the world they live in differently. Historical experience suggests that political self-determination in this sense is a possibility, though it is quite rare and fraught with dangers. And naturally it is hard for a conservative political order like the British, proud of its continuity, to contemplate deliberate change which would challenge that very continuity. Yet this may be preferable to the dangers inherent in accepting a process of decline in which social tension is exacerbated, economic folly perpetuated, and in consequence the authority of political institutions dissipated.

This brings me very close to the main preoccupation of these reflections – the character and capacity of British political institutions. It is because institutions have to operate in a specific social context, acting as mediators of social realities, that it has been necessary to spend so much time on some of the dominant features of this context. The next stage is to consider the manner in which understanding of the traditional political concepts has weakened, so that the political order itself has come to express much of the confusion which has accompanied the pursuit of social and economic ends.

CHAPTER 3

The Waning of Constitutional Understanding

I have so far expressed the British predicament chiefly in terms of the pursuit of illusions, a failure to grasp the nature of the economic problem and a refusal to recognise the likely consequences of a particular view of social claims and of the conventional modes of state action by which they have been satisfied. To fall victim to illusions is to forget reality — to turn a deaf ear to the necessities of the world. But nothing can be built on a refusal to acknowledge that the world subjects us to its own necessities: creative freedom has to start from this insight. When a society collectively refuses to recognise reality, it is in great danger. The individual who retreats into illusion may survive, protected perhaps by kind friends. Not so the society. There are no friends who will save it out of a spirit of pure charity, whilst the consequences of error which is collective will be magnified many times over.

Up to this point in the argument the emphasis has been on mistaken judgements in the sphere of economics and on a distorted understanding of social justice. These errors have compounded the constraints within which many issues of common concern have to be resolved, and as a result the demands made on the political system have steadily increased, so much so that often enough political solutions are sought which cannot conceivably be found in a society which still professes to have limited government. Persistent inability to find solutions to practical problems of living together indicates that the society no longer has the political means at its disposal which are required if it is to maintain that degree of cohesion and unity without which it will drift into a war of all against all. To say that the political means of solving problems are inadequate is to say that the political procedures and the institutions embodying these no longer have the capacity to mobilise the authority needed to sustain consistent policies and courses of action. It is also to suggest that at least some of those who act through the institutions may be at fault. Not surprisingly there is always a reluctance to contemplate the possibility that the political institutions of a society may be defective, for to do so is to raise fundamental questions and to challenge deeply entrenched interests and opinions. It is always easier to put the blame somewhere else, typically on social or economic forces which the political institutions are allegedly unable to control or influence. But this is to take a naive view of the relationship between political principles and practice on the one hand, and the world in which they manifest themselves on the other.

The authority of institutions rests finally on the acceptability of the principles and procedures which they express. But institutions can retain this foundation of consent — and, *a fortiori*, their ability to act — only if there is some reasonable correspondence between the manner in which they are actually used and the justification which it must always be possible to give for the terms on which they operate. In other words, the theory — or the principles — of the institutions must not diverge too far from the reality of how they are used. The case which I want to put forward now is that the gap between the theory and the reality of British political institutions and procedures has assumed serious dimensions. Later I shall try to sustain this argument by looking at particular institutions. But on this occasion it is a more general case which will be advanced — the contention that the root of the political difficulty is to be found in a refusal to recognise that much of the traditional language of the British Constitution, that is to say of the framework within which the political institutions and political activity are enclosed, has lost its vitality. It has become merely formal, still adapted to the sustaining of myths, but for this very reason unable to contribute effectively to the establishment and maintenance of authority. The search for durable solutions to practical problems is unlikely to be more successful than it has been of late, until we show some signs of being ready to contemplate changes in political procedures and rules designed to counteract this weakening of institutions and those who act through them.

One might then ask why it is that there has been so much reluctance to envisage measures of genuine political change in Britain, and why we have been so addicted to believing that the political methods evolved over the years are still perfectly adequate to the demands made on them. The issue of political change has to be seen in the context of a general dislike of change, and particularly of change which is explicit and deliberately intended to alter the terms on which particular relationships rest. The rejection of principled change has been pervasive and one can find examples of it in practically every sphere of social and political organisation and activity. No matter what it is proposed should be done, one can be certain that someone or other will discover a vested interest in stopping it. Virtually the whole of the opposition to the European Economic Community, for example, was founded on the fear that if Britain were to join and remain in this association, then we might one day actually be required to behave differently. Many of the difficulties in the economy and in social relationships stem from an underlying belief that things cannot really be arranged differently and that there is no escape from what has emerged from tradition. This is not to decry the significance of tradition nor of an awareness of the past. But surely an understanding of the importance of tradition can coexist with an appreciation of the need to change and of what change might imply. For change is a response to challenge, a recognition of reality, a willingness to see life as a continuing exploration.

What has just been said might appear to be contradicted by two fairly obvious facts. One is that the social character of the country has changed quite a lot in the past quarter of a century or so, leading in turn to marked changes in moral attitudes. For example, the ethic of work with its justification of rewards by reference to work performed, has notably weakened. The other is that there has for at least ten years been no lack of institutional change in Britain: we have indeed been very busy "reforming" structures of public life. Surely these points count against the alleged aversion to change.

Appearances are, however, deceptive. Social change generally happens without a deliberate effort to bring it about, and certainly with few exact conceptions of the kind of relationships being sought. Consequently, it is perfectly possible for substantial changes to take place in social structure, in income distribution, in the manner in which people divide their time between work and other activities, and in the culture of which they are part, but without such changes having much direct effect on existing patterns of organised social co-operation and political behaviour. Of course, when this kind of social evolution occurs there is the risk of a growing gulf between social attitudes and expectations on the one hand, and political structures and methods on the other. In Britain, for example, one sees evidence of this in the increasing remoteness of the parliamentary style of politics from the behaviour patterns of the society at large. This is but one case of what can be deduced from a careful look at many of the formal structures of social and political co-operation in Britain — remarkable stability in the midst of a fluid and uncertain context.

As far as the spate of institutional reform goes, it is easy to show that much of this has been directed to pseudo-change. Have we really altered the character of the central government bureaucracy, the Civil Service, as a result of the superficial diagnosis of the Fulton Report[1] and the rather selective reform treatment which the service then received after 1969? Has the smoothness of the rhetoric in the Redcliffe-Maud Report[2] done anything to modify visibly and substantially the political irrelevance of British local government? Has the proliferation of state agencies of economic intervention of one kind or another over the past ten years or so succeeded in improving our economic prospects? Did we not try to establish a civilised and binding framework for the anarchy of industrial relations (thus initiating real changes),[3] only to find that the electorate took fright before the unrelenting hostility of the oligarchs who are determined that here above all there shall be no change? Has the so-called parliamentary reform of recent years made one iota of difference to the basic relations between Parliament and Government? Has the administrative upheaval in the Health Service decreed in 1972 done anything to improve the manner in which individuals are treated? Do the dogmas of educational reform offer the firm promise of a society which will value more highly those qualities of intellectual and moral discipline without which a creative response to the dilemmas facing it is impossible? I fear that the answer to all these questions and to many more like them is "No", or at best, "Hardly at all".

[1] *The Civil Service*, Cmnd. 3638, Report of the Committee 1966–8; chairman: Lord Fulton.
[2] Royal Commission on Local Government in England 1966–9, Report, Cmnd. 4040; Chairman: Lord Redcliffe-Maud.
[3] Chiefly through the Industrial Relations Act 1971, subsequently repealed in 1974. This reference should not be taken to imply that the legislation of 1971 represented a wholly satisfactory way of handling the problems in this field. But it did constitute an attempt to introduce certain principles for the ordering of relationships in employment on which it would have been possible to build constructively had the interests hostile to change been less adamant in their opposition.

The reason for the hollowness of so many of the claims made on behalf of "reform" and "change" is that those who make them rarely pause to examine carefully the principles upon which the changes they praise are actually based. If they did this, then perhaps they might see that most of the changes made conceal a refusal to revise the principles and procedures according to which people are supposed to act. As a result of this crucial qualifying condition imposed on change there are plenty of differences in the organisational scenery, but little new in the play which is acted out on the stage. This has happened over and over again in Britain, and indeed a considerable number of intellectuals have become professional apologists for the building of such Potemkin villages. Perhaps that is the fate of the incautious social scientist who gets caught up in a political milieu which finds him useful for legitimation but for little else.

If we seek to explain why genuine change is viewed with such suspicion, we can discern reasons of two kinds. There are vested interests which oppose change for selfish reasons. But I will not pursue these any further at present. Lying deeper is the weakening of an understanding of the justification for institutions which can be seen at work. No doubt there are signs of this tendency in the political life of many of our neighbours: they too have their propagators of Utopia who believe that collective good can be built upon the foundation of individual anarchy. In Britian the disease manifests itself in the atrophy of any language in which we can talk of constitutional issues, of rules, or of the principles of public law. There is plenty of argument about co-operation, participation, voluntary action, social harmony and that sort of thing. But we no longer see that institutions must have their rules, that they exist in order to express a perception of the rules by which we will shape our behaviour, and that there must be an appropriate language in which to express the terms in which they confer obligations on those subject to them. So we are left floundering in a world of pure pragmatism, in which those who should know better turn to the business or management consultant for advice on how to design or re-jig the institutions of the polity — as if anything could be more ridiculous! For people of such provenance rarely understand institutions, the scaffolding of a political order. Usually all that they can offer is more machinery, leaving untouched the conditions and the terms on which people are expected to work together in the pursuit of shared purposes. As I have said already, this is how the scenery is changed, and perhaps the costumes of the actors too. But the parts they read remain the same.

Let me come now to more specific aspects of our political and constitutional order. There are two features of the political development of Britain which make it different from other mature political societies. There is first an extraordinary and basically unbroken continuity of conventional political habits. Its constitution *is* these political habits and little else. Then there is the fact that the political élite has been produced by broadly similar means for a very long time now, and that on the whole it has shown a high degree of adaptation to shifts in the distribution of social and economic interests in the society. In other words the élite has been produced by parliamentary means and its character has changed in many subtle ways as the context of social interest which it has to represent has changed. So in essentials we have continuity of constitutional behaviour and continuity in the evolution of political élites.

Yet perhaps there is another aspect of British experience which is so obvious that one almost forgets how crucial it is. This is the complete dominance of one particular body of ideas about government, namely what we usually call the idea of parliamentary government. Since the end of the seventeenth century there has in England been no substantial challenge to this idea. This means that there is no alternative or competing political tradition to fall back on, no different view of the basis on which political authority might rest. Now this is usually considered a great blessing, a happy state of affairs which preserves us from the tensions and conflicts likely to be experienced in countries in which there is no such dominant political tradition. This is a reasonable point of view, or certainly it was when there were no reasons for suspecting that the British interpretation of parliamentary government might be defective in some respects. The peculiar problem now presented by the very supremacy of one particular way of looking at the establishment of political authority is that those who may be anxious about the future, sceptical about the continuing vitality of this doctrine *alone* as a support for a satisfactory political order, have no other tradition to appeal to. They are compelled to think in terms of political precepts and values which have, on the whole, either been rejected in this country, or at best treated with insular condescension. This certainly does not make the task of recommending political change an easy or rewarding one: the reproach likely to be met is that of importing alien ideas and of pressing for change where, almost by definition, change cannot be made.

But let me come back to the first of the two main points which I have mentioned — the continuity of constitutional ideas and practice. At a later stage I will turn to the political élites. It is well known that Britain has an "unwritten Constitution" and that this intangible and somewhat nebulous entity has lasted a very long time. What exactly is meant by the Constitution being "unwritten"? Is it a fact that this is a peculiar benefit, conferring on our political arrangements a flexibility and resilience unknown elsewhere?

To a certain extent the description of our Constitution as "unwritten" is misleading: there are clearly some statutes which look like constitutional law, such as the Parliament Acts, the Ministers of the Crown Act 1937 or the Crown Proceedings Act of 1947. What is really being said about the Constitution when it is described in this way is that it is not formalised. There is uncertainty about what counts as a constitutional provision, there is a grey area between particular constitutional enactments and political convention and habit, and there is no special procedure by which constitutional provisions are to be made, amended or repealed. This, of course, means that constitutional law in Britain is a tenuous and elusive subject, and that a great deal of what passes for constitutional practice is no more than conventional political habit. Britain is quite exceptional in all this. Practically every other developed political society[4] has a written or formalised constitution which attempts to define the structure of political institutions, to guide the manner in which political life is to be conducted, and to define the rights and obligations of citizens in relation to the state. All this we lack! It is because a written constitution does these things — or tries to — that there is always a trace of that problem which is identified in German as the gap between *Verfassungsrecht* and *Verfassungswirklichkeit*, between the law of the Constitution and the political reality of it. The English have flattered themselves that under *their* Constitution such a problem can never arise. That may logically be so, yet it is not necessarily an unqualified blessing.

The attractiveness and perhaps the strength of an unwritten or

---

[4] Israel might be considered to be one of those states without a formal constitution, though this could be disputed.

unformalised constitution depends upon the continuing awareness of a particular insight which that kind of tradition reveals. This is that all formalised constitutional ideas can be realised in practice only if supported by appropriate conventions and understandings: in other words a large part of the reality of any constitutional order must consist in the traditions of behaviour which sustain it. This, too, is what underlies the criticism often made of too great a preoccupation with achieving an exact correspondence between *Verfassungsrecht* and *Verfassungswirklichkeit*, between the "ought" and the "is" in constitutional relationships. The uniqueness of the British Constitution is to be found in the fact that it has erected that very insight into a dominant feature of the Constitution itself. It appears to eschew rules and principles as far as possible, proclaiming instead that the rights and procedures which it claims to protect have their security and continuance in particular political habits and understandings, and only there. Unfortunately, whilst the Constitution may have rested safely on such a basis in the past, and more particularly in the last century when such theory of it as we still have was elaborated, there can be no guarantee that it will always be so. Nor do we need to look far for reasons to account for the uncertainty and dangers which stem from a total reliance on convention and habit. The distribution of power in a society is never static: it can change in ways which strain and dissolve the conventions; the role of government has vastly increased, bringing dangers for the protection of individual rights undreamt of half a century ago; political values and attitudes change, weakening particular conventions and blurring such understanding as may have been present of the purpose of earlier constitutional understandings. But most serious of all, the uncritical acceptance of flexibility and adaptation as the supreme values of the Constitution expresses an unhistorical view of the conditions in which such values come to play a major part in the definition of that very Constitution.

I have referred to an unhistorical view of the role of convention and habit. This merits a little more explanation. The contemporary account of the Constitution of this country still owes nearly everything in it to the writers of the last century, and notably to A. V. Dicey.[5] For it was he who

---

[5] In particular, *An Introduction to the Study of the Law of the Constitution*, first published in 1885.

gave such a large place to convention and attempted to explain how it operated as an indispensable complement to constitutional law proper. But the crucial point is that the power of Victorian constitutional convention was incomparably greater than that of any contemporary convention of the same kind. In saying this I am to some extent doing no more than pointing out how much more seriously our forefathers were committed to the firm observance of a range of moral and political conventions far wider than would be conceivable today. In contrast it is a hallmark of our age that virtually every aspect of social life is caught up in a process of change, is open to challenge, and has lost the kind of predictability which it once had. But for the builders of the Victorian theory of the Constitution there was no need to question the reliance on convention or to believe that they were not building on solid ground. The large place then given to convention was precisely the result of a belief that it was founded on habits and traditions expressive of the genius of the people which, like the rock of ages, would endure. (It is immensely important to remember how keen a sense of the force of opinion in society was expressed by Dicey, the constitutionalist.)[6]

When we begin to think about the character and role of convention in our present political life we can see that this confidence was misplaced and over-optimistic. There is no longer that degree of commitment to particular procedures, that respect for traditional values and habits, nor that breadth of agreement about how political authority should be exercised and for what purposes, which would justify the belief that convention alone is a sheet-anchor on which we can rely for the protection of civil rights or for the survival of a particular form of government. Flexible and adaptable the Constitution remains, but these are qualities which can be used for different purposes, and increasingly it becomes clear that they serve chiefly to justify the relentless extension of public power and the erosion of such notions as may survive of the limits within which it may properly be exercised. Thus what was a valuable element in the British constitutional tradition, a sign of political wisdom, has been perverted: it has begun to absorb all else and to obscure the very sense of a constitution.

---

[6] Vide *Lectures on the Relation between Law and Public Opinion in England during the 19th Century*, 1905.

What we all tend to forget nowadays is that most elementary truth about a constitution, that is to say that it is a means of establishing limits, constraints or boundaries for the exercise of power both by office-holders and by one citizen against another. A constitution is a kind of corset for us all: if it is not that, then it is nothing, it is degraded to pure formalism. This was still understood in the late nineteenth century and on into our own. But now that sense of what it means to conduct political life within the framework of a constitutional order has passed away. We no longer seem to appreciate that having a constitution entails setting limits to the exercise of powers. The very categories of constitutional reasoning have atrophied. And as I shall try to explain later, many of the procedures subject to which the executive arm of government operates have ossified. This is true, for example, of many of the charades played out in Parliament, the miming of procedures which no longer impose the constraints which was their original justification, though their survival itself may ironically be a powerful obstacle to genuine constitutional innovation. Meanwhile, the virtues of trusting to convention are extolled as the vital principle of the Constitution by those whose chief interest it is to maintain just such a state of affairs. There is indeed nobody to watch over the guardians of our Constitution.

No doubt there are some people in Britain who will grudgingly agree that perhaps the flexibility has been overdone a bit, that may be nowadays our politicians and administrators are inclined to stretch the old Constitution just a bit too much. But, they will suggest, must we not recognise that it is a sign of great strength and adaptability that "the Constitution" can be modified so easily, and that we are spared the difficulties and strains of real argument about whether it can or should be done at all? I doubt whether such an argument has ever been a good one and certainly there is little to be said for it in present conditions. Nothing in the experience of the post-war years suggests that the ease with which the Constitution could be pulled and tugged this way and that has brought us substantial and identifiable benefits. The chief effect of this famous flexibility, of course, has been to spare us some of the conflict which might occur under more formalised constitutional systems when proposals for change are under debate, and thus to deprive us of the stimulus of having to argue seriously about the principles on which we claim to be acting. To call this pure gain is naive; it is yet another way of blurring issues and choices, of staying within the bounds of cosy illusions.

The conclusion then is that the present crisis must be seen as having a constitutional character because there is no longer any large measure of confidence in the terms on which political authority is to be established and exercised. The challenge is constitutional because we have lost most of our sense of having constitutional rules. In this we are the unfortunate victims of our unwritten traditions as well as of a contemporary misunderstanding of the presuppositions on which they rested. It is constitutional too because there is growing evidence that many people no longer believe that their rights are protected, that they enjoy the benefits of "due process" in all matters affecting their rights under the law. And it is constitutional because we see governments, organisations and even individuals openly flout such principles and procedures as have been thought to govern public life in this country. The outcome is a kind of constitutional wasteland. There is no established body of thought and practice to which to appeal. There are merely fragments lying here and there, many of them having an almost antiquarian ring about them.

But our constitutional order is also weakening because it cannot contain the political pressures to which it is subject. It is bypassed by the active political forces in the society and begins to look obsolete. This condition has been drawing nearer over the past generation. Competitive two-party adversary politics and the universal belief in the inevitability of "big government" have burst the bounds of the constitutional shell supposed to contain them. (Let me admit that the criticism of party is no new theme: echoes of it are to be found, though with a different tone, in the constitutional arguments at the end of the last century and before 1914.) Yet our dominant mode of politics and the great expansion of public powers have found no new legitimation: no revised constitutional consensus has arisen to give support to these features of the polity. Perhaps even that gap might have been tolerable had the political order not revealed the one shortcoming for which in the long run there can be no pardon: failure to vindicate itself by results. It is in the persistent inability of our rulers and our institutions to solve in an acceptable way some of the problems with which the society is confronted that a crisis of government is revealed. Political failure cannot be blamed indefinitely on the intractable world in which the politician labours, for if that were so the talk of political freedom would be meaningless.

Understandably people are reluctant to admit the possibility of a political and constitutional crisis. And it has to be granted that there are few of the conventional signs of it. The familiar institutions still appear to work. But that the machine ticks on can hardly conceal the fact that far fewer people seriously believe that it ticks to good purpose: there is a widespread lack of faith in the future of the country and in the ability of its system of government to guide it forward. Political involvement in national elections has on the whole declined over two decades; support for the major parties has also declined and recently fallen dramatically; there are clear signs of the breakdown of the political unity of the "United Kingdom"; indifference towards local politics is monumental, whilst irritation at the remoteness and cost of local government rises; respect for the law (and I mean public rather than criminal law) declines and there are those in the Labour party who have openly encouraged defiance of it; British public law, that is to say statutes conferring powers on public bodies, has assumed more and more the character of a mere technical requirement, the translation into arcane terminology of the immediate political and administrative demands of those in power and with little or no regard to structuring principles; the country's respect for its international obligations has slipped too, as can be seen from an ostentatious indifference towards the risk of a serious breach of treaty commitments which was implied in having a referendum on Common Market membership; there is the strident intervention of trade union bosses, not merely in industrial and economic matters but far more widely, an intervention which often looks like a claim to exercise a veto over whatever the legitimate government may propose to do; and here and there are manifestations of violence which at the very least demonstrate that the British are not immune to such dangers.

I suppose that few would disagree with the argument that a record of persistent failure, combined with declining faith in the capacity of the system of government to produce positive results, creates the basis for a political crisis, that is to say, for a situation in which it is manifest that the formally responsible institutions are no longer capable of asserting their authority effectively. Where there would be disagreement, of course, is on the question whether we in Britain have yet gone far enough along this road: how much more failure can the social structure absorb? How much more faith in the established political procedures can the society afford to lose? Most probably there are no straightforward answers to such questions, and certainly not answers of the kind which social scientists claim to offer when they wear their professional hats. Institutions and the habits associated with them have extraordinary staying-powers even when they no longer command widespread assent and suffer from a record of failure in the achievement of substantive ends. They may even endure simply because nobody knows (or nobody agrees) what might be put in their place.

So perhaps it is more useful to put the question in another way. If there are grounds for believing that the institutions of a political order are losing their hold and no longer sustain the authority of those who act through them, what general conditions have to be fulfilled in order to reverse such a process? Here I would suggest that the answer must lie at a point of intersection between a recognition of the constraints imposed by reality and a perception of the limits imposed by particular concepts of the kind of political relationships people wish to create and maintain. A political order and the institutions in which it is embodied draws its authority and its capacity to endure from its ability to define and illuminate such points of intersection. The expression of these must always contain a judgement of practical possibilities and at the same time confine decisions within the bounds of what is compatible with the character of the political association itself. But the judgement of what is possible can be set high or low, or somewhere in between. Where the challenge is set depends on many things — on the obstacles, constraints and advantages in the world around us as well as on such faith as people have in their capacity to find acceptable ways of pursuing purposes which in some degree they share, though never completely and to the exclusion of their separate interests. And almost the whole of the constitutional element in politics lies embedded in the word "acceptable". The tyrant's solution is easy. So is that offered by politicians who, by flattering the people, deny their own responsibility and persuade their followers that all can be achieved at no cost, material or moral. What remains immensely difficult is to find solutions to practical problems which take account of realities — e.g., that many kinds of resources are not available in unlimited quantities — and at the same time can be achieved by political means which sustain the notion of a *res publica*, a public realm in which all are entitled to a part and to which all are bound by the ties of obligation. The maintenance of *that* kind of political order presents a very difficult challenge which certainly cannot be met without careful attention to the terms on which its institutions rest and are used.

This is to touch upon much wider issues which affect all liberal constitutional states and which might well assume a more serious shape in the years to come. But to come back to the British context, we have advanced far towards a condition of political lassitude and frustration. We have lost much of our sense of political institutions as creative instruments, as the means by which we impose on ourselves the rules which define our freedom and establish the authority needed for the achievement of substantive ends. No doubt we can go a long way towards diagnosing the economic and social causes of many of our problems. There will, too, be no shortage of schemes demonstrating how resources and organisation can be manipulated in ways which will supposedly help us to overcome our problems. But the fact remains that the achievement of collective purposes depends on a political will being present and on the acceptance of an idea of political authority. It is these conditions which are hardly fulfilled any more in Britain, and the absence of which has meant that so much of the political effort of the past ten years has resembled a gigantic charade.

Inevitably this vision of the situation suggests the conclusion that there can be no way forward, no escape from the steadily more constricting circles imposed by the pursuit of illusion, without a measure of political reconstruction. We need to re-think some of the political rules under which we live. We need to regain some sense of institutions as the means by which authority is created and made effective, and to escape from a world in which institutions have been degraded to "machinery of government", "management and organisation" or simply "dignified scenery", lending respectability to the demands of those with the loudest voices. We need to recognise once again that we are not powerless in determining where the point of intersection lies between our understanding of political freedom and our recognition of reality. If we continue to behave as we have done in recent years, then that point of intersection will be set so low that we try to escape all political challenge and set our faces against reality. That means not only crisis, it means decay. But the alternative is there, painful though it may be for many. We can set the point of intersection high, we can embrace the challenge of finding the political means of accepting reality and of reconciling ourselves both to its constraints and to the opportunities it still offers.

I have felt obliged to go into these matters in order to make somewhat explicit the philosophical ground for what will be said later about the condition of politics in this country and about some aspects of the working of its political institutions. I hope by so doing to avoid confusion, but also to escape from that condition of being suspended in thin air which seems endemic in so much contemporary political writing. And it is done, too, because what follows is intended to suggest some of the questions of political choice with which this country is confronted. For surely it is the chief concern of the discipline of politics, the study of political ideas and practice, to define the nature of the choices and to explain the consequences of them. In few passages of political writing is this insight more vividly communicated than in Max Weber's great lecture on the vocation of politics, *Politik als Beruf*, and it is worth recalling what he said. In a remarkable passage he characterises two of the deadly sins in politics as *Unsachlichkeit* and *Verantwortungslosigkeit* — a lack of respect for the facts of life and irresponsibility.[7] In essence, the argument advanced so far is that both these sins flourish in Britain: we want to pretend that the world is other than it is and yet we do not want to live with the consequences of such foolish behaviour. But what Weber is arguing in those grim purple passages is that the exercise of power, which was for him part of the very meaning of politics as an activity, always becomes irresponsible and dangerous precisely when these sins are committed. The only kind of politician who deserves respect is one who thinks of the consequences of his actions for those for whom he *necessarily* bears responsibility. (Necessarily, because there can be no adequate notion of political office without a concomitant conception of *some* responsibility of the officeholder on behalf of those he acts for.) Institutions are failing when they no longer call forth men ready to bear responsibility for their public acts. But equally men can fail their institutions: they can grow insensitive to the logic these impose on political life, and blind to the perpetual challenge to use and develop institutions creatively. This has begun to happen in Britain. There are too

---

[7]Max Weber, *"Politik als Beruf"*, in *Soziologie, Weltgeschichtliche Analysen, Politik*, Kröner, Stuttgart, 1956, p. 169.

few people in all sectors of public life willing to accept responsibility and ready to stand by the consequences of what they do.

According to conventional judgements all this strikes a pessimistic note. Yet there is nothing to be said for the optimism which consists in persuading ourselves that there are no difficult choices to be made and no losses to be sustained. It is that optimism which has in Britain bred a kind of paralysing inertia. (It is sometimes still called pragmatism or a spirit of compromise. It is nothing of the sort: it is sheer political escapism.) A serious optimism is akin to cautious hope. It springs from an awareness that at least we can try to determine our future. We can recognise the limits within which we must live, we can discern what then might be achievable, and we can shape the rules of political life according to a judgement of how authority should be constituted. We do not thereby avoid conflict, difficulty and tension. There is certainly no guarantee that all problems become soluble. But at least we can raise our eyes and look ahead.

This brings me to the point at which it is necessary to leave these general considerations in order to look more closely at particular aspects of British political institutions and to ask some questions about the principles on which they now appear to be based. At first sight it may be thought that this means drawing something like Bagehot's distinction between the dignified and the efficient elements in the Constitution[8] and identifying matters which today could be held to belong to the dignified sphere, though ostensibly still regarded as efficient. But that is not really so. The distinction which Bagehot drew is of dwindling relevance in contemporary conditions, acceptable only if it is understood as an injunction to be careful to try to distinguish the formal from what happens in reality. However, the weakness of Bagehot's analysis lay in his relative lack of interest in the terms on which even the efficient parts of the Constitution rested. He was anxious to describe what happened, but more or less indifferent to the problem of making sense of this by reference to the principles guiding the actors. One long-term consequence of this was, of course, that the very pragmatism of that analysis helped to

---

[8]Walter Bagehot, *The English Constitution,* first published 1867. The distinction between the efficient and the dignified is made throughout the work, and was similarly followed in the introduction by R. H. S. Crossman to the 1963 Fontana edition of the essay.

prepare the way for the weakening of the understanding of constitutional categories to which I have just referred. It reduced the British Constitution to pure description. Whilst it is clear that a definition of principles has to be extracted from what is rather than from what ought to be, it is nevertheless important to recognise that the present point of departure differs from that accepted by so many who have followed in Bagehot's footsteps. The objective is not to elicit "the secrets of the Constitution", but rather to outline the logic of particular relationships expressed in certain institutions. And this means that one must be careful not to take at their face value the reports of those engaged in the game of politics. Bearing that in mind it is appropriate to turn now to Parliament, the core of the traditional Constitution.

CHAPTER 4

Parliament: The Mirror of the Nation

There are many in Britain who profess to believe that only the British Parliament is a genuine species of the genus "parliament". The assertion is, of course, absurd. Yet it has an odd plausibility about it if we consider the way in which we in Britain talk about Parliament in everyday speech. The sophisticated will talk about Parliament being "sovereign"; the perplexed and worried might think about securing redress from Parliament, and the indignant might suggest that the will of Parliament is being flouted. The serious point here is that the English often refer to Parliament when other people might well talk of the law, or the people, or the State.

This has happened in part because Parliament has its roots so deep in our history, in part because it was in the name of Parliament that war was once waged against the Crown: to the extent that we ever had a revolution, it was a parliamentary revolution. It was on those events that the claims of Parliament to be the place where sovereignty is located in our political order were later founded. Though in strict constitutional terms sovereignty rests with the Crown in Parliament, the picture in the popular mind of the place where ultimate authority resides is still of that pseudo-Gothic pile alongside the Thames. In comparison the Crown has faded into no more than a vague and beneficent symbol of the national family.

So in the political imagery of the country, or at any rate of England, Parliament – and essentially this means in modern times the House of Commons – occupies a unique place, an institution which deeply influences our very political vocabulary. This is why it is not quite outrageous for Englishmen to talk as if all other parliaments were somehow or other like degenerate progeny or pale imitations of their own. For indeed there is probably no other country in which Parliament occupies such a special place in the political structure and in the language of politics. Nevertheless, as I shall argue in a moment, this is not to agree that a "special place" is still equivalent to the possession of decisive influence on political decisions, nor even to a clear understanding of the political functions of Parliament.

In the light of the history of Parliament during the twentieth century it is legitimate to discuss the political significance of the institution in terms of the elected chamber, the House of Commons. The House of Lords has been pushed to the margins of political life and survives in its present attenuated form chiefly because there is no basis for agreement on how an alternative revising chamber might be constituted. There is reason to believe that a revising chamber is useful, if only to provide opportunities for the technical improvement of legislation, and it might be held, too, that the facility of appointment to the Upper House affords to governments a degree of flexibility in finding suitable personnel which they would lose if dependent solely on the elected chamber. Yet in essentials the character of parliamentary government in Britain is now little affected by the survival of a bicameral legislature: it is the Commons which must stand at the centre of any account of what Parliament means for the British pattern of government.

There is no need here to recapitulate in full Bagehot's theses about the House of Commons and what it is said to do. But it is worth making some mention of the manner in which he characterised Parliament — his famous catalogue of functions running from the election of a cabinet through expressing the mind of the people, teaching and informing the people, to legislation — if only to underline certain crucial changes that have taken place. Too many writers are still ready to hark back to the eternal verities of Bagehot and fail to recognise the extent to which the conditions which gave support to his analysis, have long since gone.[1] Bagehot finished his work just before political parties in something like their modern form emerged and whilst the political public was extremely small. Can it make much sense to talk about the educative and informing functions of Parliament in the way in which Bagehot understood these terms, now that the small and relatively articulate public of his time has been replaced by a mass public, consisting chiefly of that very working class of which Bagehot

---

[1] Admittedly contemporary writers tend to concentrate on Bagehot's view of cabinet government. But his analysis of parliamentary functions in *The English Constitution* (1967) is also regularly taken as a point de départ. The most relevant chapter is V.

was so suspicious? After all, most of this mass public is unaware of Parliament and probably indifferent to what it does. Not even *The Times* nowadays devotes on average more than one page to reports from Parliament, whilst in most of the newspapers with a mass circulation there is either no mention of Parliament at all, or at best the occasional headline-making report and such snippets as are thought to have "story value". As for the radio and television, they do little to communicate what Parliament is doing, though to be fair Parliament has not been particularly helpful in providing facilities for their kind of reporting.

Again, Bagehot attributed such a subsidiary role to legislation simply because there was relatively little of it, and a large part of what there was consisted of measures of an essentially administrative kind, that is to say, of private acts. In the high Victorian summer there was a case for holding that it was declarations of general policy and specific executive and legislative decisions in pursuance of these which constituted the core of the work of government: it was on these and the principles they expressed that Parliament had to assert itself by expressing public opinion. But by the end of that epoch the situation had changed a lot. Dicey, for example, had at the end of the last century no illusions about the rapid growth of statute law and its significance as an instrument of change and of collectivist reform. And by his time it was already prudent to take a less optimistic view of Parliament's capacity to express public opinion: party was becoming dominant in the shaping of opinion in Parliament in a manner which would have shocked Bagehot. Yet the odd thing is that in the discussion of Parliament we are still more or less stuck with Bagehot's view of its functions and with his rank-ordering of them. There is still a presumption that Parliament is the sole mentor of the nation, whilst legislation is firmly relegated to the bottom of the list. Only in relation to the so-called "elective" function have commentators moved with the times. At least we accept that that has been claimed by the electorate, though as the 1974 elections showed they may not always wish to oblige.

Of course, there is another misleading aspect of Bagehot which lingers on in subtle ways. This is his oddly negative view of party. He wrote before parties as we know them had emerged (though he was on the brink of that change) and his experience was essentially of twenty years of party confusion. Though he did assert that party was inherent in the House of Commons ("bone of its bone, and breath of its breath"), he saw party ties chiefly as a kind of organising principle for enabling people to do business in the House. For Bagehot Britain was ruled by the broad band of opinion in the middle, the sensible people who did not take the ties of party and the commitments entered into on account of these too seriously. Thus, whilst acknowledging party in a vague way he was able to build up a picture of the working of the House of Commons which assumed that it was full of backbenchers, independently minded but ready to co-operate under reasonable leaders. Astonishingly enough a great deal of this mythology still survives. With hardly an exception the formal procedures of Parliament do not acknowledge the existence of parties (though early in 1975 the House of Commons quietly voted funds for the support of the work of its Opposition parties).[2] Above all, if one looks merely "at the face of the record", the on-going flow of words in *Hansard*, then one is easily tempted into believing that the Commons consists only of backbenchers and ministers (with shadow ministers occasionally bracketed with the real ones), and that the art of being a minister consists in paying a kind of ironic deference to all these independents on the backbenches.

All this is really to say that in trying to understand the role of Parliament, and more particularly the House of Commons, Bagehot should no longer be taken as a starting-point since many of his views on Parliament have been rendered obsolete by changes in the party environment and in the position of government. Most notably, the character and quantity of legislation has changed dramatically. It now expresses essentially the administrative requirements of governments and is the flesh and blood in which their policies are clothed. For this very reason it is surely a mistake to set its examination and approval so low in the scale of parliamentary functions. So I would argue that we should try to escape from the inherited categories and frame the questions we ask about Parliament with reference to the kind of world in which the institution actually exists and to the political needs and relationships to which it is now subject.

There are obviously three decisive factors at work shaping the conditions under which the British Parliament has to survive. The first is

---

[2] The voting of funds for Opposition parties in March 1975 was followed by the setting up of a committee to examine the case for subsidising parties in their extra-parliamentary work. This was an official committee presided over by an ex-Labour minister, not a parliamentary body. It reported in 1976, Cmnd 6601.

the dominance of the executive, not so much in the sense that a government can always do just what it wants, but that at any rate there is a presumption that most problems can be handled only through the direct involvement of the Government. In other words the demands facing Parliament flow insistently from the Executive. The second is the strength of party discipline: the institution of Parliament as such can very rarely assert an opinion which transcends party ties. And the third is the importance of organisations outside Parliament as representations of social interest. As we know, some of them can behave in ways which render the claims of Parliament to sovereignty a bad joke. But even if they refrain from doing this, their position is such that much of the work of government is dependent on agreement with them, despite what this might imply for the conventional claims of Parliament.

Clearly the conditions which I have just outlined are not peculiar to Britain. They exist in most advanced industrial societies and have for some time thrown a question mark over older ideas of parliamentary and representative government. But there are grounds for concluding that these conditions are most sharply defined in Britain and weigh more heavily on Parliament, not least because the claims made on its behalf have always been of such an extravagant nature. As has been said before, there is an intense commitment to the virtues of executive action in this country: we accept like sheep the providential view of the role of the Government. The governmental structure is markedly centralised, and this, too, is something which has been encouraged by the blind pressure for uniformity which has gone out from Parliament itself. The result is that the Government directs Parliament in an insistent and overwhelming manner for which there are few analogies in countries which lay serious claims to operate parliamentary government. This is in part because Government and Parliament are intertwined one with another in Britain in so intimate a way. There are relatively weak legislatures elsewhere whose situation is rendered tolerable by the distance which separates them from the Executive.

As far as party discipline goes, there too it seems that we suffer from an excess of it as compared with many other parliamentary democracies. It is true that by resorting to roll-call analysis and such techniques of measurement, it is possible to show that there are other countries in which parties are just as tightly disciplined, at any rate if the matter is judged in terms of voting cohesion in relation to the end-products of parliamentary activity. But that by no means tells the whole story. What is most important is the extent to which the internal structure of parties and the terms on which they determine their policies permit a genuine arbitration between different points of view and interest before final decisions are taken. The problem in Britain is that the formation of opinion in the parties – the *Willensbildung*, to use an evocative German expression – rarely amounts to a process of constructive intra-party negotiation in which there is some give and take, and out of which a reasonably firm consensus emerges. In the case of the party in office policy is either laid down from on high in virtue of a presumed mandate, or there is a noisy public argument in which usually the Government wins because it has most of the big sticks, but in which sometimes particular groups inside the parties may win because the Government and the official party leadership fear to oppose them.[3] Either way, there is a rigidity about intra-party policy formulation and a tendency towards the over-simplification of issues. A major consequence of this situation is that many important policy decisions in this country rest upon a very narrow base of consent, even within the party which happens to bear the responsibility for them. If the question is put why people generally seem prepared to accept such unsatisfactory ways of handling affairs inside the parties, then a substantial part of the answer has to be found in an inability to escape from the influence of an adversary conception of political relationships and argument. In other words, even when the results of an intra-party argument are wholly unsatisfactory, people continue to believe that they must never break ranks because to do so is to let in the adversary.

As to the role of interests outside the parties, the crucial problem here is the extent to which the latter are capable of expressing the former, yet without this going so far that the parties merely become the mouthpieces of particular interests. Here in Britain we again face a remarkable paradox. On the one hand, there are many interests whose links with parties are weak and tenuous and who to some extent feel thrown back on the benevolence of the Executive because they lack real influence inside this

---

[3] A notable example of this was the withdrawal in 1969 of the then Government's proposals for legislation on labour relations in deference to pressures inside the Parliamentary Labour Party and the trade unions.

or that party. Increasingly it can be seen that this is the case with business, and that its ties with the Conservative Party are far looser and more fragmentary than has usually been supposed. On the other hand, there are interests which have become so powerful that they can afford to ignore parties, or in the case of the trade unions simply to treat the Labour Party as a piece of property. At the very least the effect of these divergent conditions is to undermine such public respect as the parties might enjoy. People begin to realise that either the parties are unable to ensure that particular interests are recognised in the making of public policy, or that on some occasions they are merely like the dog on the gramophone label. Either way it is to the Executive rather than to Parliament that the interests in society must turn.

Such in outline is the background against which questions about the purposes now served by Parliament have to be asked. Later on some attention will be paid to the kind of political élite we have in this country and the effects on it of parliamentary experience. Perhaps this will throw more light on the extent to which Parliament is still a satisfactory representative body. But I want at present to concentrate on some of the things that Parliament does and in this way try to reach some conclusions about what sense we can still attach to the notion of "parliamentary government" in Britain.

When talking about things that Parliament does, I am referring primarily to the functions of control. And provided one takes a sufficiently broad view of control, then virtually all the active functions of a parliament can be brought under that heading. For what we are concerned with is the extent to which executive activities are influenced and the decisions of a government modified by the part played by the legislature.

What the House of Commons achieves by way of control will have to be summarised in a brief and somewhat dogmatic way. But the essential points are quite clear. Its influence over proposals for expenditure is virtually nil, and has been for many decades. It has a marginal *post-facto* influence on spending procedures through the Public Accounts Committee, but all attempts to strengthen its position before financial commitments are given statutory force have failed.[4] The impact of the

[4] This appears to be true of the post-1970 Expenditure Committee which has achieved little more than its more modest predecessor, the Estimates Committee.

House on taxation is not quite so vestigial, largely because of the survival of procedures which impose time constraints on governments and afford to members of the House substantial opportunities to oppose tax measures. The result is that tax proposals do get modified in detail, though rarely in principle. The changes are usually a kind of concession to exhaustion and, of course, do little to improve the general quality of an extremely complex and frustrating body of tax law. As to ordinary legislation, the House has similarly no effective and continuing influence on measures to which the Government is committed. There are the rare occasions like the House of Lords reform proposals of 1968–9 on which a government miscalculates and faces criticism from both sides which forces it to abandon its schemes. But the general rule is that immense legislative schemes, often hastily and badly prepared, are steam-rollered through the procedural hoops in Parliament and become law unaltered in all essentials. For practical purposes the legislative process, long and worrying though it may be for party managers, achieves remarkably little.[5]

However, the defender of the *status quo* will come along and say that this is to misunderstand the whole business of Parliament. Of course, Parliament is weak in the manner just outlined, but this is because it is not an executive body. It does not share power with the Government, it exposes the Government to criticism and to the judgement of public opinion. So we are told to look at the critical function of the House of Commons, the opportunities it enjoys for telling the Government what the public will not stand and for exacting from it an account of its actions. It is true that on the face of things the House has rather unusual opportunities for subjecting governments to scrutiny and pressure. On average there are over 30,000 questions per year, an even greater number of letters from members to ministers, adjournment debates on matters of constituency interest at the end of every sitting, many other procedural pegs on which to hang demands for information and justification of executive action, an increasing number of select committees which are entitled to poke into many corners of executive activity, and yet other inquisitorial procedures. Moreover, if we look carefully at the bulk of debates (including such dreary occasions as the interminable Budget

[5] A very judicious study by J. A. G. Griffith, *Parliamentary Scrutiny of Government Bills*, 1974, seems to bear out this view.

debates and those on the Queen's Speech) we find that between the ritual performances of the Front Benches, there are hours given over to the narrow preoccupations of back-benchers; the confrontation of policies is followed by the accumulation of specific pleas and complaints. In particular, the defender of the House of Commons as it is will underline the importance of debate and of the debating tradition. He will argue that the very life-blood of Parliament is the idea that virtually anything can be the subject of debate and of talk there. Yet what is being forgotten in this contention is that debate as we now understand it is largely (though not wholly) a nineteenth-century development. It expresses a particular style of conducting the political argument which may have been well adapted to the relatively intimate relationships of mid-nineteenth-century politics and to appealing to a small and for the most part educated public. But the style means little today: it cannot allow participants to reach out to the larger world on which they depend and, more important, it no longer expresses the manner in which problems are discussed and issues resolved in contemporary society. It is rather like trying to maintain a highly sophisticated literary style against the onslaught of a vernacular which prefers simpler and more direct modes of address. In fact, of course, much that passes for debate now bears no resemblance to conventional ideas of debate: it has become merely desultory talk, the conditioned reflexes of party competition and the often mechanical obedience to inherited procedures. Nevertheless, it is because of all the opportunities for debate and for demanding "the redress of grievances", so runs the traditional argument, that British government remains extraordinarily sensitive to public opinion and to Parliament as an institution.

Despite all the shortcomings it would do violence to the evidence to dismiss as quite ineffective all the efforts which the House of Commons makes to assert the accountability of government and to maintain an environment critical of this overgrown executive apparatus. Indeed, the relationship between ministers and Parliament remains important and has, too, major implications for the character of our central bureaucracy. What has to be appreciated is the contradictory nature of the reality with which we are confronted. True, Parliament has all these opportunities and holds on to them with remarkable tenacity. The parliamentary environment *does* make an imprint on British government. Yet at the same time much that Parliament is trying to do in the enforcement of accountability is now futile and misguided: it has literally no effect other than the immediate burden it throws on ministers and officials who have to respond. But Parliament has to continue to behave in this way because to abandon *these* efforts would be to run into an open confession of impotence: the populace would see that the Emperor has no clothes on. It is this paradox, this contradiction, which now has to be explained and justified.

At the heart of the paradox lies the British belief that government should be in the hands of ordinary men. The rationale of a Parliament is to ensure that this is so, both by guaranteeing that a considerable proportion of those who eventually become members of a government are indeed "ordinary men" (and women nowadays) and by ensuring that government remains subject to the criticisms of "ordinary men". Sometimes, of course, Parliament has been defended on the grounds that it encourages the best and the cleverest to aspire to govern. But on the whole this argument has mainly been advanced by the clever people — John Stuart Mill, for example. The more worldly-wise students of Parliament have preferred to argue that human abilities are but thinly distributed, and that Parliament is in this respect very representative. Therein lies its strength. There is little doubt that the view I am talking about retains much of its vitality. This is why Parliament in fact spends so much time expressing grievances, voicing complaints, pursuing hares. It does this because there persists an opinion that such is the natural stance of "the ordinary man" towards government. He must remain suspicious and rebellious, otherwise his liberty is endangered. It is irrelevant that we are here faced with another bundle of illusions, or that this attitude overlooks a vast contradiction contained in the British passivity in the face of the advancing claims of government to act for the common good. The fact is that Parliament survives here because it expresses the principle of complaint. And it is that which matters: not the fact that Parliament is a kind of omnipresent impotence, not the reality of many of the complaints put forward, nor the actual chances of ensuring that anything useful is done as a result of the complaints having been voiced.

Thus we have an activity pursued in Parliament which has many of the characteristics of ritual. And yet it is not mere ritual. There is a certain respect paid by the Executive to the continuing stream of parliamentary pressure. This happens because generally the Executive too (and remember that all its members are themselves parliamentarians and know the conventions) believes that it is in its interests to show deference to the demands put forward in Parliament. Little may be conceded, perhaps on many occasions little *can* be conceded, since the complaints are ill-informed or misguided. But the gesture of listening must be made, the vanity of Parliament must be flattered. And it is precisely because the Government acknowledges the presence of Parliament in this way that we can regard the continual demand for explanation and information, for justification and promise of action, as having a real effect on the behaviour of governments. It puts them on the defensive, gives them the feeling of being always under an obligation to justify their actions, and teaches them the value of a political exposition which will quieten the fears of our "ordinary man". So they spend a lot of time on political self-defence, far more than do governments in most other democracies. If as a result of this situation much goes undone and much is done badly, then that is the price we pay for maintaining the belief that Parliament in some mysterious way symbolises the British people, assembled there to give grudging assent to the acts of government.

If the matter is looked at unsentimentally, it cannot be doubted that much of the critical activity of Parliament is misguided and without practical effect: it is kept going in deference to a myth and up to now the myth has not quite lost its grip on the popular imagination. It retains a certain efficacy. But my argument is that the British Parliament teeters dangerously on the brink of discovering the truth about itself. Even its more traditionalist members hardly bother to disguise the weakness of the House of Commons in all the substantial activities of control — finance, law-making and the like. The threat that now hangs over the institution is that very soon faith in its ability to maintain the responsiveness of government will collapse, the ritual will become mere ritual, and questions will be asked which have not been asked for a very long time. The threat is there only in part because of the irrelevance of much of the critical activity of Parliament and the lack of specific results flowing from it. It is there, too, because the ties of party have become so rigid that they begin to subvert any sense of the institution of Parliament as something distinct from the parties which work in and through it. So, increasingly, the claims which are wearily made on behalf of Parliament have a hollow and mechanical tone about them: we know that Parliament as such has become a shadow.

However, in spite of all this, we have not quite reached this breakdown of faith, as indeed I accepted right at the start. What then keeps Parliament alive? I have already alluded to one of the answers, and that is the absence of any alternative tradition of how to constitute political authority. So pervasive has been the role of Parliament in our history that we have hardly any idea that perhaps the people might themselves constitute authority by giving themselves a basic law, a constitution. Only once did this idea of the people as *le pouvoir constituant* find expression. This was in the course of the seventeenth-century constitutional conflicts. But it savoured then of extreme radicalism and succumbed to forces already strongly entrenched in British institutions. It was, nevertheless, to wander off to the American colonies, where later it served as the foundation of a new state.

But to come back to the question about the survival of Parliament, narrower answers can also be given to it, more closely tied to contemporary political life and practice. We have a peculiarly tenacious faith in the idea of having members who represent constituencies, of people who are chosen to represent a locality in the national speaking-place. The odd thing is that this conviction coexists with the practice of carpet-bagging, and with a situation in which many seats are virtually put up for auction and go to the man who best pleases tiny and often unrepresentative selection committees. Belonging to the locality has usually been of little importance, though it is an interesting sign of the times that rather more constituencies seem now to be showing some preference for candidates who either do have some local ties or promise to act very much as spokesmen for local opinions and interests. (There are shades of the imperative mandate about here, at any rate in the Labour Party, as well as the influence of an idea of community politics). Anyway the continuing strength of the idea of constituencies being represented in the House of Commons means that many members — almost certainly a majority — discern their first role as being that of an ombudsman for their constituency and quite often for particular pressure groups too. Of course, at the same time many members share a common ambition to become a minister of some kind or another, whilst there is still a substantial number who pursue a profession and thus remain half-time politicians.

What happens in practice is that over time members then divide into two categories. There are those who gain office and for that very reason become less dependent on their local ombudsman role, and there are those who fail to get office (or do not seek it) and in consequence concentrate mainly on attending to the matters referred to them by constituents and others. The expansion of government and its centralisation has tended to strengthen the ombudsman role of members, or at any rate to make it appear more important. The range of complaints they receive has widened and their readiness to pass them on to the central government has increased *pari passu*. Bold indeed would be the Member of Parliament who would encourage his constituents to look after themselves, to address their complaints to the local authority or such other public agency as may be appropriate and competent, or to engage a lawyer. The disposition is to accept the complaint and to pass it on to the all-seeing and all-caring central authority.

Then, too, we must not underestimate the importance of the idea that Parliament is a continuing presence. It is a fact that the House of Commons sits for more days and more hours than the legislature of any other major democracy. It is a regrettable fact, too, that its hours of work are not only long, but remarkably inconvenient, as if calculated to make the life of members intolerable and to drain away their energies. The extraordinary thing is that as the powers of government have expanded and as the demands imposed on the House of Commons have increased in range and complexity, there has been no noticeable change in the manner in which the House uses its time. Obviously it would be absurd to extend the sitting time. The alternative is to make more efficient use of the time already available. But since nobody can be in two places at once, the only way in which the House of Commons could accommodate many contemporary needs would be by shifting away from the doctrine that the House as a whole must always be in session. In other words Parliament would have to take on board the idea of specialisation, accept that for most members politics is a full-time professional activity, and recognise that much of what goes on in plenary sessions would have to be abandoned.

It is not intended here to make yet another contribution to the arguments about committees which have been so fashionable for the past ten years or so. The notable thing about them is that so many of the exponents of more and more committees seem to have believed that a man can be in two places at once! In other words, the case for more committees has been made without any recognition of the necessity of making a sacrifice in other directions − another case of the reluctance to make a choice. But it is reasonable to hold that the House of Commons can benefit from greater specialisation (whether for legislative scrutiny or for administrative inquiry) only if it stops doing other things: this is the way in which priorities would be changed and members made to realise that they could achieve something in directions now barred to them. We are, however, a long way from such a change of outlook, as was shown, for example, in the discussions which have surrounded the setting-up of committees to scrutinise the output of EEC instruments from Brussels. Here is a formidable scrutiny task. But the House managed to persuade itself that it can and should be taken on as a net addition to everything else. The result was that the House later found itself having confused and sometimes quite pointless debates in the early hours of the morning on matters which the House as such could not understand and on which as a rule it can have no influence.[6]

A final point needing emphasis is that the survival of Parliament, notwithstanding its current weaknesses, depends extensively on the simple fact that it is, with rare exceptions, from this source alone that the personnel of government can be recruited. Those who aspire to govern must first pass through this funnel. The British often fail to see how unique they are in this respect. It is true that there are many other countries which are governed by what can roughly be described as "parliamentary élites". However, the character of such élites is modified and diversified by many structural factors, e.g., by the presence of provincial or regional levels of government, by ethnic or religious influences, by the fact that many countries tolerate much more movement between politics and administration than we do in the United Kingdom, or by a preference for candidates for political office who have first picked up

---

[6]From late 1972 until early 1974 both Houses of Parliament considered what kind of committees should be set up to scrutinise European secondary legislation, with the result that eventually both Houses set up scrutiny committees, the Lords in February and the Commons in May 1974. The committee set up by the latter was affected by political differences as much as by the backlog of work it faced, and by late 1974 was recommending plenary debate on a considerable number of draft regulations, etc. The difficulty of finding time to debate them on the floor of the House then became obvious, as well as the limited value of the debating opportunities themselves.

substantial experience outside politics in some other sphere altogether. Whatever the variations may be, the main point is that there are few countries in which the parliamentary élite is shaped so completely and so exclusively by the experience of its members from an early age inside the national Parliament. This is our peculiarity and, so long as it escapes challenge, a great bulwark of the House of Commons.

Whoever reflects on the unchallenged role of the House of Commons in shaping those who govern this country is faced with a puzzle. Life in that institution is not really attractive. The working facilities are poor, the hours long and inconvenient, and much of the activity there of appalling boredom. For some it is a life of great uncertainty and, for most, of relative penury. There is for many a reasonably good chance of achieving some kind of public office, though only a few can hope to join the group which enjoys high office. The average member disposes of virtually no patronage and his own hopes of reward must not be pitched too high. Why then are men and women attracted into such a way of life, and why above all are they so keen to stay there once elected?

Part of the answer must be found in the inertia of the political system. This is how the membership of governments has been recruited for a couple of centuries or so (longer if we bring the House of Lords into the picture), and it is hard to imagine any other way. So those who aspire to political office accept the burdens of apprenticeship with as good grace as possible. There is, too, some lingering prestige still attaching to the position of a Member of Parliament, though it is hard nowadays to assess the quality and significance of this. But what appears to be very important is the sheer personality of the institution. It has an extraordinary capacity to absorb people and to make them ready to accept all its own peculiarities. More than that, it can turn most of them into devoted defenders of the procedural accretion of centuries which is the very definition of the British Parliament.

Why this is so presents a perplexing problem, the explanation of which would go far beyond the scope of these considerations. Undoubtedly the English are remarkably susceptible to the charms of institutional continuity: they reveal this in all sorts of ways, often quaint and endearing, outside the bounds of conventional political institutions. Perhaps even the grandiloquent pomposity of Barry's Gothic palace has something to do with the phenomenon in question: the building is like some gigantic stage set, meant for ritual and the acting out of an unending play. But it is not meant for business and management of the practical affairs of life, at any rate not in our present world.

Yet these are but fragmentary explanations. We have simply to accept the fact that the institution of Parliament still succeeds in imposing itself on those who become members of it whilst relatively young. This is an observable phenomenon. Strikingly enough, it is particularly those who enter Parliament as young men who are nearly always completely absorbed by it. Those who have made their lives elsewhere and have perhaps achieved much in other spheres rarely adapt themselves fully to its peculiarities. In a negative way this suggests that the impact of Parliament is not so unique as I am suggesting: there may be antidotes to it. However, as a rule, members are nearly always ready to defend its methods and to question the very possibility of changes in them. And since there is no other tradition of politics, who can gainsay them?

The picture which has been painted of the condition of the House of Commons and of the part which it plays within our political arrangements has highlighted many of the weaknesses of this vital element in the institution, Parliament. Yet it has to be accepted that parliamentary government in a certain sense of that term survives. Parliament is the channel through which ruling élites are maintained and renewed. The Government in this country still presents itself and its policies extensively within the parliamentary context, and for that very reason has to defend itself according to the procedures and conventions of Parliament. And no matter how weak the House of Commons and its members may have become in practice, no matter how subject they are to the requirements of party competition, they retain some sense of possessing the sovereign authority in this country. One feels that perhaps, in an extremity, the House could assert itself and embody the people of Britain. (Maybe that is to express a view of sovereignty which sits uneasily in contemporary societies, as well as to hint at a general will for which pluralism can have no place. But if sovereignty in a Hobbesian or Austinian sense really is a myth in the pluralist society, then at least there are some claims which certainly should no longer be made on behalf of the House of Commons.)

The British system of government retains then a core which is obstinately parliamentary in something like the senses just indicated. For the rest Parliament suffers from the weaknesses which have nearly everywhere affected parliamentary institutions in some degree, but which affect Westminster in a particularly acute form. This is fundamentally because traditional views of the role of Parliament have combined with the structure and behaviour of parties to exclude Parliament from any longer exerting a significant influence on the shaping of powers and their exercise. There is little that can be directly and visibly attributed to the action of Parliament or of forces and structures within it. This makes it more difficult to invest the decisions of government with a genuine parliamentary authority, despite all the appearances which are still preserved. This in turn contributes to the political weakness which is now apparent. However, given the dominance of the parliamentary tradition, the vital practical question is then whether this country is still capable of innovating within that tradition. Is that tradition and the procedures in which it is embodied still capable of accommodating the kind of radical adjustments in institutional relationships which are required if political authority is to be strengthened and Parliament to be seen to be making an effective contribution to that end? It is hard to give an affirmative answer with confidence. Nevertheless, it is equally difficult to envisage as a practical possibility any re-invigoration of the principles on which the political order rests except within the framework of familiar institutions.

   This line of argument implies that there is still some sense and value in the pursuit of the reform of parliamentary institutions. But this must be done seriously and with an understanding of the issues of principle at stake and of the ends which such reform should serve. Unfortunately, during the past decade there have been so many naive attempts at parliamentary reform that the whole effort has been brought into discredit. Many of the changes have been a tribute to the blindness and even the frivolity of the reformers rather than evidence of their realisation that what is at issue is the survival of parliamentary government in something more than a merely formal and ritualistic guise.

   To refer critically to recent parliamentary reform is not to be taken as a rejection of change. The fact is that these reforms have reflected sometimes self-deception and sometimes deliberate attempts to deceive others. Many of the protagonists of more select committees of scrutiny, for example, have just failed to see that as such committees have no real powers and are detached from party interests, they are thus committed to fundamentally academic exercises. And experience shows that the House of Commons — by which one means both the Government in the House as well as the House itself which has absorbed the guidance of government — will then take practically no notice of what they do. Scrutiny therefore becomes an activity which keeps a growing number of back-benchers out of mischief: its end product is a growing quantity of paper, voluminous reports and evidence which constitute quarries of great importance for future students of government, but impinge only slightly on current action. This is where self-deception takes place, with people pretending to results which can never in fact be attained. As to deliberate deception, there are ministers who have practised this, preaching reform and yet dedicated to enhancing Executive powers. It can be assumed, too, that successive chief whips of both parties have nearly always leaned in this direction. What we have had as a result has been a variety of "reforms", the purpose of which has been to satisfy the voices on the back-benches calling for a bigger role, and at the same time to ensure that the supremacy of the Executive is in no way infringed. In the playing out of this game select committees have been one of the principal counters, though there have been other expedients like morning sittings, smaller standing committees, relegation of much of the Finance Bill to a standing committee and some increase in the chances of securing debates on matters of urgency.[7]

The net result of ten years of institutional tinkering in the House of Commons is plain to see. No changes have taken place which have altered significantly the manner in which the House operates nor the influence which it can exert. Perhaps the only development which potentially may gradually change the character of the place is the very proliferation of committees: inevitably this has taken members out of the chamber and done something to weaken the sense of the importance of the whole House. On the other hand, the unremitting pressures of party discipline

[7]Many of the procedural changes made between 1966 and 1970 are commented on in A. H. Hanson and B. Crick (eds.), *The Commons in Transition*, Fontana, 1970. There is a substantial post-1970 literature on various aspects of parliamentary development. Notwithstanding what is still regarded by many as a decade of "reform" the Government still found it necessary to announce in late 1975 that it wished to arrange for "a fundamental review" of the procedures of the Commons. This seemed to suggest either that the "reform" had been illusory or that it had been carried out on the wrong principles.

still enforce attendance in the chamber for frequent votes: members cannot vanish entirely into committees.

Though the various reforms which have taken place have had little effect — as was testified to by a 1975 government promise of a major review of procedure — this does not mean that the manner in which we structure institutions is of no importance. On the contrary it is possible to discern structural changes in the House of Commons which would have profound consequences. An obvious example would be a radical change in the manner in which legislation is handled in committee.[8] At present standing committees are essentially the chamber in miniature, operating a debating procedure which is unsuitable for the work in hand and controlled largely by ministers. If instead bills were handed over to specialised (and quasi-permanent) committees which operated through an amalgam of select and standing committee procedures, then the balance of power in the House would begin slowly to shift. Again, if the House used its power to adjourn on Wednesdays or abolished Questions on two days a week, these measures too would have a big impact, forcing the House gradually to reassess its rationale. Indeed, the problem is not the impossibility of devising effective institutional changes, it is the difficulty of securing assent to such schemes. For of one thing there can be no doubt whatsoever. Experience in the House of Commons breeds an intense institutional inertia, and in particular develops in members a very keen sense of what kind of changes will damage the customary relationships and procedures. So it is not easy to persuade the House to accept genuine reform, let alone to gain the support of a government for such a course.

This leads to the final point: what would be the basic condition of genuine change in the manner in which the House of Commons operates? The answer is obvious, of course. The House can change only to the extent that it accepts a redefinition of the terms on which parties interact in it, and to the extent that the parties themselves acquire a different understanding of themselves and the purposes they serve. *A fortiori* this means that we must be prepared to accept some redefinition of the relationship between the Government and Parliament. All else risks being

---

[8]It is worthy of note that the White Paper, *Our Changing Democracy: Devolution to Scotland and Wales,* does recommend for a Scottish Assembly permanent subject committees empowered to examine all aspects of legislation, a model which has always been rejected at Westminster. Cmnd. 6348, paragraphs 76—9 refer.

an exercise in self-deception. When I talk about a redefinition of the relationship between Government and Parliament, I have in mind the achievement of a more balanced relationship in which Parliament would more often be a counterweight to the executive power. This in turn could come about only if there were in Parliament political forces willing and able to impose restraints both procedural and substantive on a government. That would imply either of two possibilities. One is a shift to a multi-party situation in which single-party majority government becomes impossible, the other (and this is less likely) is a shift towards much more internal diversity inside the present major parties.

What all this implies is that a drastic change in one of the key concepts of British politics, the idea of adversary politics, has to be contemplated. We should have to turn away from asserting the value of a two-party system and the virtues of a constant competition between Government and Opposition, and recognise that the continuance of this mode of politics is the basic reason why no serious change can be made in the manner in which we manage our political life. In other words, it is adversary politics and the two-party syndrome which are inexorably destroying the political vitality of Parliament itself. There are grounds for holding that all prospect of real change is sacrificed on the altar of preserving these relationships.

This already signalises the next theme to be discussed. So far an effort has been made to establish a link between the institution, Parliament, and the dominant ideas which are expressed in the way in which it has developed and operated for most of this century. It will, however, not have escaped notice that so far next to nothing has been said about Opposition, and the question arises how such a grave omission can be justified. The reason is that to see Opposition purely as a parliamentary phenomenon, a facet of parliamentary organisation and behaviour, is to see the idea in too narrow a context. For the idea of Opposition is not merely something which is enshrined in the institutional arrangements of the House of Commons and in its daily behaviour. It is expressive of a particular way of thinking about the kind of relationships which it is desirable to maintain in the political life of the country. These relationships are held to be adversarial, and the preference is justified by an appeal to democratic values as well as to the argument that such relationships offer a good solution to the problem of how to control government and guard against the abuse of power. The notion and practice of Opposition is but the institutionalisation in Parliament of this adversary mode of politics.

The next stage is, therefore, to examine the character and consequences of adversarial politics. That in turn will allow me to indicate what is the obvious alternative within a parliamentary framework, a mode of coalition politics. This is not to deny alternatives outside the parliamentary mould, e.g., a presidential solution (or in this country should one say, Cromwellian?). But since for the present most people seem reluctant to move at all, it seems that little advantage can be gained from contemplating the even more remote possibility of their breaking with the parliamentary tradition as consolidated by the end of the seventeenth century. Prescriptive argument too must acknowledge some of the constraints of history.

CHAPTER 5

Adversary Politics and Institutionalised Opposition

It is the exaggeration of a political concept which often brings about its own decay. This is what has happened in the pursuit of an adversary relationship in British politics. Competitive two-party politics has been developed to such a point that success in the competition is all that matters. The sense of there being a common good or a public interest to which all parties might contribute and in which the whole society has a share has for practical purposes atrophied. The institutionalised expression of adversary politics has, of course, been the practice of Opposition, That, too, has been developed to an extreme, so much so that the activity of opposing often enough risks tipping over into something indistinguishable from the mere negation of government. Certainly this appears to have been the interpretation of the function of the Opposition most often put into practice by both major parties in recent years.[1]

Regrettably, few people appear to recognise how serious are the implications of such a view of opposition for the very survival of democratic politics. In the Labour Party the strengthening of ideological opposition has served to whet the appetite in recent years for an accentuation of the negative elements in the role of institutionalised Opposition. On the Conservative side of the political spectrum there are still traces of a reluctance to push the practice of opposition to destructive extremes, as indeed the attitude of the Conservative Party leadership on a number of issues arising after the party's relegation to Opposition in 1974

---

[1] There might appear to be a precedent for this view of Opposition in the conduct of the Conservative Party between 1908 and 1914. But this is hardly so. No matter how much later generations may disapprove of the causes motivating Conservative opposition at that time, they constituted for many of those involved genuine issues, so much so that they were ready, though no doubt in part for selfish reasons, to turn opposition to the Liberal Government of those years into a *guerre à outrance*.

showed. Yet the Conservative Party, too, has often enough been a victim of the competitive pressures of the relationships which are supposed to exist between Government and Opposition, blowing up criticism of government measures simply because that is what the conventions are thought to demand. To criticise, to argue against, to act against – all that can be a positive and constructive view of opposition. But merely to deny because the rules require it, indeed to deny by conditioned reflex, to act in this way is ultimately to question the foundations of the political community. This is the danger which is immanent in the concept of institutionalised Opposition.

It is necessary to develop further this critique of adversary politics and of the idea and practice of Opposition associated with it. But before starting on that it is worth remembering that the results of the two elections of 1974 have already put a question mark over the survival of the habits under scrutiny here.[2] It is true that after a few months of a "no majority" situation the country returned in October of that year to something which looked slightly like a normal majority government. But, of course, this would be a superficial view of the position. The fact is that neither major party commands anything like a majority in the electorate, nor has much prospect of so doing. Between those supporting the two larger parties there were in 1974 about seven million voters who had chosen one of several other parties; in the House of Commons itself there are nearly forty members elected in October 1974 who belong to third parties; in some parts of the United Kingdom loyalties have clearly shifted right away from the Labour and Conservative parties to nationalist groups; and in England in particular the Liberal Party appears to have the support

2 The results of the elections of 1974 were as follows:

	February 1974		October 1974	
	Seats gained	Percentage share of vote	Seats gained	Percentage share of vote
Conservative	297	37·9	277	35·8
Liberal	14	19·3	13	18·3
Labour	301	37·1	319	39·2
Scottish National Party	7	2·0	11	2·9
Plaid Cymru	2	0·4	3	0·6
Northern Ireland (all parties)	12	2·3	12	2·4
Others	2	0·5	0	0·4

Source: *British Political Facts*, D. Butler and A. Sloman, 4th edition, 1975.

of a large and heterogeneous block of voters who, as far as their representation goes, are the victims of an electoral system which increasingly looks like a device for shoring up the *ancien régime*.

So the behaviour of the voters suggests already that the two-party system is cracking up. But it will be argued that no firm conclusions can be drawn from recent experience: perhaps people will soon return to their customary allegiance and all will be well. This seems very implausible. On the contrary, there are grounds for believing that the fragmentation of the two-party pattern which became so visible in 1974 is but the expression of a long-standing frustration with the effects of what has been essentially "government without consensus", to adopt the title of Richard Rose's book about Northern Ireland and its politics.

It may seem bizarre indeed to suggest that over the past fifteen or more years Britain has had government without consensus. But the idea is by no means as perverse as may appear at first sight. There is the obvious fact that for a long time there has been no underlying agreement in the society and between the parties about the principles governing the management of the economy and the development of the social services. In real political terms the broad centre spanning both parties has proved unable to articulate or sustain a consensus on these matters, and increasingly often pertinacious minorities have called the tune. We have an electoral law which seriously exaggerates the effects of small movements of opinion and by so doing has a marked impact on the competitive character of political life. Though at one election after another party preferences have shifted only marginally, this has not prevented the formation of governments which have claimed a mandate for measures which, by no conceivable stretch of the imagination, can be said to have had the support of a majority within the electorate. And in addition there is the internal structure of the major parties which, as I have suggested already, is peculiarly hostile to the building of a soundly based consensus even within a single party, let alone to the creation of an agreement which extends beyond the bounds of party. So it by no means outrages experience to suggest that our so-called majority governments have in recent years acquired more and more the real character of minority governments, and that this has happened because the structure of parties and certain dominant conceptions of how political relationships should be expressed have conspired to obscure a serious understanding of the conditions of achieving a genuine consensus. And the supreme irony is that we now face a condition in which, precisely because there is no majority in the political community, there is no authority which a government can claim to wield when faced by the demands of recalcitrant minorities.

Let me come back, however, to adversary politics and to the meaning I attach to that term. Briefly this amounts to the maintenance of relationships of political competition through a mode of argument which assumes that political questions can best be resolved if expressed in terms of two and only two contrasting alternatives. Furthermore, it is held in Britain that by a happy coincidence such alternatives are normally voiced by two competing groups of politicians. For this reason adversary politics becomes more than a way of conducting political argument: it becomes a mechanism of choice too.

What appears to be eccentric about this particular conception of adversary politics is the belief that all serious political argument ought, *from the beginning to the end,* to be cast in terms of two competing and mutually exclusive alternatives. It seeks to make pervasive the convention that debate can take place only on a motion which, by definition, has to be accepted or rejected. But it is absurd to try to confine the life of a society within a procedural straitjacket which is useful only for very specific and restricted purposes. The issues which come up for resolution are hardly ever as simple as this convention pretends, and anyway we know well enough that there are always many interests to be accommodated and many different ways of achieving particular purposes. So at any rate in the process of formulating policy, of moving towards a situation in which there is some agreement on what is to be done, it is plainly irrational to force matters into the Procrustean mould of "either/or". To do so is to narrow the basis of consent and to increase the chances of taking decisions which are both unsound in practical terms and resented by those who are overriden. As to the conventions of debate, what is apparently forgotten is that not all debate needs to follow the stereotype of a grand clash in the House of Commons. Debate may take the form of discussion and can end — or be replaced — by a recognition that decisions need to be founded on something like a consensus of opinion rather than on the triumph of a simple and often slender majority. And after all, many bodies in Britain proceed in their domestic affairs precisely on such a principle, thereby confirming that formalised, ritualised debate is by no means always the best procedure for resolving many questions.

For many, however, it remains hard to imagine that politics can be conducted except through what are held to be the great traditions of public debate. Many foreign legislatures are regarded with disfavour because their members are said to be far too willing to bury themselves in the more or less executive tasks of legislative and administrative scrutiny, and by so doing to let pass the opportunities to simplify and dramatise issues by talking out through the windows to the public beyond. But the Westminster ideal of a debating Parliament as contrasted with a working Parliament is now better worshipped from afar. True, it is an ideal with a touch of nobility about it, evoking the image of enlightened and responsible representatives appealing in serious argument to each other's hearts and minds before a public opinion alert and responsive to the deliberations of its representatives. But all this is far from the reality. The cult of continuous debate is obsolete. The mistake consists in the exaggerated attempt to live up to the ideal day by day. In contemporary conditions this is impossible: debate is not an appropriate procedure for forming an opinion and reaching a decision on so many of the questions which require public action. Instead, by sustaining the crude notion of adversary politics which has been outlined, the cult of debate has encouraged irresponsible competition between parties, over-simplification of problems and issues, and a depressing waste of human energies. There is no necessary reason why a mode of political argument appropriate to one age should suit the needs of another. The time has come for this country to recognise the price it pays for clinging to the adversary mode of politics and the procedure of formalised debate in which it is embodied. Where conflict does not exist, adversary politics manufactures it; where genuine conflict is present, adversary politics will exacerbate it and may in the end frustrate its resolution; and where there is a many-sided and complex pattern of interests involved in the political argument, adversary politics imposes on it its own crudities and dogmatism.

Such are some of the consequences of retaining a particular understanding of how to conduct the political argument. And, incidentally, let us not forget how few are the countries in which the British view of adversary politics actually prevails: even in parts of the old Commonwealth like Canada it is heavily modified by provincialism and linguistic-cultural differences. I shall come back in a moment to the relevance of electoral reform as a method of counteracting this view of political relationships. But before turning to that possibility it is necessary to discuss the idea of Opposition, the very institutionalisation within the State of the concept of adversary politics.

If we consider the matter historically, it seems reasonably clear that the modern notion of Opposition stems not so much from conflict between parties as from the idea that political responsibility cannot be divided or shared out. The Crown must have a council or a cabinet (as it became in the course of the eighteenth century), and this cabinet must show collective responsibility both towards the Crown itself and towards Parliament. Perhaps it is this idea which is really expressed in the famous quip attributed to Lord Melbourne, that it did not so much matter whether the price of corn went up or down so long as the members of the cabinet all said the same thing. After all, party in the modern sense did not then exist, but the idea that a cabinet must speak with one voice obviously did. Even before party took its modern shape the idea of Opposition as an alternative set of ministers able and willing to serve the Crown had struck root. Gradually, in the course of the nineteenth century, the dominant commitment which held cabinets together ceased to be the ideal of service of the Crown — carrying on the Queen's Government — and became instead party allegiance and loyalty. As parties became more coherently organised, so Opposition came to mean that a party in Parliament was prepared to provide the alternative government, and in turn as party discipline strengthened, the power of choosing such an alternative passed from Crown and Parliament to people. Inevitably the role of Opposition tended more and more in the direction of seeking to discredit a government in the hope of thereby convincing the electorate that a change was needed.[3] Both government and alternative government became victims of the rules of that game which is best described as "adversary politics with institutionalised Opposition". The contemporary consequences of this — to which I have already referred — is that Opposition becomes on occasion the negation of government. In the minds of the people the

[3]One of the truisms of contemporary electoral behaviour research seems to be that Oppositions do not win elections; instead Governments lose them. The exact status of such an assertion is obscure, but British experience provides some examples which seem to support it.

impression is created that there is not, and indeed cannot be, a public or common interest which it is the duty of the Government to try to express and in which the critics of the Government have a stake. Instead, even on the gravest questions, they have the spectacle of the prime minister or some other senior minister declaring government policy, only to be followed the next day by the shadow prime minister or some other shadow minister who attempts *on similar terms* to put the "official" alternative. Few systems of government can have institutionalised the role of Mephistopheles as effectively as the British.

To question the wisdom of "Opposition" in this special sense is not to question the rights of opposition as such, nor the value and necessity of critical public argument and discussion. Nor is it to dispute that a country needs to have alternative groups of personnel who can assume the responsibilities of government if the electorate so wish or the needs of building up agreement so dictate. It is instead to question whether any country can in the long run be governed according to a convention which virtually denies the possibility of there being a public interest and the need for office-holders who, *pro tempore*, are entitled to try to express this interest. Perhaps in certain small and tightly-knit societies where stable over-arching conventions of social and political behaviour play a large part, it might be possible to carry on public affairs on this basis. But it is hard to take an optimistic view of such a possibility in a society in which parties are rapidly losing public respect, in which the understanding of constitutional rules is in decline, and in which sectional socio-economic interests have suddenly discovered the enormous power which they can wield. In such conditions the forces of disintegration have become so strong that a countervailing power is needed. In a free society it is hard to discern where this can be found other than in an idea of the public interest, in an agreement that there are values which transcend particular interests. It is then the duty of a government to protect these values and to seek to ensure that the public interest is formulated on particular occasions in a way which does justice to the individual and partial interests which it must respect and embody. It becomes illogical, therefore, to maintain procedures and conventions which encourage a mode of opposition destructive of that very common interest. The challenge is to find a more rational understanding of those rights of opposition to which a free society must remain committed.

Much that has been said contradicts the received wisdom about the way in which the British political system works. It does not accept that under the adversary mode of two-party competition with institutionalised Opposition coherent and stable governments are always and automatically secured, nor that these are always disciplined by the need to moderate their policies in order to compete successfully with the Opposition for the "middle ground". It questions whether the practice of Opposition any longer does much to enforce the accountability of government other than in an empty, dramatic sense, and it disputes whether this form of competition has such beneficial effects in terms of maintaining effective leadership groups as have conventionally been attributed to it. And, finally, it challenges the widely held belief that under prevailing British conventions there is any longer a flow of authority from people to the majority in Parliament which legitimises the pattern of government more directly and more surely than is possible under a system of institutional checks and balances or of coalition.

This critique of adversary politics and the practice of Opposition can be pursued further through some reflections on coalition as an alternative principle in the British context. Though unfamiliar to the British in practice, coalition is at least not such an uncomfortable idea as might be the concept of public interest to which reference has just been made. That after all raises the spectre of the State, the need to have some conceptual understanding of what it means to embody an idea of public interest in the life and institutions of a society. Rather than tackle at the moment such a difficult prospect, let me proceed obliquely by a consideration of coalition.

The idea of coalition and the prospect of more than two parties are supposed to worry the British greatly. In fact we do not really know whether this is so, though there are many whose professional interest leads them to assert that it is so. As far as coalition goes the British have no experience of genuine coalition. For just over a century this has been true. What there has been on some occasions, notably during two world wars and to a large extent in 1931–2, is a suspension of party politics in favour of a "national government". This was the essential meaning of such coalitions as we have had. Parties gave up their normal competitive activities in order to combine for very specific and easily understood purposes. Now this is certainly not coalition as understood elsewhere, whether in the United States or on the continent of Europe. Genuine coalition is a species of power-sharing by groups. They enter into such arrangements in order to secure a majority and to serve such interests as they represent. And, of course, no time limit need to be set to coalition arrangements: in Switzerland at least they appear to be eternal.

There is, however, an odd fact about British blindness to coalition. This is that we are perfectly well able to understand its applicability and utility in other circumstances than those we fondly imagine to be our own. The best recent example of this is the adoption of a policy of "power-sharing" in Northern Ireland, initially by a Conservative Secretary of State, but then (one of those rare recent cases of bipartisanship) confirmed by a Labour government.[4] This was never officially called coalition, and indeed it is an interesting speculation that perhaps power-sharing might have become more acceptable to the dominant majority in Northern Ireland had it been interpreted as a doctrine of coalition in the interests of securing a concurrent majority. However, that is of no particular relevance to this argument. The crucial point is that an understanding of coalition is not wholly unattainable in Britain: maybe all that is required to make it a familiar experience is an electoral arrangement which will make it clear that Britain too cannot tolerably be governed without a form of power-sharing which binds to the decisions of public authority broader majorities than can any longer be bound by the mechanism of adversary politics.

To suggest that coalition as a principle of government might have something to recommend it is to run the gauntlet of many objections in Britain. I shall have to mention some of them, if only to set up a foundation on which to present the argument that one of the major structural changes which needs to be considered seriously is a reform of the electoral law, in other words the abandonment of the principle of relative majorities in single-member constituencies. What then is alleged against coalition?

[4] The White Paper, *Northern Ireland Constitutional Proposals*, Cmnd. 5259, March 1973, committed the Government of the day to the condition that any scheme for self-government in the Province must bind the majority and the minority alike (para 52 of Cmnd. 5259 refers). This has been stuck to by subsequent governments. But it should be noted that this condition need not entail "power-sharing" as vulgarly understood.

It is argued for the present system that it renders the electorate sovereign. There is a choice of parties, of policies and governments. The voter makes his cross, and, hey presto! he gets what he wants (or at any rate he does so long as his preference coincides with that of the majority!). In contrast, under a multi-party system with a fairer electoral law, the voter rarely knows for certain what kind of government is likely to emerge from his particular decision: the search for a majority and the construction of coalitions have a logic of their own. But the argument that under a relative majority system the voter always knows what he is choosing is highly artificial. The contestants in a British two-party competition nowadays offer a large slate of policies, many of which are designed to placate vocal minorities within or behind the parties. Increasingly the sheer pressure of competitive two-party politics in an era of welfare statism has meant that parties commit themselves to policies which are unrealisable — carelessly thought out, founded on ignorance, too expensive or merely sectarian. The result is that the voters nearly always find that in "choosing" a government they have landed themselves with some policies which they actively dislike and others which cannot be realised. Their choice is rapidly soured.

Similarly it is held that two-party competition guarantees responsible and responsive government. This, too, appears to be an exaggerated claim. A government in the early years of its majority rarely worries too much about electoral defeat, but is more concerned to keep quiet those of its own supporters who have special demands to make. To show responsiveness to the pressures of the Opposition is thought to be a confession of weakness. Instead it is customary to present every policy decision as an expression of the most perfect and balanced wisdom on the part of those who have been set over us as our rulers, and beyond any need for improvement. The fact is that traditional ideas of the mechanism by which a government was held responsible and responsive depended very much on the assumption of an intimate relationship between ministers and a sensitive and critical House of Commons, in which certain standards transcending party loyalties and commitments were held to apply to the behaviour of governments. But these conditions have gone: in consequence the term responsibility loses much of its content.

Another argument always wheeled out against coalition is that it must mean weak government. To a substantial degree this view expresses little more than ignorance and insularity, a kind of "foreigners regrettably do as they do" outlook. It is perfectly well known that in liberal and constitutional states coalition forms of government are more common than something on the British model. But are we seriously to argue that in all such countries government is always weak? The truth, as any student of politics knows, is that coalition is sometimes strong and sometimes weak. Multi-party systems may be beset by factionalism, by extremism or by the strength of local and individual interests. But equally many examples can be found of stable multi-party systems and of their beneficial interaction with institutional procedures and habits directed to coherent and broadly based government. That this is so is borne out by the experience of many countries in contemporary western Europe, not to speak of the special case of the United States of America. Why should it be assumed that in Britain the conditions are present which have on occasion undermined government in countries where many parties seek and secure representation?

The misunderstanding about the weakness of coalition government abroad is accompanied by corresponding illusions about the strength of government in Britain. A superficial acquaintance with the experience of the past couple of decades suggests that British governments have become steadily weaker. There is no need to invoke any of the conventional explanations for this trend: for example, the veto power of certain pressure groups, the undue influence of minorities within parties, the inadequacies of the governing élites, or the strength or weakness (according to one's judgement of these matters) of the Civil Service in relation to transient politicians. Instead, it is time that we recognised that highly competitive politics are likely, in contemporary conditions of a mass public and a media network dedicated to the purveying of sensational news stories, to result in parties committing themselves to increasingly unworkable policies. This danger has been magnified by the growing sharpness of the ideological divisions between the parties during the past few years, divisions which owe most to the persistent efforts of the Left, both inside the Labour Party and on its fringes. Another factor is the straightforward impact of economic decline: the parties become fearful of telling the truth and, like Mr. Micawber, always on the look-out for something to turn up, they succumb the more easily and the more quickly to the temptations of irresponsible competition. Nor does this apply only to the two major parties. There are plenty of signs that the Liberals are exposed to the same pressures, and indeed that the Scottish Nationalists too have not hesitated to promise the Earth when they must know that all they can offer is a mess of pottage. The outcome of this process is that political parties are in the van of the flight from reality. They offer bread and circuses to the crowd; in office reality catches up with them and their hastily concocted policies either have to be abandoned or are revoked by their rivals. Can anyone seriously argue that the bonfire of the preceding Government's policies and legislation which has now become quite normal in Britain is a tribute to strong and stable government? Or the turning of the ministerial carousel which has given us fourteen Chancellors of the Exchequer and sixteen Education ministers in thirty years? Eventually the voter (who admittedly is by no means blameless: *caveat emptor* applies in politics too) is left cynical and resentful. Of strong government there is no trace. All that remains is posturing government, trying to create the illusion of success and achievement for as long as it can get away with it.

But if the harm done by adversary politics in a two-party situation is held now to outweigh the benefits it might once have conferred, it is necessary to consider how the situation which has been described might be remedied. Political societies have always faced two opposite and conflicting dangers. One is that they fall victim to governments which cannot be controlled: there is a danger of tyranny. The other is that they become ungovernable and run the risk of falling apart: there is the danger of a Hobbesian state of nature. For a long time the British could reasonably claim that they had been very successful in devising modes of political co-operation and of government which avoided these contrasting dangers. They solved the problem of how to change rulers without disorder and conflict, they evolved a form of government which has been coherent and generally competent, and they managed to provide a mass electorate with some elements of a choice. At the same time, though they retained a generous view of the privileges of the executive arm of government, they subjected those in authority to the demands of public opinion and to the need to justify their actions in Parliament. Such roughly is the ideal of responsible government and opposition in a two-party situation.

My contention is that that particular model has had its day. The English no doubt performed a great service by inventing the notion of "loyal

Opposition".[5] But they now suffer from the exaggeration of their own invention. Their situation begins to resemble that which Hegel attributed to the Germans when he wrote (referring in fact to the concept of representation) that "there is a higher law that the people from whom the world is given a new universal impulse perishes in the end before all others, while its principle, though not itself, persists".[6] For the time has come when this model needs to be drastically re-shaped. Reality falls too far short of the ideal, and there is no reason at all for believing that we can somehow or other return to the political conditions of late nineteenth- and early twentieth-century England, nor even to that balanced final movement of the years from 1945 to about 1960. The adversary mode of politics encourages a condition of ungovernability because it steadily destroys that belief in the existence of common interests and values without which a political community cannot survive. It achieves this destruction through the very irresponsibility of the competition which it encourages. But equally the adversary mode erodes and weakens the instruments for the control of government which were so carefully developed in the course of the evolution of parliamentary procedures. For it is a curious and often neglected fact that some part of the practice of parliamentary control presupposes that Parliament as an institution can perceive itself on some occasions and, for some purposes, as being distinct from the Government and Opposition which sit within it. Even within the British parliamentary tradition there is — or there must be — at least this element of separation of powers. If there is not, then there is the certainty that much of the activity of Parliament will be reduced to the level of an elaborate charade, for in the final analysis government and party will combine to defeat Parliament.[7]

[5] The term "loyal" is rarely attached to "Opposition" now. It used to mean "loyal to the Crown". With the decline of the Crown as a ground of political loyalty, one might well ask: Loyal to what?

[6] G. W. F. Hegel, "The German Constitution", in *Political Writings*, edited by T. M. Knox and Z. A. Pelczynski, p. 206.

[7] It is of some significance that the opposition of institutions has tended to emerge in periods of party coalescence, e.g. during the Second World War, when occasionally the Executive found itself opposed by Parliament as such on matters affecting civil liberties and the use of emergency powers. See J. Eaves Jr., *Emergency Powers and the Parliamentary Watchdog: Parliament and the Executive in Great Britain 1939–51*, Hansard Society, 1957. Much of the argument on delegated legislation and its control in the period 1920–50 also assumed the possibility of an institutional separation between Parliament and Executive.

It would be idle to pretend that there are any easy and quick remedies to these problems. In the life of the political institutions of a society so much depends upon a spirit of moderation and realism. It is all too easy in a period of decline and of growing weakness to accept the dangerous argument that institutions impose no constraints and have no logic of their own. Those engaged in political life persuade themselves that the only obligation which weighs upon them is to listen to the voice which shouts the loudest and to satisfy the appetite which opens its mouth the widest. But to behave in this way is to conspire in the destruction of institutions and to render nugatory the normative directions they impose. Men are, of course, always free to do this. But if they are prudent they will at least recognise that they have to pay a price for so doing. One of the symptoms of the malaise which affects Britain is that fewer and fewer political figures are willing to recognise such truths publicly. Instead they pretend that politics is easy, a game in which there are prizes for all and in which the rules — that is to say the institutions — can be changed as easily as they were in the Red Queen's game of chess.

The conditions and consequences of adversary politics in the two-party mould would undoubtedly be profoundly affected by one major rule change which has so far been resisted doggedly. This is a change in the electoral law. It is not of particular interest or importance to discuss here the kind of alternative system which might be adopted. In British conditions there is much to be said for some form of single transferable vote in multi-member constituencies, a system which would retain constituencies, ensure fairness of representation and yet would not strengthen unduly the central party organisations. But the precise nature of electoral reform is not of crucial importance. What matters is the principle, and here it is obvious that no change is worthwhile which does not facilitate a more equal representation of political opinion, that is to say, of parties. The effect of any such a reform would, of course, be a Parliament in which most probably no party would for the foreseeable future ever have an overall majority. The consequence of this would be the destruction of the two-party alignment, the weakening of adversary politics, and perhaps eventually the emergence of a practice of coalition government. It is unlikely that the transition to coalition politics would be rapid, and no doubt there would be first a period of minority government. But once it were known that there was to be no return to the simplicities of the two-way swing of the pendulum, the seeds of coalition would have been sown.

It would be possible to devote a lot of space to discussing the benefits which might be associated with coalition government. But to do so would take me irrelevantly far from the effort to delineate present realities. However, it must be said that it would be foolish to claim that a transition from adversary politics to coalition and power-sharing will usher in a new Heaven. The most that can be hoped for is that such a change might open certain gates. First, politicians, all those engaged in political argument and negotiation, and ultimately the electorate would be exposed to that discipline of reality which comes from knowing that the basic rule of *Do ut des* applies. Decisions would have to rest more often on broadly based and negotiated agreements. That large appeal to party loyalty and to the obligation not to rock the boat would have lost much of its force. And in particular, for it would be disingenuous to disguise the point, the trade union movement of this country, as the major source of veto power over the decisions of government, would probably be compelled to come to terms with majorities which, unlike the Conservative Party at present, it could no longer hope to replace by its pliable political arm, the British Labour Party.

Second, the way would slowly be opened to changes in the political élite of this country. It is true that major and early changes would require many measures additional to electoral reform, and indeed it is conceivable that electoral reform by itself might have only a small effect. But at any rate the conditions which candidates for elected office have to meet would change, the criteria governing selection might be substantially revised, and perhaps there would eventually be a place in politics for people of a kind currently unwilling to contemplate such a career (e.g. the serious subject specialist).

Third, the prospects for significant institutional innovation might well be improved. One need consider only the example of parliamentary reform to recognise that changes would become possible which are at present ruled out by the interests of the Government and its shadow. Nor need such prospects be confined to the central Government and Parliament: changed political relationships there would reveal possibilities of devising new ways of managing our political affairs at other levels of the structure of government too. Finally, the developments under discussion would have an effect on the public and on public opinion. The temperature of politics might be lowered, the febrile excesses of those in television, radio and the press who are concerned only with what titillates most and sells best might be curbed, and slowly political comment might become more cautious, more qualified and better informed. With luck the overall effect would be less heat and more light, hopefully more tolerance and a more critical view of the prejudices of the age into the bargain.

Naturally a price would have to be paid for the kind of transformation contemplated here; much of the simplification, the dramatisation and the colour would go out of political life. But just as the Oxford Union is slowly but inexorably dying out as a cult amongst Oxford undergraduates, so we should have the courage to recognise that the mode of politics which such a debating society symbolised, is also dying on its feet. It is no longer adequate to the condition of complex interdependence which characterises our world and no longer capable of channelling into the structure of political authority the diversity of interests which needs to be recognised. But equally the adversary mode no longer gives us any protection against those who would destroy a liberal political order, nor against those who are so maddened by their appetites that unwittingly they too act in ways which undermine that order. Acceptance of the inevitability of power-sharing in Ulster came only after blood had flowed and violence had taken its toll. Even now there are some in Ulster nourished, it must be admitted, on a garbled version of British democratic principles, who have not reconciled themselves to such a conclusion. Must the rest of Britain wait until the political order begins in a visible manner to break down before the courage is found to contemplate the kind of genuine changes which might bring hope of renewal?

After Parliament and adversary politics it might seem appropriate to pass to the character of the British political élite, the actors within the institutional setting. But that must wait some while yet. In particular, the problem of our rulers and their qualities needs to be considered against the background of the demands made on them and the worries which beset them. This means that the next theme will be the centralisation of governmental power, a consideration of the great Leviathan which has been built up in the land of the night-watchman state. And in a dialectical manner the antithesis must subsequently be contemplated too, the possibility that we are on the verge of the dissolution of the United

Kingdom, the breakdown of the unitary state outside England. From that vantage point it is not hard to discern the synthesis which alone might save a kind of unified state; a re-shaping of the Constitution and the setting of the institutions of that unified State on a new foundation.

CHAPTER 6

The Leviathan at the Centre

The study of politics is beset by paradox. Though there are many who choose to overlook this source of perplexity, the exploration of paradox remains one of the conditions of our understanding social and political life, signifying recognition of the readiness of human beings to pursue different and contrary courses at the same time, to struggle forward without entirely destroying their past, and to pursue ideals of which the consequences are incalculable. This reference to one of the major philosophical difficulties in the explanation of political relationships may serve as an appropriate introduction to some remarks on an aspect of government in Britain which is in many respects paradoxical: the centralised state. Much of the traditional literature about our politics and government barely acknowledges centralisation, or if it does, then merely to accept it as a beneficent and natural condition. But the theme which runs through so much of the writing on British government from the middle of the last century down to this day (though admittedly the theme is wearing thin now) is one of freedom from the oppressive burden of a centralised state. There was diffusion of power, so it was argued, and the scope of the central political authority was severely limited by the rights of individuals, the autonomy of associations and the healthy independence of local communities. In addition there was the watchful vigilance of the courts and the vigorous tradition of self-help and voluntary action.

The paradox with which I am now concerned lies in the fact that despite the continuing influence of these traditions, and despite such residues as they have left behind in our contemporary public life, Britain has now become subject to an unusually centralised state, this being in part a natural consequence of the providential view of government. The story of the French Minister of Education of many years ago who looked at his watch and told his visitor exactly what books all the children in all the schools of France were reading at that moment, is a well-worn source of amusement which has long provoked complacent commiseration with the French on their centralisation. What we fail to grasp is that there are several possible modes of centralisation, and that though we may have left our school-teachers free to follow their own whims and fancies, we may in other ways have arrived at a condition of governance from the centre every bit as burdensome as that which is associated with the deliberately planned centralised state. Indeed, as a very few perceptive observers have pointed out in recent years, it is arguable that the centralisation of the Napoleonic state has usually been moderated in a variety of ways, e.g. through the interposition of political parties or through the very structure of field administration embodied in the prefectoral system itself, and that the outcome is in some respects a state *less* harmfully centralised than that which has taken shape in Britain.

However, my purpose is not to pursue comparisons but to explain what I take to be the nature of centralisation in contemporary Britain, in other words to characterise in some way the centralised state. One has to begin with a few remarks on the history of the matter. We are perhaps the oldest centrally organised state in Europe, or rather England is. The impact of a vigorous and continuous monarchy, working from a capital city which steadily came to dominate to an unusual degree not only the political life of the country but culture, commerce, trade and the professions was profound. Well before France, England became a centralised state. But, of course, England did not become an absolutist state nor did it acquire a ruling bureaucracy: these were the great differences between the political development of England and that of its continental neighbours during the centuries when the modern European state was emerging. We did not acquire a structured centralisation under which the instruments of public power became exercisable in a uniform way. But the political foundations for the Leviathan were well and truly laid, and we had but to wait for the advent of a different notion of the proper sphere of governmental action for that Leviathan to come into existence.

Two closely related constitutional concepts have served as the driving force behind the process of centralising governmental power in modern Britain, that is to say in the course of the past century and a half. One has been the idea of the sovereignty, or what might be better characterised as the omnicompetence of Parliament. The other has been the doctrine of ministerial responsibility.

In the case of parliamentary sovereignty, there are at least three points to be stressed. The first is that Parliament is not merely the representative, authorising body; it is equally "the Crown in Parliament", the executive power supposedly fused with the expression of the popular will. This explains why even now the ambiguity of such a phrase as "it is for Parliament" to decide is happily tolerated. From one point of view it reserves the sovereign position of Parliament, and in the first place of the House of Commons. From another it legitimises the decisive voice of the Government as the Crown's agent in Parliament. The second is that the legal aspects of the doctrine of parliamentary sovereignty are important, though not the end of the story. But in the legal interpretation of parliamentary sovereignty the significant point is not so much that Parliament is the sole source of statute law,[1] rather the notion that a Parliament cannot limit itself by binding its successors.[2] It is this argument which stands as a formidable barrier in the way of establishing a genuine constitutional framework for the exercise of powers. Finally, stretching beyond the legal definitions of parliamentary sovereignty is the idea of omnicompetence, the belief that there are no matters, legislative or executive, which are in principle outside of the reach of Parliament. And that means, too, the Government in Parliament. The efficacy of this part of the doctrine as reflected in the results of the activity which goes on in the institution "Parliament" is not of vital importance. What matters is the fact that the claim is made and upheld, and that this has been a great engine of centralisation. For in the twentieth century no group of people have been more dedicated to extending the powers of government than Members of Parliament, and they have done this not only in virtue of their authority but because they have believed that they could then really control the use of these powers. Enough has already been said to suggest that this belief rests on very dubious foundations.

[1] This statement has now to be qualified by reason of the British accession to the European Communities and the European Communities Act of 1972. Both lawyers and politicians disagree about the extent to which the legal sovereignty of Parliament has been qualified: my view is that it has been so qualified, and that the desire to find arguments to deny this stems partly from political motives, and partly from a realisation that to accept the conclusion openly is to acknowledge a decisive breach in traditional constitutional doctrine. And if Humpty Dumpty once falls down, he cannot be put together again in the same form.

[2] This part of the doctrine too is questioned by some: for a perceptive discussion of "auto-limitation" see G. Marshall, *Constitutional Theory*, OUP, 1971, Chap. III.

The idea of ministerial responsibility is the counterpart of parliamentary sovereignty, though of much more recent origin. For a few years in the fourth and fifth decades of the last century there were signs that this country might develop an administrative structure, part of which would escape the control of ministers and acquire some autonomy under the law. This happened under the influence of utilitarian thinking and in the establishment of new agencies, often in the form of "boards", for the exercise of regulative powers made necessary by the emerging problems of an industrial society. But the parliamentary élite was already strong enough to choke off such a development and instead the new powers were gradually all concentrated in the hands of ministers or under the supervision of ministers.[3] Similarly, the central bureaucracy which began slowly to emerge in the second half of the century understood itself as "the servants of ministers", though that is another part of this argument. The important point at this stage is that powers, whether discretionary or statutory, were vested in ministers and they were held to be responsible to Parliament. It was on account of this relationship of responsibility – which incidentally was never defined as a doctrine of public law – that it was believed (and still is by many) that there could be no danger in the steady extension of public powers.

In the discussion of ministerial responsibility in our day one can often read remarks to the effect that the doctrine is dead, that it has no effect, is a charade and so on. If we are thinking of responsibility in the sense of a liability to render account and, if found wanting, to suffer penal sanctions in the form of dismissal or enforced resignation, then, of course, these strictures are justifiable – or nearly so. And even if we think of the doctrine as requiring the collective responsibility of the Cabinet to Parliament, there are now many signs that it is wearing thin. But to understand the doctrine as if it only had to do with the responsibility of ministers individually or collectively to Parliament is to misunderstand it and to run the risk of failing to discern the immense impact which it still

[3] There is unfortunately no comprehensive account of the triumph of the ministerial principle of organisation over the principle of autonomous boards and agencies favoured by many early Victorian administrative reformers. Important aspects are, however, dealt with in D. Roberts, *The Victorian Origins of the Welfare State*, Yale, 1960. See also S. E. Finer, *Life and Times of Sir Edwin Chadwick*, Methuen, 1952.

has on our political life and on our structure of government. For it is fundamentally a doctrine about the manner in which public powers are to be established and located: it defines who is responsible for what rather than who is responsible to whom. And if the British have any notion of the State, then it is to be found in this doctrine of ministerial responsibility. Interestingly enough it was a German, old George II, who grasped this very well when he murmured once to Lord Chancellor Hardwicke, "Ministers are Kings in this country".[4] That is the core of it all.

The enduring effect of the doctrine of ministerial responsibility has been over the past century or so that powers have been vested in ministers and on a relentlessly increasing scale. This can be demonstrated with ease by looking at any volume of the statute book. Here are to be found powers vested by the cartload in named persons, ministers. The overall effect is strikingly different from continental public law in which it is so often the practice to adopt what is best described as a declaratory style, one in which the powers are simply defined and stated to exist, being there to be used by whatever organ of that eternal corporation, the State, is able and qualified to exercise them. For the sake of underlining this point of contrast I am exaggerating the differences somewhat: in German or French public law powers will often be precisely attributed to specific bodies, even to ministers on some occasions; and equally in British law we may sometimes see the minister retreat into the background and a more general statement of rights and duties emerge. Moreover, I recognise well enough that many powers have been vested in local authorities, in public corporations and in a variety of other agencies. Yet it must never be forgotten that practically all the powers conferred on agents other than ministers are in some degree conditional and qualified: the nature of these other bodies as creatures of Parliament is underlined and the exercise of their powers in nearly all cases is subject to a wide and flexible supervision by those who are directly agents of the Crown, the ministers of Her Majesty.

The centralising force of this doctrine needs no emphasis. And indeed in modern Britain nothing has so far been able to stand against it, neither

---

[4] Philip Yorke's *Life of Hardwicke*, quoted in W. C. Costin and J. S. Watson, *The Law and Working of the Constitution, Documents 1660–1914*, vol. I, p. 376.

Parliament (in whose name ministers claim to act), nor the bureaucracy (the obedient servants of ministers) nor the courts. It is a strange blindness, partly attributable to the separation between the study of law and that of politics, which persuades many students of British government to ignore its importance and to underestimate its formidable influence on the way in which matters of public concern are dealt with in this country. They have bothered too much about the niceties of ministerial responsibility in its individual and collective senses (and of even the latter only shreds survive after Mr. Wilson's temporary abandonment of cabinet responsibility in 1975 for the sake of party unity),[5] and for this reason they have not appreciated how powerful is the doctrine in itself as a mode of conferring and maintaining powers. And let us not forget that when the objection is raised that this or that constitutional change would affect the powers of Parliament, as often as not this is but a form of words: what is really meant is that it would diminish the scope of ministerial responsibility by withdrawing power from the hands of our contemporary kings and their servants in Whitehall.

There is one other condition which has grown out of British history which ought to be mentioned as one closely related to what has just been said. This is the unimportance of the courts in relation to the interpretation and control of public powers in Britain, one might almost say their subservience before the Executive. To put it another way, it is permissible to talk of the insignificance of our system of law as a source of regulative ideas applicable to the shaping of public powers. At the moment it is not my intention to justify these statements and to embark on a discussion of the place of law in the structuring of a political order, chiefly because some aspects of this subject along with the problem of rights in our society will be considered later. The main point now is that as a consequence of the settlement of 1689, which *inter alia* guaranteed their inviolability, English judges accepted the supremacy of Parliament and a

---

[5] Shortly before the referendum on EEC membership collective responsibility was suspended far enough to allow ministers to campaign for one side or the other of the argument. But the practice of collective responsibility is in decline, partly due to changes in moral behaviour (e.g. the late R. H. S. Crossman's readiness to publicise in his Diaries the weaker characteristics of his colleagues) and partly to differences of political purpose which can no longer be bridged by a willingness to accept *and* subsequently to act according to a consensus reached in Cabinet. *Pari passu* the willingness to resign on principle has atrophied.

self-denying ordinance in respect of their claims to make political judgements. In their own field of the common law they remained supreme, and from time to time they have sallied forth to check the abuse of public powers, either on procedural grounds or when power was plainly being exceeded (and not always even then). But by and large they have not been able to develop doctrines which would allow them to challenge in the name of constitutional principle what Parliament has enacted, and *a fortiori* what ministers claim to do in Parliament's name.

This is not the place to discuss the merits or otherwise of this situation. All that is necessary is to emphasise the importance which is to be attributed to the absence over the centuries of any doctrinal challenge from those whose profession is the law to the claims made in pursuance of the two key concepts which have just been examined. This is one of the features of our experience which helps to explain the crumbling away of all notions of constitutional rules at the present time: there is no nourishment for such ideas in the British legal tradition, nor do the courts possess sure means by which they can compel those involved in a disputed issue to recognise the questions at stake as "constitutional". The contrast between the situation in Britain in these matters and that in many other countries is, of course, remarkable. Whether we look to the American experience or to that of many of the nations of continental Europe, or to that of some parts of the Commonwealth, nowhere do we find such a poverty of judicial interpretation and of public law concepts. To make good such a deficiency is indeed a hard task: it calls for nothing less than a new science of justice.

I must come back now, however, to more mundane questions and in particular to the centralising impact of the doctrines examined. Before the growth of public powers and responsibilities in the later years of the last century, the potential for centralisation within our political order was not, and indeed could not, be realised. Political direction in matters of war and foreign policy rested firmly with the central government, whilst what we must call administration (though much of it then was in the guise of judicial action by lay judges, i.e. magistrates) rested with local notabilities or was regarded as entirely within the discretion of freely interacting individuals. But with the emergence of the idea that collective regulation and public administrative action must be invoked for the provision of services to the citizen, the process of centralisation as it is now known got under way. In purely quantitative terms, the growth of the state has not been much different in Britain from the same pattern elsewhere: it is in its special structural characteristics that it is distinguished from the experience of many other countries. A central bureaucratic system of formidable size and power was shaped; the administrative structure at other levels expanded rapidly too, a trend which has become even more marked in recent years; the quantity of legal instruments of one kind and another — statutes and administrative orders — has grown into an immense flood, the bulk of them being no more than the necessary formalisation of the administrative demands of the central power; the hold of the state on individual and corporate wealth has steadily been strengthened, so that now something like a half of the annual national product (more according to some calculations) is disposed of in one way or another by government or public authority; and relentlessly the boundaries between public action and those spheres which have usually been thought of as private, or at any rate within the bounds of self-imposed social co-operation and regulation, have been broken down so that all come to believe that they have a claim on government. And in Britain that means nearly always "the Government" in London, for it is the central political authority which not only attempts to supervise the whole of this immensely complex administrative state, but in addition constantly claims a right to do so.

It has been stressed several times that the doctrine of ministerial responsibility results in powers being conferred on ministers and being made exercisable in their name. But it is also necessary to remember that this does not mean that central government and its administrative services are themselves regularly the executive agents. Far from this being the case, it is a fact that many of the most important powers possessed by the central government are supervisory rather than original or executive. It is true that there are important services such as pensions and numerous social benefits which are provided directly by agencies of the central state. There are others like hospitals which *de facto* are provided in the same manner, but in which an appearance of the voluntary co-operation of the relevant professions and of local interests is preserved. The most common pattern, however, is to confer powers and responsibilities on administrative agents who have in some respects a kind of autonomy, but who in the exercise of their powers must work according to the requirements of ministers and subject to the supervision and control exercised by them and their agents.

The classic example of this is local authorities, Nominally autonomous in virtue of their representative quality, in practice local authorities have become little more than the agents of central government, confined within the policies determined by ministers and the resources allowed to them. In the case of many other administrative agencies — the public corporations administering nationalised industries, for example — there cannot even be the protection (such as it is) afforded by the possession of some degree of democratic legitimation: they must accommodate themselves as best they can to the demands which flow from the controlling rights of ministers. The advantage of all such arrangements from the point of view of the central government is that its power is safeguarded, whilst the responsibility for action is blurred.

The acceptance of a providential view of the role of government has already been identified as a major influence on the rise of a centralised state, and in commenting on the effects of centralisation there is no need to go over that ground again. There has been an accumulation of central powers and we must try to understand the various consequences of this. One of these, which is of great practical significance, is that the British mode of centralisation has imposed an immense burden on the central governmental system which it is now beyond its capacity to sustain. It is unreasonable to expect that ministers and their agents should be capable of discharging effectively *both* the tasks of conception and design of policy and powers *and* the supervision of executive action by such an enormously diverse range of subordinate authorities. Moreover, they are expected to do this under the watchful eyes of a Parliament which tolerates no limit in principle to its own claims to intervention. In the conditions of the modern state such a form of centralisation is self-destructive. Yet the only ways in which it could be changed would involve a serious breach of the very concepts which were set out at the beginning of this analysis. One way would be to accept a degree of political and administrative decentralisation — dispersion might be a more accurate term — against which Parliament and ministers will always fight, for it would imply real limitations to their powers. Another way would be to learn from the Napoleonic model and re-design the state considered as a structure of executive action, that is to say, to give to the various administrative agencies of government far wider powers to act autonomously in the execution of policy determined at the centre. But that, of course, would require us to re-draw the boundaries between ministers (politicians) and officials (bureaucrats), and that, too, is not something of which there is much sign at present. Moreover, to go in that direction would be tolerable only if the institutions of the state were set within a coherent framework of public law which would itself provide the means of confining the action of those institutions within acceptable limits.

May be once again the peculiarity of the British mode of centralisation can be made more vivid by noting some of the ways in which it differs from patterns of government elsewhere. It goes without saying that there is nothing which resembles the political diffusion of a federal constitution. The experience of Northern Ireland might be thought to qualify this assertion, but this is to be doubted. The striking fact about the autonomy which that province enjoyed until 1972 was that for half a century the British Government did not wish to know of its existence: Stormont was a convenient way of getting rid of a tiresome problem. Similarly, there is a level of elected local government which is (and always has been) politically insignificant. The self-government of municipalities is highly qualified and there is no flow of strength from local politics into national politics. The two levels of political action are strangely separated in contrast with the position in Germany or Italy or Holland, and there has not even been that interdependence which in France has done so much to qualify the character of French centralisation. All this does not prevent us from maintaining an official ideology which affirms the importance of local institutions as a school for democracy.[6] But it has long had a hollow ring about it, scarcely capable of masking the fact that we have but a feeble grasp of the potential relationship between territory and power. Turning away from elected bodies (and ignoring the interesting topic of the involvement in public action of appointed lay persons, volunteers) it must also be noted that there is really nothing by way of an operational and co-ordinating middle level of the state administration, in a prefectoral or

[6]This view is regularly put forward in official reports, statements, departmental circulars, etc. But its roots lie rather more in John Stuart Mill's somewhat condescending argument that local representative institutions are a useful means of qualifying people for the larger national scene than in the opposing tradition of his contemporary J. Toulmin-Smith, who started from the assumption that free institutions depended essentially on the capacity of local communities to govern themselves.

provincial governor, type of organisation. Of course, this is not to question the existence of regional and local offices of the central administration, nor the manner in which many specialised and quasi-autonomous administrative bodies have to run field services in consultation with such offices. What is significant is that there are no effective organs of co-ordination and initiative below the level of the central ministries, which have the kind of discretion in matters of policy implementation which would be regarded as quite normal in a French *préfet*, a Swedish provincial governor or in a German *Regierungspräsident*. The consequence of all this is a gap between the centre and all below it: the power to decide gravitates to the centre, whilst there is hesitation and inhibition at the peripheries.

Furthermore, as has been suggested before, Britain is distinguished from most other comparable societies by having no genuine concept of public law, and thus no proper public law structure which defines powers and by so doing creates barriers. This may seem a strange thing to say, for after all what do most modern statutes do if not establish powers? The justification for this remark lies in the doctrinal poverty of English law. Such ingenuity as it has shown has lain in the devising of remedies against the misuse of powers, remedies external to the powers themselves. It has failed to understand that within the terms in which powers are defined and distributed and in the principles governing their use, there are possibilities for the maintenance of justice conceived as a distribution of countervailing powers and the recognition of constraints. As a consequence of this failure (which admittedly has expressed deeply held social sentiments too), we find that English statutes reveal an extraordinary mixture of the narrowly casuistic specification of powers (on which ironically the appetite to create more then feeds) and the conferment of discretions on ministers so broad as to be virtually unlimited. Indeed, it is often counted as a great merit by those who design it that law conferring powers on public agencies and ministers is as a result largely judge-proof, inaccessible to challenge and interpretation by processes of law. It is such conditions which then help to explain why all institutions other than ministers and their servants are so weak: they may have powers, but they know that they exercise them on a kind of sufferance and that if they were to stand on their rights against the political imperatives of ministers, their wings would soon be clipped. As I have said, powers are in Britain rarely barriers.

So far this has been chiefly about the anatomy of the centralised state and the principles which appear to have permitted the structure of executive action in Britain to assume the shape it now has. Centralisation has, however, wider political effects and these have become of increasing, though perhaps half-hidden importance in recent years. Frenchmen who criticise their own traditions of centralisation often bewail the manner in which Paris is said to have made a desert of the French provinces. The price paid for the dominance of the capital city has allegedly been the political, social and cultural impoverishment of the provinces and local communities. Whilst I have no wish to embark on a discussion of how far this is a true description of what has happened as a result of centralisation in France, it does seem to be important to recognise that much the same criticism can be made of centralisation and its effects in Britain.[7] The pattern of centralised government which has been evolved has steadily sucked into the centre a great part of such political energies as the country generates. At the same time all that is not at the centre is stultified and cramped, and the sense of there being opportunities for creative political action outside of the shadow of the Leviathan is dulled.

It would be an interesting and difficult enterprise to trace historically the progress of this condition of political encephalitis. I certainly cannot attempt to do so here and must restrict myself to a few sketchy remarks. The roots of the malady lie deep in the past. But not until the years since the end of the Second World War has the disease assumed dangerous dimensions. Several factors have made this so. There has been the rapid expansion of the powers of government of which no more need be said, except perhaps to underline the discretionary central control of financial resources which this inevitably brought in its train, a control, moreover, which operates very differently from the centralised allocation of finance through federal law and constitutional provision with which some federal states are familiar.[8] There has been the standardising and unifying impact of nationally provided means of communication, in particular radio and

---

[7] The point was once put to me tellingly by a Frenchman whom I heard lecturing in Germany about the debilitating effect of centralisation in his own country, and to whom I remarked that everything he said could have been said with equal reason with the substitution of "la Grande-Bretagne" for "la France": "Monsieur", he sighed, "nous sommes tous les deux fossilisés".

[8] For an example of this difference see the author's *Federalism and Decentralisation in the Federal Republic of Germany*, Commission on the Constitution, Research Paper 1, HMSO, 1973.

television, which has encouraged a sense of dependence on opinions and values shaped centrally. There has been the gradual disintegration of established social interests outside the orbit of the metropolitan capital which has weakened a source of countervailing influence to that of the governing inner circle. Of immense importance, too, has been the sheer failure of economic enterprise which has eroded the confidence of those who ought in large measure to have represented the productive and forward-looking interests of the society. And perhaps, too, we should not discount the complacent absence of any genuine political education in the country at large which might have served to cultivate in people's minds some awareness of their own individual potentialities for helping to determine the conditions of their lives.

The enervating effects of centralisation are seen most seriously in the weakening of the national political élite, in its gradual detachment from the active forces in the society and in its consequent inability to perform effectively the tasks which of necessity fall to it. But that is a topic in itself which will be taken up later. There is nowadays one fashionable objection against these criticisms of the effects of centralisation which needs to be disposed of. It will be argued that there are now on all sides signs of a new demand for participation and involvement, that the sense of community is being revived, that distinct national or cultural groups are reasserting themselves, and that in industry and even in public administration workers are claiming a new kind of self-determination. The reality of some of these stirrings is not to be denied, even though their scale and significance may often be exaggerated. And indeed these developments are to some extent an expression of the frustration caused by the rigidities of central control and direction, particularly when that control does not result in the benefits expected of it. Nevertheless, these stirrings of discontent with the centralised pattern of government have to be viewed with some caution and for two main reasons. One is that most of those who express such ideals of participation, involvement and so on do not in general show any sign of appreciating the implications of their demands for the existing order of things. They seem hardly to realise that the demand for self-government — for that is what it amounts to — makes no sense unless it is grounded in a readiness to accept the responsibilities and consequences of such self-government. Unless this dual understanding is present the only outcome must be participation and self-government when it suits those concerned, followed by an appeal to the beneficent central authority when things go wrong. Unfortunately, too, it is apparent that many of the advocates of self-determination in its fashionable modern senses are so committed to their own substantive political ends, that they are really centralisers in disguise. Participatory democracy is but the ante-room to new kinds of tyranny. The other reason for caution is that as yet there are few signs to be seen of that willingness to tolerate diversity, difference and inequality which is a condition of a wide diffusion of powers. Seen under one of its aspects, the modern state exists to promote equality of human conditions. How then can it be taken apart if this, one of its chief purposes, is not challenged?

My conclusion on this particular matter is, therefore, that there are certainly protests against some of the effects of centralisation, but that so far they do not add up to any kind of coherent argument against it, still less have they shown understanding of what would be implied by a serious effort to institutionalise such aspirations. The most that these stirrings and protests have achieved has been to reveal the growing weakness of the political authority, its inability to fulfil the promises which its representatives so foolishly make. Of a revival of interest in what was once a question of great importance, the proper limits of government action, there are but few signs.

Let us turn now to another aspect of centralisation. The modern state is inescapably a bureaucratic state, and the centralised state in Britain is no exception, though some of our mythology would have it otherwise. So it would be most appropriate to say something about the bureaucracy, or some parts of it, within the context of these reflections on the theme of political centralisation. Moreover, there is a good practical reason for this. The bureaucracy in the service of the central government, though silent and withdrawn from the world of political argument in public, is one of the most powerful props of centralisation. Indeed, it is more than that. It is the very model of that network of informal communication without which a centralisation so arbitrary in its political will as that of Britain, would be rent apart by dispute. The corridors of Whitehall lead out to the interlocking worlds around it, and there are few in these worlds outside the central administration who are not susceptible to the style and manners of Great George Street, the home of Her Majesty's Treasury.

What follows refers chiefly to the Civil Service as we call it, the bureaucracy of the central government. There is in Britain no such thing as a single common public service — no *Beamtentum*, no *fonction publique*. It is true that some of the characteristics of the Civil Service are reproduced in other branches of public service, e.g. in local administration. But equally there are great differences, and the same is true if we were to set the Civil Service alongside the increasingly numerous public services which have grown up as the number and scale of agencies has increased which are neither part of the central government (i.e. of a central department or ministry) nor of local government. In fact there is now a remarkably heterogeneous and little-studied range of public services, some of which show little sign of a lively recognition of their public status and of the obligations stemming from that. However, there can be no doubt that it is the Civil Service which has been and still is politically the most significant and influential segment of the public bureaucracy, and this is why I shall be concerned chiefly with it. Nor do my remarks even refer to the whole of the Civil Service: janitors and typists, research scientists and tax collectors, such people do not figure in my argument. The group which is of political interest is small, no more than the three or four thousand people who constitute the group which advises ministers, supervises the execution of policy, controls the administrative machine, and hopefully finds time to look ahead. It is this group which, through its administrative skills, contributes most to holding the centralised state together.

A few years ago it would have been precisely definable as the administrative class of the home Civil Service, but after the changes consequent on the reception of the Fulton Report (1968) these higher levels of administration have become vaguer and looser in outline. But the majority of the members of this controlling group are in fact still general administrators brought up under the old dispensation: so we do not need to worry too much about the effects so far of the winds of change.

It is commonly thought that England shares with a few other countries such as Prussia and France the distinction of having invented a loyal, neutral and apolitical Civil Service. This very idea is, however, highly misleading. The basic error in the comparison is that in such continental countries the bureaucracy was at its higher levels never really apolitical — its mission was to serve a particular view of the state and of its purposes. In virtue of this it shared in varying degrees in the authority of the state.

In contrast the British bureaucracy, as it emerged in its modern professional form in the service of a parliamentary leadership which controlled the central government, was intended to be genuinely excluded from political authority. And it eventually became so excluded. In this respect the British Civil Service is almost unique: if the model is to be found anywhere else in the world, then it is perhaps only in India where it lives on as an echo of empire.

What I have just said would be taken by many as a compliment, a commendation of the British view of the proper understanding of the place of a civil service in the structure of government and politics. But my intention is not so complacent. It is often forgotten how relatively recent is the detached, politically neutral and anonymous higher official. True, the conception of the official as the detached and impartial adviser is certainly present in the ideas of the founding fathers of the British Civil Service, in Trevelyan, Northcote, Macaulay and others. Yet this idea assumed flesh more slowly than is often believed. For many reasons which I cannot go into, but amongst which the close social intercourse between higher officials and political personalities was certainly very important, the upper reaches of the Civil Service remained only imperfectly detached from politics and party until the end of the First World War. Until then there was an intimacy between the worlds of politics and of administration which even permitted politicians to exercise a small amount of patronage, not on behalf of family friends as earlier on, but by way of securing the support of men of ability whose services they needed. It was after 1920 that the Civil Service as it is now known rapidly took shape, largely under the influence of the Treasury whose official head also became head of the whole Service, and for that reason was able to claim within the bureaucracy a centralising influence with which there is nothing comparable elsewhere. In a social sense the spheres of politics and administration then drifted apart (though that rupture was not complete until after 1945), and the Civil Service cocooned itself within the ethos of the anonymous, impartial and politically indifferent servants of political masters. The Service accepted its servitude to ministers, but for that bargain the politicians had to pay a price. This was that they accepted the ultimate irresponsibility of their servants and agreed not to meddle in the internal affairs of the bureaucracy. This is why ministers have today negligible influence *in* their departments as opposed to influence *over* what they do; it explains why the Civil Service has become a closed corporation, a contemporary equivalent to the medieval church whose members, moreover, enjoy "benefit of clergy".

The contemporary criticism of the bureaucracy which has been voiced most often is of the generalist, non-specialised, amateur character of those who make up its central and directing core. This has always struck me as a somewhat confused and muddle-headed criticism which misses the main point, besides overlooking the important fact that the logic of our governmental arrangements has required that ministers should be served by people who have certain qualities in common with them. And the traditional administrator with an education in the humanities was undoubtedly well adapted to understanding the political needs of ministers. But the crucial thing is that the administrative Civil Service (to use for a moment the old expression) has indeed its own expertise and special skill, and that is in the manipulation of the administrative system in the service of ministers: the civil servant is the master of the machine. If we then remember that the price paid for the neutrality and loyalty of officials was the withdrawal of the politicians from interference in the affairs of the machine, and if further we take into account the manner in which the powers of government have expanded, then we can understand without difficulty the pervasive influence which the Civil Service acquired. And, as I have already remarked, in a very real sense the Civil Service remained irresponsible. For success ministers take credit, for failure ministers (if any one at all) take blame. It is rare indeed for the civil servant to be identified with any act of commission or omission, or until recently even to be known to have any views of his own at all. But for this complete self-abnegation he gains complete security.

There is a kind of deadness at the heart of the conventional doctrine defining the position of the Civil Service in British government. It denies commitment and encourages indifference; it sets the preservation of form far above the expression of purposes; and it keeps alive an idea of the contribution which administration should make to the life of the society which is narrow and restricted. In saying this no judgement is being made of the qualities of individuals who compose or have composed the directing part of the Civil Service, and indeed on other occasions and at other times I have acknowledged the abilities and virtues which such people possess.[9] What we have to do with here is an institution, or part of an institution, which has assumed certain characteristics as a result of the postulates on which it is founded. It follows, of course, that there would only be some prospect of changing these characteristics (or some of them) if we were ready to look critically at the postulates themselves. But the so-called reform of the Civil Service which has been in train since 1968 was founded on a firm refusal to disturb any of the postulates, all of which are, of course, of a political and constitutional nature. So there has really been very little change in respect of the characteristics of which I write — it has been another case of refurbishing the scenery and moving around the furniture.[10] (For the sake of a balanced judgement let it be said that there are a few changes taking place in the Civil Service which may in time have important effects. But for the most part these owe less to the impulse of the reform movement as such than to the impact of such factors as the proliferation of agencies, the expansion of governmental functions and the changing character of university education.)

One consequence of what has been argued is that it is hard to attribute to the Civil Service any concept of the public interest, any consciousness of having to serve such an interest. This was recognised rather cynically, yet very truly, by Sisson in his essay on British administration some years ago, though as a man of an older generation sensitive to the dilemmas of politics, he tried to rescue at the end some notion of service of the Crown, arguing that if political circumstances were to provoke a crisis of conscience, then *in extremis* the worm, the creature of ministers, might turn and reveal a scruple.[11] But to invoke the Crown hardly carries much conviction nowadays: the symbol has become too vapid. Interestingly enough there are here and there a few younger officials who discern this problem, and who wonder whether their obligations are quite exhausted by meticulous compliance with the transient political wills of ministers. [12]

[9] For example in Memorandum No. 133, submitted to the Fulton Committee on the Civil Service, published in vol. 5 (2) of the evidence to the committee, pp. 939–76.

[10] An interesting example of this is the Civil Service College, founded in 1970. It was in 1974 the object of an inquiry by two retired gentlemen (the Heaton-Williams Report) and then later of an internal Civil Service Department review. What was seen as a great innovation has obviously not given satisfaction. But as set up, was it really an innovation?

[11] C. H. Sisson, *The Spirit of British Administration*, Faber & Faber, 1959, p. 24.

[12] See *Professional Standards in the Public Service*, a Report by a Sub-Committee of the First Division Association, in Public Administration, Summer, 1972.

Perhaps they sense that there is no guarantee that there will always be a happy coincidence between the political will of ministers and the public interest as embodied in the principles of the political order, and that if this condition were manifestly not fulfilled, they would face a crisis of conscience not different in nature from that which has faced officials under other régimes which have been called into question. Yet, again, it is hard to see how any way can be found through this thicket without re-thinking some of the ground rules of the constitution itself. I will come back to this possibility in a moment after interpolating a few remarks which might be made in vindication of the *status quo*.

The argument of principle for the neutral, anonymous and non-political Civil Service is familiar and straightforward. We have an elected, representative government of politicians. If that government is to be able to do the things it proposes to do, then it must have a reliable administrative organisation working in support. But the popular will can change and governments with it. There is, therefore, some advantage in having a civil service ready to serve equally well any government, regardless of its political colour. The British Civil Service is designed to meet this requirement and in doing so subserves the ends of representative government. In other words, a particular idea of democracy is thought to entail a permanent administration detached from the commitments of political argument in that democracy and laying no claim to any original authority in virtue of the part it plays as an institution in the state. Moreover, one could supplement the theory of the relationship by considering the historical evidence which suggests that the British Civil Service has indeed fulfilled its particular role with a fair degree of success. As permanent bureaucracies go its standards have been high: there has been remarkably little corruption, the Civil Service has usually dealt with the public in a fair and even-handed way, its members have on the whole worked hard and efficiently at their different tasks, and at the higher levels it has had a generous share of the intellectual talent available in the society. Finally, there are grounds for believing that the administrative group at the centre has over the years lived up fairly well to the ideal of the objective and far-sighted adviser, serving ministers loyally but at the same time explaining to them the changing limits of what is possible within the different constraints operating.

Put like this the traditional doctrine defining the place of the Civil

Service in the constitution is persuasive. Nevertheless, it is inadequate, partly because it rests on an out-dated view of the separation to be made between the functions of ministers and those of officials, and partly because the very transitoriness of ministers means that the total subordination of officials to the demands of their political masters can make sense only if it is believed that they are in some degree custodians of an experience and of interests which transcend the preferences of particular groups of politicians. But, of course, in practice the difficulties which can arise from the limitations in the doctrine do not present a problem in relation to the bulk of the Civil Service: their task is to administer policies within clear guidelines and to provide services within conditions often prescribed in some detail by law. In such circumstances the case for the retention of a permanent and properly qualified bureaucracy, bound to observe the policy needs of different governments and sensitive to the demands of the legal framework within which it works, can hardly be disputed. The problem which I see arises from the exaggerations in the application of this principle in respect of the relatively small groups of officials who in virtue of their functions must be in fairly close and regular contact with the political leadership. It is, however, a problem of some magnitude precisely because such groups occupy an important position in our centralised state (and, indeed, do in any kind of state) and wield great influence, even if it is often enough an influence of a negative kind.

The character of this problem can best be identified by asking a question and by considering some of the consequences of the too rigorous application of what I will call for short "the neutrality principle". The question is simple and crude: is it really sensible to believe that in the task of determining policy — setting the guidelines of action and establishing objectives — a man can with *equal* dedication and ingenuity support any politician, regardless of his party and of the kind of commitments he wishes to pursue? Or to put the question another way, would Machiavelli have believed that the ideal secretary could and should give equally good service to any kind of prince? The British doctrine answers both forms of the question with "Yes". Defenders of that doctrine would argue, too, that experience shows that the Civil Service has successfully lived according to an affirmative answer: have we not had secretaries to the Cabinet who have served many prime ministers, officials who have nationalised an industry one week and de-nationalised it the next, and men who have been for a statutory incomes policy one month and have defended its termination the next? All this is true and, indeed, psychologically plausible if we imagine the official at this level of responsibility to be like a lawyer who explains the legal conditions to his client and then asks for instructions. But what we should not forget is that a heavy price must be paid for the affirmative answer. This price is a certain cynicism towards values and perhaps a certain corruption of the mind. Officials become so used to furthering any policy that often they lose all faith and interest in the possibility of there being a good or a better policy.[13]

It should be remembered, too, that Britain is very exceptional in maintaining this extreme interpretation of the impartiality attainable by officials: everywhere else (or nearly so) the doctrine I am talking about is qualified in some degree or other, often by recognition that at a certain level of the bureaucratic organisation the political sympathies and affilitations of officials become relevant, that ministers are entitled at the very least to ensure that some of their senior advisers are personally sympathetic to them, and that officials are after all men with opinions and preferences which must affect the manner in which they work. Where such qualifications are accepted the outcome is not necessarily a spoils system and rampant party patronage. In some countries – France and Sweden for example – retention of the idea of a permanent state service has been reconciled with recognition in practice that there are positions in respect of which the officials must be expected to have a relationship with the

---

[13] This remark should be seen in relation to yet another paradox, which is that the ostensibly neutral official may identify himself strongly with an agency or departmental policy, pressing this on unwilling or uncertain ministers. An example frequently cited is the consensus which appeared to emerge in the 1960s within the Department of Education and Science (formerly the Ministry of Education) on the desirability of a non-selective structure of secondary education, and which had a major influence on government policy, regardless of the party in power. Yet though such an example appears to bear out the opportunities for policy initiatives enjoyed by officials, it has to be recognised that such influence could be exerted successfully only because the Department was expressing opinions which were steadily gaining ground in society and in the teaching profession: it was to a substantial degree the voice of an emerging popular consensus. In addition, the officials' ability in this case to determine the pace of advance towards non-selective education was strictly qualified by many factors, including ministerial opposition, e.g. between 1970 and 1974.

politician which goes beyond mere service. All this means that in many countries there is at the higher levels of the bureaucracy less perfect security of tenure in posts of their choice than our officials enjoy, and that often the preferences of ministers in the selection of their advisers must be respected. And it means, too, that there must be some kind of public identification of officials, or of a few of them, with particular points of view and policies. Against all this the closed corporation which is the British Civil Service maintains a tone of frowning disapproval.

Some of the consequences of the isolation of the Civil Service within its own world have already been mentioned: a certain indifference and tiredness of spirit. There are a few further aspects of this which are worth mentioning. The very security of officials breeds complacency and something like contempt towards those outside (well-mannered and restrained though the expression of this may be). It is very difficult for the academic and even for the professional man in some practical area of life to have an easy relationship with senior officials. Rules about keeping official secrets are an impediment here, and of course the political servitude of officials in relation to ministers is held to impose an absurd degree of spinsterish discretion on discussion and the exchange of ideas. But to my mind it is the very exaggeration of the official's neutrality which is most productive of this inability (which sadly grows with advancing years) to communicate freely with the world outside and to appreciate what can be gained in that way. At its worst this failing assumes the guise of a self-righteous claim to omniscience, the effect of which can be disastrous. At the other extreme is a tendency to flatter the vanity of politicians. Sometimes no doubt the official is guilty of this quite deliberately and he can justify it to himself on several grounds, those of prudence and necessity as well as on the principle that he is there only to serve the ends of ministers, no matter how misconceived these may be. But to be fair to the civil servants, this particular consequence stems more from the ruling doctrine itself than from their obsequiousness. For the doctrine is intended to sustain illusions about the omnicompetence of ministers which are undoubtedly highly flattering to such poor mortals, though totally misleading as a guide to the complex relationships between political direction and administration in the contemporary state.

This brings me to an effect of the British view of the position of the Civil Service which has far less to do with the moral characteristics of that body than with our understanding of a rather difficult problem, the relationship between policy and administration. This is not a treatise on administrative theory (the existence of which is any way rather suspect), and so I will not try to explicate this relationship. But it does need to be said that the ideas under discussion here rest upon a somewhat crude and over-simplified view of the relationship, according to which policy is roughly equivalent to determination of political ends, and administration whatever is involved in then putting the policy into effect. Policy is, of course, the peculiar province of ministers, though the Civil Service is said to help them in this, whilst administration falls to the civil servant. And it is on this distinction – or something like it – that his claim to be able to achieve impartiality and neutrality has been founded.

But the whole thing is far too simple-minded. Lines cannot be drawn clearly between policy-making and administration, and the more senior official is inevitably involved in a lot of policy appreciation, policy development policy change and so on, in the course of which his judgements of value must be brought into play. And sometimes these value judgements are bound to reflect particular political preferences. Moreover he works within complex organisations which acquire a momentum of their own – their own departmental philosophy. However, I do not want to use the complexities of the interaction of policy-making and administration as another argument for admitting that ministerial preferences should influence far more than they do particular official appointments, though that would be an argument with some force. I want rather to make the point that the country at large would benefit if the fuzzy character of this distinction were admitted, and if as a result more senior civil servants more often gave some cautious expression to their opinions on policy. Sometimes this already happens – e.g. before a House of Commons Select Committee. May be, too, as the number of agencies separated from the central departments and direct ministerial control increases (as is the organisation tendency now)[14], we shall gradually hear

[14]In the wake of Civil Service reforms following the 1968 Fulton Report and of the 1970 White Paper, *The Reorganisation of Central Government*, Cmnd. 4506, it became fashionable to look for opportunities of "hiving-off" functions from the central departments. More recently this trend has been reinforced, not by organisational theory but by the extension of government functions, particularly in the economic sector. This appears to have prompted the establishment of many new agencies outside the traditional central department structure and subject to varying degrees of control by it.

from those in charge something more of *their* views as the responsible officials of how policy should develop, despite the preferences of passing politicians. What is needed here is more realism and a more open recognition both of the policy preferences which officials must have and of their duty, from time to time, to defend them in public.

The last consequence of the neutrality principle which needs to be sketched briefly is in some ways the most serious. It is the impoverishment which the application of this principle imposes on British political life. This point calls for some explanation.

As has just been said, we in Britain still draw a sharp line between administration and politics. The former is seen as a service provided by permanent, anonymous and professional officials, removed from party affiliation and sympathy, and withdrawn from public argument and discussion. The latter is seen as the pursuit of elected office by people committed to parties and ready to plead their case in public. To help maintain the separation we impose a variety of legal and conventional constraints on the ability of civil servants to become involved in party political activity, let alone to stand for office. Indeed, comparative study suggests that in no other country is it anything like so hard as in Britain to pass from administration to politics or back again. (This applies, though with slightly less rigour, to other areas of administrative activity than the Civil Service, but oddly enough has never been quite so true of industrial workers in public employment. Is there here yet another tribute to the power of the trade unions over the years?) Another contingent fact of some importance is that the extent of public service has widened immensely, so that today something approaching one-quarter of the labour force is in some form of public employment, though of course the number in the central Civil Service is but a fraction of this. But clearly very many people are subject to this limitation of political rights to which I refer.

The overall effect of the separation which is made between administration and politics and of the rules by which it is maintained, is that we exclude from political life and from engagement in party politics at all levels a very significant part of the available talents and experience. It cannot be claimed that this loss of ability which might otherwise in various ways find some expression in political life and in political commitment is quantifiable. One can go no further than to suggest that it is very hard indeed to believe that the society has such abundant energies and abilities within it that it can afford to narrow and restrict the reservoirs of political recruitment in this way. Nor is it only a matter of recruitment into politics in the classic way by entry into Parliament: the problem affects political service and commitment to policies expressive of political preferences in a much wider sense and at all levels of co-operation and endeavour in the society.

The absence of administrative experience and knowledge can be read off from a cursory examination of our political élites, nationally, provincially and locally. To the effects of this impoverishment on the political class I will come back later. As far as the Civil Service and other sectors of public administration are concerned, it would naturally be difficult to persuade their members (and especially at the higher levels which are at issue here) that the effects of this situation are so disadvantageous. After all, when we look into the mirror we are loath to express dissatisfaction with what we see. But there is a wider interest at stake than that of the administrative corporations in which the state abounds — that of the nation as a whole. The time has come to contemplate the possibility that the decline which has taken place, the weariness and the lack of energy which have come upon the country, and the temptation to retreat into mere words, owes just a little to a refusal to modify an antiquated view of the relationships between bureaucracy and politics. Maybe the windows need to be opened more widely in Whitehall and perhaps just occasionally an official should have to raise his voice and say where he stands. And were he to do so, the politicians would do well to remain silent.

This begins to probe difficult questions affecting political authority, to whom it should be attributed and on what terms. And I have given more than a hint that we would do well to look again at the notion that the official can never be more than a nullity in the authority he enjoys. To disturb the relationship between bureaucracy and politics, between the official and the politician, is certainly a difficult thing to do and fraught with dangers. Nor must the popular sentiments against "bureaucracy" and the misunderstanding of the complexities of the political side of an official's life be underestimated. It is at this point that I come back to the matter which was left in suspense some pages back about the absence in our Civil Service as well as in other sectors of public service of any clear commitment to serve a public interest and to have an obligation not merely to their political masters, but to the community they serve. Seen from one perspective this is an unjust reproach and a mis-description of relationships. Yet from another it is justifiable, for a state is held together by interests and procedural values which do transcend the particular wills of this or that group of party politicians.

For an official to claim too much authority in the interpretation of substantive interests is dangerous, though if he is honest and conscientious he can often add a dimension to this which the politician may miss. But in relation to the maintenance of the procedural values of a state, the official surely does have a peculiar responsibility. For it is his very condition of permanence and his commitment to public service which imposes on him an obligation to sustain these values. This is the public interest which he ought to serve and on some occasions it may be his duty to set this above other, more problematical statements of that interest. The difficulty with this solution in the present British context is that our understanding of what are these procedural values has become attenuated: we no longer have any agreement about what are the constitutional rules. Only if this situation were changed and these defects made good, could there be some prospect of resolving the dilemmas of the official who has a scruple.

These reflections on the Civil Service and administration have moved rather a long way from the doctrinal core of political centralisation, the claims of Parliament and the responsibility of ministers. Yet in reality the distance separating the two sets of considerations is not great. It is the permanent administration in action which gives continuing reality to the political centralisation which emerges from the competition of parties and the structure of political institutions. And in the complex administrative state which now exists it is the bureaucracy which shapes behaviour and expectations far beyond the public realm in which it operates. This has been particularly true of the central Civil Service, if only because of the prestige and reputation which its higher levels have for so long enjoyed.

It might be thought that these criticisms prepare the way for a total rejection of centralisation, perhaps for a plea to return to a pattern of small and self-governing communities. But that, I fear, would be mere romanticism. The wheels of centralisation cannot be turned back so easily, nor should one underestimate the benefits which can flow from a firm and vigorous central structure of government. The problem is rather to escape from an overbred, even degenerate centralisation, expressed at its worst in the arrogance of politicians and in the pervasive interference in nearly all sectors of activity of a self-satisfied bureaucracy, and to pursue *per contra* a situation in which the centralised state is disciplined and restrained by a diffusion of political initiative and administrative responsibility. Such a condition certainly implies more decentralisation than we have ever been prepared to contemplate and most probably it depends very much upon a willingness to expect less from the central government. And in addition it means accepting that at any rate some parts of the administrative structure are also in the political sphere, exposed to its pressures and subject to its sanctions. The myth of the official as always a political eunuch should go.

The purpose of this chapter has been chiefly to consider the concepts underlying the central political and administrative authority in Britain, concepts which I venture to think go a long way towards explaining why the Leviathan at the centre has assumed the character and structure which it now has. If little attention has been paid to such topics as the Cabinet and how it is supposed to operate, to the Prime Minister and his position within the Executive, to the structure of government departments and the allocation of functions amongst them, to the problems of ministerial policy-making and so on, this is because it does not seem to be strictly necessary for the purpose in hand to go over such well-trodden ground again. What is more important is to elucidate the concepts tying together the whole.

My conclusion is that it is essentially a particular view of unlimited parliamentary authority which finally elicited a doctrine of ministerial responsibility as a congruent solution to the problem of controlling the equally unlimited authority of the Crown. In this way powers came to be vested in ministers and there was no need to conceive of the State as a legal entity or corporation. This was – and substantially still is – the British notion of responsible government, and in a certain sense it is – or it was – a genuine alternative to the State conceived as strictly a rule of law, as a *Rechtsstaat*, to use the German expression. Barely a century ago the structures of party interest began to conform to these institutional concepts, and then in turn gradually came to sustain them. As the need for public powers grew, so inevitably did the central Leviathan. The instruments through which the national political authority became effective as its responsibilities expanded was a bureaucracy which was also most successfully shaped by the values inherent in the dominant institutional relationships, a civil service pliant to political preferences, yet protected and strengthened by its very remoteness from the commitments of politics. Out of these ingredients a formidable structure of centralised political and administrative direction has been built up, one which still possesses an impressive internal logic, no matter how unfortunate may be some of the consequences of its application to the tasks of government.

It follows from this view that there can be no easy ways of loosening up or modifying the centralisation which is so dominant a characteristic of the British polity. Mere administrative changes can have but little effect. What matters crucially are the underlying political habits and modes of political action as well as the concepts and values which the institutions express. Only if changes are made at this level does it become reasonable to expect that there might be some prospect of moving in new directions.

It is not, however, intended at the moment to contemplate how, if at all, significant changes in the British centralised state might be brought about as a deliberate measure of re-shaping or reconstruction. Indeed, it is tempting sometimes to conclude that the pressures for centralised direction and initiative have become so insistent, increasing with every step in the weakening of the economy, that such an enterprise could have no hope of success. However, there have recently been signs of a new and unfamiliar political challenge to the centralised state which it would be worth looking at more closely as the next stage in these reflections.

I refer here to the demand for some kind of political autonomy being put forward in those nations which came into the English orbit to form the United Kingdom — Scotland and Wales. And in that context one can hardly avoid some mention of that other troubled part of the United Kingdom, which alone offered an example of a kind of autonomy — Northern Ireland. In effect, therefore, what follows is a consideration of the antithesis to centralisation, the stirrings on behalf of a decentralisation of power. Yet that may be too mild a way of defining the theme: in reality my concern is with a possibility which only a short time ago would have been dismissed as fanciful — the dismemberment of the United Kingdom. Perhaps Leviathan has come near to overreaching itself.

CHAPTER 7

Challenges to the Unitary State

People outside these islands often talk about "England" and "Britain" as if they were interchangeable and equivalent terms. The failure to understand that they are not is remarkably widespread. And indeed it is sometimes the English themselves who assume that there is here a distinction without a difference. Nevertheless, the confusion is to some extent pardonable if one thinks of the history of this country and of the impact of the British Empire on the world. At the apogee of empire there was even in Britain itself little need to worry much about the question of identity, the issue of Ireland apart. It was plausible to claim that the separate national sentiments of the component parts of Britain had been absorbed within a wider identity which understood itself as British, even though the character it bore owed rather more to England than to her neighbours to the west or the north.

A striking change has taken place within the last few years. There has been a revival of national feeling in Scotland and Wales which has given to political nationalism a strength which it has not had before, whilst at the same time the "out of sight, out of mind" solution to the problem of Northern Ireland has broken down, compelling the British Government to assume complete responsibility for that part of the United Kingdom. The results of these shocks administered to traditional loyalties and political ties cannot yet be foreseen. But two immediate consequences are quite evident. One is that the party landscape has already been radically changed. The complete dominance of the two established "British" parties in the House of Commons was breached in 1974, and for the first time for many years there are groups there whose purpose is essentially to demand the right to exercise political authority elsewhere. The other is that the constitutional structure of the United Kingdom has been called into question in a manner not experienced since the bitter argument over Home Rule for Ireland before the First World War. In short it is not unreasonable

108

to wonder whether the United Kingdom — with the emphasis on the word "United" — can much longer survive, at any rate in something like the form with which we are familiar.

This is of itself an extraordinary turn of events. Only a few years ago anybody who might have raised such a question would have been dismissed as being quite out of touch with reality. Yet now this is not so: there are thoughtful politicians who in private will admit that they doubt whether the unitary state in its present form can be preserved. So it seems worth giving some thought to the reasons why this change has come about and what it may portend.

In the last section I considered some of the characteristics of centralisation in Britain, both the ideas of a constitutional and political nature which sustain it and its structural expression in our pattern of government and administration. The growth of nationalism is both a challenge to and a protest against that centralisation, though as I will try to explain there are other factors which are at least as important as causes of this phenomenon. But in describing nationalism as at least in part a protest against centralisation, there is one misunderstanding which must be guarded against. In its strict sense centralisation denotes a particular structure of government, a certain way of distributing the executive and law-making powers in the State which may — or may not — be supported by a parallel centralisation of the expression of political opinion in a country, that is to say of the parties and such other means of voicing political preferences as exist. Now strictly speaking nationalism in the different parts of the United Kingdom may only be a very qualified challenge to the notion of centralisation in these more comprehensive senses. And indeed some of the evidence from its expression so far suggests that this is so, for the movements calling for autonomy have not on the whole made any serious and coherent plea for a different structure of government which would demonstrate that they understand what might be implied in a genuine dispersion of powers within the United Kingdom. Admittedly there is much talk of community and that kind of tning, especially from the Welsh nationalists, but it reveals naivety and is not the stuff of which states are constructed. Moreover, in England there is nothing to show that there is a strong body of opinion which understands the price which is paid for centralisation, and the pleas which are regularly made for local and regional autonomy have at present no political foundation worth speaking of. So what the qualification made here amounts to is that the demands for autonomy can certainly be seen as a challenge to the "United Kingdom" and to the dominant position of the Government in London in our pattern of centralisation. But it is so far doubtful whether they are a challenge to the idea of the centralised state as such — perhaps an independent Scotland would be ruled from Edinburgh or Glasgow — in much the same way as England is from London. And certainly there are many in Northern Ireland who would run that province as the very model of a tiny tightly centralised state. All this means, therefore, that the real significance of the signs of separation lies in the effects they might have on England, on the shock which the achievement of some of the demands now made would have on the political consciousness of the English and on the ability of its structure of government to survive in an unfamiliar and strange situation.

Let me outline in a rough and ready fashion what appear to have been the principal reasons for the growth of disenchantment with the idea and practice of a unified state in Britain. There have always been national and cultural minorities alongside the English majority in Britain — the Scots, the Welsh and the Irish — and there are even smaller groups too, though these represent folklore curiosities rather than potential political entities. The Irish largely maintained their separate identity, and it is not necessary to describe the manner in which the larger part of them finally achieved political independence. Ironically, those in Ireland who did not want independence fought their cause in the name of Britain and for the sake of staying British, but in the very achievement of that aim were pushed into a kind of isolation which is the underlying reason for the collapse of Northern Ireland over the past five years or so. Though the cultivation of their special national characteristics by the Scots and Welsh can be traced back quite a long way, it is only recently that it has begun to take a serious grip on the imagination of larger numbers of them. And that, of course, was a precondition of it acquiring a political character.

It seems not unreasonable to regard these national revival movements as being influenced in some degree by the process of nation-building which has gone on throughout the world during the past quarter of a century: the forging of new national identities has helped to stimulate the rediscovery of old ones. But whatever may be the influence of this broader trend in the world at large, there can be little doubt that awareness of it has brought hesitation and perplexity into the reactions of the British Government and the political élite at the centre towards this phenomenon. The outcome is a mixture of pretending that the new challenge barely exists and may amount to no more than a passing mood to be followed by a brave return to old loyalties, and a slightly panic-stricken search for concessions through which it might hopefully be placated. These range from the construction of pseudo-constitutional schemes for institutional changes through the promise of additional material benefits to the appeasement of vociferous minorities within a minority by such gestures as decreeing that road signs in English shall be duplicated in Welsh, a language relatively few understand even in their own country.

This revival of national feeling has been stimulated, and especially in the last three or four years, by the weakening of the British economy. Throughout the centuries England's dominance over her neighbours rested essentially on her greater wealth and resources, and indeed for much of the past on the more advanced stage of her civilisation. The impression of the power derived from wealth and technical skill was, of course, at its strongest in the last century when the expansion of empire was taking place. And it no doubt lingered on into very recent times. But now all has suddenly changed. Though the nations apart from England cannot claim to enjoy great prosperity themselves — and in fact have incomes per head somewhat below the English level — it has become obvious that they cannot look forward to being swept onwards and upwards on the coat-tails of England. On the contrary, the belief spreads that they are hitched up to an ailing economy and a country no longer capable of sustaining the demands made on it. A decisive factor in encouraging something like this conclusion has been the discovery of North Sea oil and the realisation in Scotland that here is a resource on which Britain as a whole, and England in particular, are setting great hopes for future salvation — or, perhaps one should say, relief.[1] The impact of economic weakness is felt both on sentiments and material interests. It has reduced the esteem in which England is held by her neighbours and at the same time has reduced the prospects of the poorer parts of the United Kingdom continuing to receive

---

[1] It is, of course, still possible (though perhaps not probable) that North Sea oil will turn out to be a very costly investment, a source of expensive rather than of cheap fuel. To the extent that if this were to happen its value as a source of wealth for an independent Scotland would diminish.

the subsidies and support[2] to which they had become accustomed. But when those who have been dependants discover wealth of their own (or hope to), then they are likely to resent even more strongly the memory of their former dependence.

Alongside declining faith in the material advantages to be gained from association in a unitary state there has been increasing discontent over the remoteness of the central governing authorities, a progressive disenchantment with centralisation and the procedures through which it is upheld. This was something that the Kilbrandon Commission, rather misleadingly described as the Royal Commission on the Constitution (1969–73), investigated by social survey. As is usual in respect of such subtle and difficult matters the survey hardly discovered new truths which had not been apprehended before. But at least it served to confirm that in Scotland and Wales, and even in some parts of England, there is no sense of the proximity of the state and of the involvement of its institutions in the life of the people. One result of this is that the people can have little opportunity themselves for the continuing engagement of self-government. However, it is not just a question of remoteness and distance, important though that clearly is in the case of Scotland, much of which communicates in its very landscape a feeling of worlds quite removed from the preoccupations and manners of middle and southern England. There is also the feeling that the central government is just too English in its character, or to put the matter another way, that it cannot really understand and express the interests and sentiments of those parts of the United Kingdom which are not English. And after all we must remember that the share of Scotsmen, Welshmen and Ulstermen in the government of Britain has on the whole been modest in this century. One can easily recall the great individual exceptions to this, the most famous of which was Lloyd George. But despite these the characteristic condition of British government has been the preponderance of the English and of the values, styles and feelings peculiar to them. It is of no relevance for the Englishman to retort that he has not deliberately tried to maintain this

---

[2]Public expenditure per head of population in Scotland, Wales and Northern Ireland has regularly exceeded the rate of expenditure to England. Details are given in Table 15.1, p. 178 of the Report of the Royal Commission on the Constitution, vol.1, Cmnd. 5460. There are, of course, good grounds for such variations, but they need to be more fully recognised by the beneficiaries.

dominance, and that much of it can be attributed to the lack of ambition of his neighbours and the poor quality of many of those whom they have sent into national politics on their behalf. The fact of England's dominance, regardless of its causes (many of which, as noted already, have to do with the sheer size of England relative to the other nations), is enough to motivate the present discontent.

Whilst there are undoubtedly good reasons for saying that British government has been managed in a centralised fashion in relation to Wales and Scotland, e.g. in economic affairs, it should not be forgotten that Scotland has for a long time had a species of "self-administration" and that during the past decade a serious effort has been made to build up something similar in Wales.[3] Essentially what this has meant has been a voice in the Cabinet (though whether there has been a distinct "Scottish" or "Welsh" point of view as opposed to an "English" on many questions of policy must be doubted: it will be surprising if the Cabinet papers ever reveal that successive Scottish or Welsh secretaries of state have regularly made a significant contribution to the formation of opinion in the Cabinet in virtue of their particular offices and origins). In addition it has involved a provincial administration under the overall control of ministers which has had the functions of a fairly comprehensive "service of the Interior", in Scotland for many decades and in Wales during the past ten years. After the abolition of the Northern Irish government and legislature in 1972, a third provincial minister of this kind had to join the Cabinet. It is this "place at the top table" which according to received conventions was thought to meet the political needs of the Scots and the Welsh (along with a disproportionately large number of representatives at Westminster).[4] But it has been a method of meeting political claims which has never struck the imagination of the beneficiaries, and indeed in recent years has aroused criticism on the grounds that it offers a provincial administration which

---

[3] A Secretary of State for Wales, with a seat in the Cabinet, was first appointed in late 1964, his appointment being followed by a gradual transfer of various administrative services from London to the Welsh Office in Cardiff. His Scottish forerunner reaches back to 1885 when a Secretary for Scotland was appointed who came into the Cabinet in 1892 and gained the status of Principal Secretary of State in 1926, finally absorbing the powers of a variety of administrative boards in Scotland in 1939.

[4] Scotland has 71 MPs, Wales 36 and Northern Ireland 12. Proportionate to population they would be entitled to approximately 57, 31 and 17 MPs respectively.

has no need to be notably responsive to provincial opinion, because there are no provincial institutions to express this. Thus we have the rather odd situation that there is in fact a large measure of self-administration located in Edinburgh, and much the same pattern is being built up in Cardiff, but it is virtually invisible and does little to counteract the impression of a remote and disinterested central government.

There have been two major effects of this revival of national feeling in the United Kingdom. One has been the rapid growth in the strength of nationalist parties, particularly in Scotland. In other words the revival has assumed for the first time a serious political form. The other is that anxious British governments have hastily engaged in the search for suitable schemes of decentralisation – for which we use the rather unsatisfactory term "devolution" – which, it is hoped, might appease those who are now demanding some kind of home rule or self-government.

Before saying just a little more about these two effects it is worth underlining the significance of the Northern Ireland débâcle for the broader question of the survival of the United Kingdom. Northern Ireland has been similar to Scotland and Wales in being different from England, having a distinct culture of its own. And some people would say that it had the kind of self-government to which Scotland and Wales aspire. But there the resemblances such as they are break down. Ulster gained its separateness almost by mistake and because it wanted to stay British – or the Protestant majority of the people there did. The constitution which it received in 1920 had been intended for the whole of Ireland and for that reason enshrined the principle of devolution or home rule through the granting of considerable legislative autonomy and a separate executive authority or government.[5] But it did not really express the status which many people in that province wanted: they were cast into a separateness

---

[5] The Government of Ireland Act 1920 is still worthy of study from a constitutional point of view. What it did essentially was to delegate certain legislative powers to parliaments in Northern and Southern Ireland and to provide that the Crown's executive authority to maintain "peace, order and good government" should be exercised by persons appointed by its representatives in the two provinces. In the event, of course, it was applied only in Northern Ireland. The constitutional model owed a great deal to preceding measures setting up self-government in colonial territories. The Northern Ireland system before 1972 might be defined as functionally limited autonomous parliamentary government, and the constitutional categories in which it was expressed were quite clear.

which was slowly and relentlessly to isolate them from the political life of the rest of Britain and to keep alive the minority's dislike of a state which in their view had no right to exist. The troubles which swept the province from 1968 onwards and led finally to the high-handed abrogation by Westminster of all the autonomy granted half a century ago, were the outcome of the minority's realisation that it lived in a world in which many of its claims could not be denied any longer. This estimation proved to be correct: the majority in Ulster was incapable of maintaining the *status quo* through its own resources, whilst the British Government, regardless of its party colour, finally refused to give its support to preserving the position of 1920.

In important respects this reaction was right and prudent: the political arrangements of Ulster operated in a way which left much to be desired, and the substantial minority in the province had good reason for complaint, though even before "direct rule" was imposed in 1972 major reforms had been initiated which might have opened the way to a *modus vivendi* had not the resources of terrorism been so powerful. But what is unfortunate, and has a bearing on the wider issues dealt with here, is that for most of the time during the crisis British governments appeared to be the victims of circumstances rather than to have the will or desire to control the situation. There may well be many reasons why this state of affairs could not be avoided, and justifications for the twists and turns which British policy took. However, since this is not a history of what happened, the explanation of why British governments behaved as they did need not be pursued here. The point which is relevant to my present argument is that the events in Ulster did reveal the fragility of the United Kingdom and the weakness of the central political authority. Furthermore, the course taken by events in Ulster meant that the whole structure of party life there was destroyed. One consequence of this which seriously affected British politics was that the Conservative Party lost ten or eleven previously safe seats in the House of Commons. This in turn reflected the fact that the majority in Northern Ireland, which originally preferred to stay British, had become steadily more disillusioned, so that many have been tempted to think of the possibility of complete independence, no matter how unrealistic that prospect may be in economic terms.

The fate of Ulster did not, however, merely reveal the susceptibility to pressure of the British Government. It suggested too that there was a weariness and indifference towards the crisis amongst the English people, perhaps overcome only once by a bomb outrage in Birmingham in November 1974 after which there were some signs of appreciation of the kind of methods being used on behalf of the minority in Northern Ireland. But for the most part the Ulster events have stimulated no serious and continuous political argument in England. What a contrast with the situation in the late nineteenth century and on into the present one! Then virtually the whole of organised political opinion became intensely preoccupied with the question of Home Rule and its implications for the British state, and notable jurists and political writers contributed to the debate. Many of them may have been wrong-headed and too susceptible to passion: but at least there was argument and a belief that principles determining institutions were at issue, not the indifference of those who cannot see beyond the percentages of the next wage increase which they are about to demand. Again, the moral for the devolution question in relation to Scotland and Wales is clear: the English hardly appear yet to have understood what is at stake, and the prudent politician is the one who tactfully slides the issues under the carpet: Is it then entirely surprising that some of the nationalists should ask themselves whether the English really care any longer what is the shape and structure of the State to which they belong?

Coming back to the principal aspects of the challenge under discussion I shall not try to describe the nationalist political movements themselves, though the point must be made that the one in Scotland is a much more serious affair than its counterpart in Wales. Whereas the achievement of something like the majority of votes in Scotland by the Scottish National Party is in the foreseeable future quite possible, the same cannot be said of the Welsh nationalist movement, Plaid Cymru.[6] This is chiefly because it is the prisoner of the real source of Welsh cultural identity, the language. But that is the possession of only a small minority of the Welsh population and, as the experience of independent Ireland in trying to give artificial respiration to a dead language shows, there is no real possibility of changing this situation. At best the language in Wales can be prevented from dying. Consequently Welsh nationalism has difficulty in gaining

[6] The Scottish National Party gained in October 1974 the support of 30 per cent of Scottish voters, whilst in contrast Plaid Cymru had only 11 per cent of Welsh voters (gaining three seats in areas where the language is widely spoken).

support beyond the limits of those who know the language and are sensitive to all that is associated with it and its history. And there is in addition the still powerful loyalty of the industrial workers of South Wales to the Labour Party, a loyalty proceeding from the strange chemistry through which the religious life of the noncomformist chapel was transmuted into the secular idealism of a party for the "underdogs". Yet Welsh nationalism, though very much a minority movement, looks likely to benefit from the belief that nothing (or practically nothing) which is offered to Scotland can properly be withheld from Wales. Unfortunately this must mean that the majority of people in Wales run the risk of being saddled with political experiments which in reality they may not want. Such are the ironies of "democratic" politics and such is the effect of confusion of principles at the centre.

As mentioned earlier, the demands under discussion have prompted a search for remedies in London and given an opportunity for the institutional scene-shifters to demonstrate their skills. A little more attention has to be given to this aspect before passing on to the heart of the question at stake.

Many people have in recent years spent a lot of time considering what kind of schemes might best satisfy such demands as exist outside England for self-government and autonomy. They nearly all conclude that a federal solution is impossible, though most seem to think that this is because federalism is peculiarly "un-British" and unworkable rather than on account of such real difficulties as might in practice accompany a federalisation of Britain.[7] The consensus of established opinion is for maintaining the "United Kingdom", by which must be meant the supremacy of the executive power in London, though that is never said openly. But at the same time it is admitted that the demands for autonomy are sufficiently strong to require and justify concessions which are seen predominantly in the form of some degree of "devolved" political authority. In practice this is taken to mean the transfer to provincial elected assemblies of legislative and/or executive rights in particular spheres of action — chiefly those of a domestic or internal nature like

[7]Federalism is dealt with in Chapter 13 of the Report of the Royal Commission on the Constitution. Though some fair points are made about the difficulties of a federal structure, the tenor of the discussion is somewhat complacent and insular, and the view taken of federations elsewhere is too condescending.

education, health, transport and housing. But in order to satisfy the reality of maintaining the supremacy of the London Government and the form of leaving untouched the powers of the sovereign Parliament at Westminster, the powers which can be devolved have to be fairly strictly circumscribed and transferred subject to the proviso that they can be reassumed by Westminster at will. Moreover, there is nearly always in this kind of discussion a *sotto voce* assumption that any powers which are passed over to a subordinate legislative assembly will be used prudently and with due regard to the desirability of following the lead from Westminster. Such was the assumption which on the whole held good throughout the life of the assembly at Stormont: though Northern Ireland managed its own affairs, it did not legislate for differences between itself and the rest of Britain. It is assumed that Scotland and Wales would follow suit.

It is to the elaboration of schemes broadly of this kind that the Government which took office in 1974 is committed and to which in some measure all the British — or English — parties now give a kind of half-hearted support. However, in the discussion of the problem which has so far taken place it is hard to find much in the shape of a serious constitutional argument: the preparation of proposals by the Government during 1974 and 1975 proceeded with the kind of discretion and secrecy which would have been unexceptionable had it been a question of a new sewerage scheme or a revision of the law relating to graveyards, but which was remarkable in the case of matters which affect profoundly the future of the United Kingdom. An explanation of this peculiarity is, however, not hard to find. Apart from the conditioned reflexes of concealment which accompany the legislative process as a matter of course in Britain, there is the additional factor that both Government and Opposition, which after all depend mainly on English support, are committed in only a guarded and qualified way to devolution policies. Thus, their main concern has been to find a resting-place which stops short of that degree of autonomy which might seriously qualify the overriding powers of the central government and Westminster. This helps to explain why a veil was thrown over the preparation of schemes which,[8] so it was hoped, would give to at

---

[8] It is true that on publication in November 1975 of the White Paper, *Our Changing Democracy: Devolution to Scotland and Wales* (Cmnd. 6348) it was claimed that this should open a great public debate. Nevertheless, the public debate was not to hold up preparation of draft legislation.

least two parts of the United Kingdom such a degree of representative self-government as would reconcile the majority of their populations to the continuance of the British political association, and at the same time check the growth of support for the protagonists of nationalism. It goes almost without saying that for the leadership of the Labour Party a major consideration has been the avoidance of any action which might threaten the electoral advantages which it has so far enjoyed in both Wales and Scotland through the over-representation of both. Nor has great concern been shown for the possibility that under such proposals as have been made the political rights of the English would be relatively diminished. But then if the latter are content to remain indifferent in the face of what might in reality be discrimination against them, who need be surprised that there is little to be set against the yardsticks of political expediency?

By the end of 1975 a number of official proposals had been formulated and published for the achievement of devolution in Wales and Scotland. In addition unsuccessful attempts had been made to reconstruct some form of self-government in Ulster. In this context there would, however, be little advantage in examining these matters in detail. It is rather two features of the approach to the whole problem of devolution revealed by successive British governments which require emphasis. One is the preference for an extreme eclecticism in the choice of means and methods by which to meet particular claims for autonomy, and the concomitant reluctance to see the challenge in terms of a restructuring of the constitutional order. In the case of Northern Ireland some recognition of the constitutional nature of the problem has lingered on, as is revealed by the titles of various White Papers on the future of Ulster and the setting-up of a Constitutional Convention there.[9] Nevertheless, the Northern Ireland Constitution Act of 1973 expressed a significant retreat from the relative clarity in constitutional terms of the 1920 Government of Ireland Act: it represented a complicated (and as it turned out, ill-fated) exercise in qualified and guided self-government, leaving obscure the principles on

---

[9] For example, *Northern Ireland Constitutional Proposals*, March 1973, Cmnd. 5259; *The Northern Ireland Constitution*, July 1974, Cmnd. 5675; *Northern Ireland Constitutional Convention*, report presented to Parliament, 20 November 1975.

which it rested.[10] These characteristics have been reflected even more clearly in the schemes prepared for Scotland and Wales: they appear to offer certain rights of self-government, yet are replete with qualifications and reservations in favour of the tutelary authority of the Government in London.[11]

The other feature worth mentioning is the reluctance to use the word "Government" in the devolution proposals so far put forward. Even the general concept of executive authority is eschewed. There seems to have been a vague hope (not shared, be it said, by the Kilbrandon Commission in its report), that somehow or other powers might be developed in favour of assemblies and actually be exercised by such bodies, so that recognition of anything looking like a government or a representative of the Crown would be avoided. This kind of pretence has so far broken down that in relation to Scotland (and following the precedent of Northern Ireland) there was in late 1975 acceptance of the notion of an "Executive", the name given to the body which would actually exercise the powers to be conferred on it by Parliament and by a future Scottish Assembly. For Wales, however, there was to be only an Executive Committee of the Assembly, the kind of "county council" solution thought appropriate to a non-legislative assembly. It is hard to avoid the conclusion that this aversion towards recognition of a genuine executive authority stems from a failure to understand the elementary conditions of self-government. If there is to be any self-government in Scotland, Wales or Northern Ireland, then there has to be in all three territories an executive power, something in the nature of a domestic government. That condition is prior to any representative body or assembly just as the Crown preceded Parliament.

---

10 The revised system of devolution of power to an Assembly and Executive lasted only from January to May 1974. Despite its early demise, brought about essentially by a difference of opinion between the Government in London and the Executive in Belfast about the appropriate response to pressures exerted by the Loyalist Ulster Workers' Council to secure revision of the constitutional measures, the scheme did demonstrate two things. One was that a form of coalition government between the parties representing the two communities was feasible; the other that the "guided devolution" scheme tended from the start to generate a claim to an autonomy consistent with having an executive and legislative authority in the province. The Executive could not accept the role of mere agent of the Government in London.

11 *Our Changing Democracy: Devolution to Scotland and Wales*, Cmnd. 6348.

Such a contention has no bearing on the desirability one way or the other of dispersing powers within the United Kingdom: it refers simply to a necessity contained within the concept of self-government. However, to admit this necessity is to admit the possibility of an authority which might compete with London, challenge its capacity always to declare the interest of the people of Scotland or Wales, and come to exercise (as it did in Northern Ireland) an influence on the pattern of political sentiment and interest which the hitherto dominant parties would prefer not to contemplate. It is to admit also the possibility that such necessary elements in a pattern of self-government within the United Kingdom could only be contained within a genuine constitutional framework which would have something of a federal character. It is considerations of this kind which no doubt account for this strange reticence in official thinking on devolution. Yet to proceed in this way in the light of the experience of Stormont which, whatever its shortcomings, was for the people of Northern Ireland the seat of *their* Government, is remarkable. It is as if those who dominate English politics believed that there is no limit to the willingness of those they rule to be satisfied by appearances.

Let me come now to the core of the problem posed by the strains affecting the unity — or unification — of the British State. We have to ask what it is that holds this State together. This cannot be merely material interests, whatever may be the modern equivalent of the production of calico, to recall Burke's thinking on the matter. There have to be other sentiments which sustain the value of this association in the minds of those who are part of it. Of such sentiments the most powerful has in most political societies in Europe been that of nationality, the sense of sharing certain qualities in virtue of a common national identity. In the case of Britain the national identity was, however, always composite and in some degree artificial. It covered a history in which one has not to push back too far into the past to find quite separate and distinct national traditions, assuming for the moment the licence of ascribing the term "national" to perceptions held at a time before the emergence of modern political nationalism. What then was it which sustained the notion of Britain, and of being "British"? It seems that this notion is best explained in relation to the extension of England into the world. England cast its energies into the creation of an "imperium", acquiring riches throughout the world and applying the political ideas of her own people to the construction of

political communities far away from home. Gradually, in the course of the
eighteenth century, the term "British" overlaid the experience which was
"English", and more especially in their relations with the outside world
the English began to see themselves as British. But so powerful was this
process by which England projected itself into the world that it carried
along with it the energies and usually the loyalties of the Scots, the Welsh,
and even in some measure of the Irish too. Of course, in practical life the
people of these countries often had little choice: their relative poverty and
the slowness of their own development forced many of them to seek
outlets for their energies in this task of spreading English influence in the
world.

It has, however, been a peculiarity — and some would say a virtue — of
the English that they have been more interested in ruling other people
than in civilising them after their own image. Thus it came about that the
task of building a greater Britain and of evoking loyalty and commitment
to it, a task which doubtless reached its dramatic climax just less than a
hundred years ago, could take place without there being any serious
attempt to forge a British nationality at home: there was a certain restraint
in the imperialism of the English and they were satisfied if the superior
social groups amongst their neighbours anglicised themselves and so came
to perceive themselves as part of a single dominant connection. Thus, to a
remarkable extent, the symbols in which being "British" were expressed
were imperial in character and were evocative of an influence and power
exerted in the world outside these islands. The real problems of national
identity at home were put into suspense: they could lie dormant until a
future should re-discover its past.

It is something like this which has happened now. The epoch of empire
is over and Britain is thrown back in upon itself. Much of the post-Second
World War period was taken up with pretending that this had not
happened, that the so-called Commonwealth, which came to embrace such
a heterogeneous collection of former colonies and dominions, was some
kind of substitute for empire. That illusion at least seems largely to be
gone now, though echoes of it could still be heard in the argument about
membership of the European Community. Yet in returning to itself Britain
discovers that it is not really a single identity at all. England cannot claim
here at home to be co-terminous with Britain, and we find that alongside
England there are national communities which do not and cannot feel

"English". "British" they might have been prepared to be, but the England of Shakespeare and Elizabeth I, of Milton and Cromwell, of Bentham and Benjamin Jowett, is not part of *their* history. It is for this reason fundamentally that there is a challenge to the unity of the United Kingdom. Now that the substance of "imperium" has gone and the symbols associated with it, the United Kingdom can survive as a unified state only if its component parts can successfully re-define what it is in their different histories which binds them together and what it is which must hold them together in the future. These are the questions to which answers have to be found, and the answers will not be elicited from clever little schemes intended to make the relationships within the United Kingdom look different whilst in reality preserving the *status quo*. If that course continues to be followed, then the most likely outcome is indeed the dissolution of the British State.

There are few signs at present of a serious attempt at a redefinition or re-statement of the loyalties and perceived commitments on which the United Kingdom can rest in the future. It is an interesting comment on our times that loyalty to the Crown plays no part in contemporary discussion of this question: only in Ulster was that until recently a powerful symbol, and even there it now seems to have lost much of its significance. Yet in contrast the Crown was something like the British equivalent to the concept of the *république une et indivisible* in the context of the Home Rule controversy of sixty and more years ago. There are now many influences at work which make it unfashionable to assert the need for unifying sentiments, for common values, and for a shared understanding of the procedures by which the society will be governed. Instead it is vaguely assumed that every group and even every individual has the right to retreat into private worlds, untroubled by both the constraints and the opportunities which stem from belonging to a wider pattern of relationships. In this climate of opinion there are many manifestations of "separatism", not all of them with a national flavour, which it is hard to challenge. Overshadowing this situation is the factor of economic decline affecting the country as a whole, but by accident accompanied by the prospect of new sources of raw materials, especially in the North Sea, which serves to stimulate the dissatisfactions of those who seek a new identity. Any British government is inhibited from tackling this kind of problem with confidence, for after all what can it offer on present showing by way of a prosperous future? At the same time the unrealistic expectations of the nationalists have been fuelled and they are tempted to assume that the task of creating economically viable independent states would be far easier than it has ever been reasonable to suppose. Yet another factor weighing against the chances of success in this enterprise of establishing a new understanding of shared ties is the absence of a common language in which to discuss the constitutional future of Britain. There is no stock of hard-wearing concepts out of which it might be possible to fashion a shared understanding of constitutional and political values, and to re-shape institutions which together would appear then to a majority in all parts of the United Kingdom to represent something in the nature of a new covenant.

Yet even though the prospects in this matter do not look hopeful, it is hard to become reconciled to the dissolution which has been foreshadowed as a possibility no longer to be entirely discounted. What then might be the elements in what has just been called "a new covenant"? Here I am thinking not of what is likely or probable, but of what can reasonably be regarded as necessary elements in the foundation for renewed common loyalties which are what should be sought.

First, there has to be some recognition that there are benefits of a more mundane kind to be gained from a continued association of all the components of the United Kingdom, including Northern Ireland, so long as most of its people prefer to remain in the British State. This is not to argue that Scotland, and conceivably even Wales (though that is less plausible) could not survive economically as separate political units: given determination and willingness to accept sacrifices for a while, perhaps they could. Yet of the necessary determination neither has so far given a convincing sign, and both countries are every bit as much victims of the illusions which have been described as England. Indeed, it might be argued that as both Scotland and Wales are more strongly influenced by the very political forces which are in the vanguard of the impulse to live by illusions, their condition may be worse than that of England! If so, then it is hardly a sound basis on which to build prosperity in a world in which the ability to compete effectively in trade is an important condition of independent survival.

Second, there has to be a serious acceptance of the need to disperse political responsibility more widely than has been tolerated in the past.

Now in saying this the intention is not merely to echo the empty phrases which are repeated in official doctrine about letting localities and regions make their own decisions, provided, of course, that these remain tidily within the bounds of the framework which the centre lays down for us and respect the needs supposedly imposed by "management of the economy". The toleration of political dispersion has to mean the acceptance of competing and mutually checking knots of political power or influence. In a rather awkward way Northern Ireland does provide an example of what is meant here, for it is undoubtedly a fact that the representatives of the majority did have something like a veto power over the preferences of London and that there was (and is) in Northern Ireland a political life quite distinct from what we conventionally call "national politics" in Britain. It is something like this which would have to be allowed to develop in the non-English parts of Britain, and which has yet to be fruitfully accommodated to the conduct of politics at the centre. Maybe this process would be helped along and made easier if there were some willingness in England to recognise the advantages which might be gained from a diffusion of power within England itself: this is the point at which the problems of provinces become equally problems of local and community self-government.

Third, there have to be much more coherent ideas of how to federalise Britain in some way than we have so far had. In other words, the political dispersion to which I have just referred has to be given adequate institutional form, it has to be applied to tasks of government, and it has to be grounded in acceptable constitutional concepts.

The word "federalise" is used deliberately. It seems unlikely that any solution to the present crisis of the United Kingdom as a unitary state will prove enduring which is founded on the absence of special guarantees, at the least for Scotland and Northern Ireland, and on an attempt to maintain unmodified the right of the Government and Parliament in London to act at will and with complete discretion. In other words, the attempt made by the Kilbrandon Commission to present proposals for devolution without giving them any serious constitutional foundation was without sense: a Commission on the Constitution concluding that there was no need for a constitution and the kind of concepts on which constitutional reasoning might be founded, failed in its purpose. When I refer to "federalising" Britain this need not be taken to mean adopting either the American Constitution, the West German or the Swiss: there is no compulsion on Britain to turn itself forthwith into a fully fledged federal state. What is being suggested, however, is that there is little prospect of achieving a viable state within which to contain these revived nationalisms, unless courage and intelligence can be harnessed to the task of expressing through a constitutional settlement the relationships postulated by some of the claims inherent in them. Recognition of Scottish or Welsh or Northern Irish claims would, according to this view of the matter, have to be given a special status, becoming part of a new "Act of Union". To this extent we should be federalising Britain, recognising formally the different and competing claims within it as well as a distribution of rights and powers, but in a manner consistent with the survival of that central power which is the condition of any federation's existence.

No doubt many people in Britain would then rush to assert that even to contemplate such a constitutional settlement is impossible. Yet such a reaction would typify chiefly the English, speaking out of what they conceive to be their own experience. Their neighbours are, however, somewhat different, and especially the Scots and the Northern Irish majority: they have some sensitivity still to the idea of constitutionally defined relationships and the Scottish legal tradition may offer more in this direction than the English. Even British governments of recent years have, by implication at least, recognised this, as we can discern from the use of the term "constitution" and "constitutional" in the discussion of the Ulster problem. Here there has been no attempt in successive official reports to dress up what is accepted as a constitutional problem in the guise of an exercise in management consultancy. Part of the challenge is to carry this insight further afield before it is too late.

A little earlier in this discussion I alluded to the possibility that if greater autonomy could be effectively conferred on the national minorities in Britain, it might then become easier to contemplate a serious diffusion of power in England, the majority nation. Usually it has been held that this would have to mean some kind of regionalisation of England, the establishment of a small number of provincial representative authorities. But so far nothing has come of such schemes, though they have been mooted often enough: they conflict with the centralisation of administrative control in England, and just as important, there is no political foundation for them, either in local politics or at the hypothetical regional level. And indeed it is the peculiar weakness of local self-government – the one tier of representation below the national level which Britain currently possesses – which constitutes a major obstacle to devolution, whether this is to be applied solely to the national minorities or to the country as a whole.

Indeed, to suggest that the grant of some internal autonomy to Scotland and Wales might have beneficial effects on local self-government in those countries and in England too, is probably to put the cart before the horse. It is the absence of vigorous self-governing local communities which has itself favoured centralisation, and in certain parts of the country encouraged the growth of nationalist feeling as an alternative to the values of local self-government. But it is possible that schemes for devolution will prove disappointing in practice precisely because there is no strong foundation for them at the local level. As a result they may not bring that extension of democratic rights in virtue of which they are customarily justified.

It has to be admitted that local and municipal government has throughout Britain sunk into a highly dependent condition, particularly during the past quarter of a century. *Pari passu* the influence of the central authority over the provision of local services and the spending of funds locally has increased. Despite all the protestations of the reformers of local government, eager to encourage local democracy, and despite the lip-service paid to this cause by the central government itself, this drift into dependence has relentlessly gone ahead. Though the responsibilities, powers and duties of local government bodies remain substantial, they are tied down by parliamentary authority, by the supervisory and controlling powers of ministers and by financial constraints. The latter have been notably tightened in recent years, especially under the impact of government policies in the sphere of economic management which have in turn necessitated even more central intervention in local decision-making.[12]

12 In the years 1973–5 local authority spending rose by 8 per cent per year in real terms compared with GDP annual growth rates of 2½ per cent. Local spending also rose faster than central government expenditure. This phenomenon was attributable both to the principles on which the forward planning of public expenditure is controlled and to the growing volume of duties imposed by the central authority. Yet rapid growth of local spending was also compatible with wider central controls and more detailed intervention, e.g. over the level of local rate increases.

However, the crucial characteristic of British local government is not so much its dependence on the centre in relation to its executive functions, but rather its political weakness and insignificance. In very many countries there is a close interdependence between national and local politics, reflected, for example, in the career patterns of politicians, in the role of parliamentarians acting as the spokesmen for local interests in decision-making at the centre, and in the ability of some politicians to survive even against general party opinion because they have a firm local base. Equally, relationships of this kind often work to the benefit of localities, strengthening local leadership groups and bringing specific advantages to local or regional interests. Practically none of this applies in Britain. There is here a disjunction between national politics and politics at any lower level, and it is national politics alone which has been thought important. Perhaps it was only in Northern Ireland that something like a divergence from this pattern could be detected. There an interdependence of local and provincial politics, encouraged no doubt by the smallness of the province and the belief in a divided community that important interests were at stake, has been significant.

The most persuasive explanation of this peculiarity in the structure of British politics lies in the dominance over a very long period of national political élites and their relatively sharp separation from local politics understood as the maintenance of local positions of political influence. As a result, interest and influence do not flow up continuously from the base to the top in British political life. National politics has long been regarded as an altogether grander and more serious affair than local political activity, and more likely to be conducted well if freed from the ties and commitments of local communities. The social homogeneity of earlier ruling groups, the manner in which national parties evolved, the belief in the negative state held on to for so long, the strength of the national Civil Service and its dislike of any hint of dependence on those who by definition can have only narrow and local perspectives – these are but some of the factors which have conspired to confirm the subordination of local political life to the requirements of government at the centre.

Clearly the questions which arise in this manner are different from those posed by the growth of nationalist feeling on the part of the non-English populations. And indeed it has been the consistent policy of British governments to treat the question of devolution quite separately from questions affecting the structure and powers of local government. Yet there is an artificiality about this approach. The underlying problem is centralisation and its consequences. To be effective any measures intended to reduce the degree of centralisation must rest on a solid political foundation at the bottom. This means that they would have at least to tolerate, and perhaps to encourage, a genuine diffusion of power rather than offering merely the appearance of autonomy. All recent attempts to achieve through local government reform a greater measure of local independence have failed precisely for this reason. They have concentrated on administrative structures and relationships, neglecting the fact that as long as the disjunction between national and local politics persists in its present form, it is hard to see how the weakness of local self-government can be overcome.

These characteristics of the local level of political life have some bearing on the demands for autonomy put forward in the devolution argument. Firstly, though the nationalist movements in Scotland and Wales profess some concern for the revival of local political life, they may not appreciate sufficiently well that any self-government which they achieve will qualitatively depend very much on how far a fruitful relationship can be achieved between local and national (i.e. "sub-national") interests within the structure of "home rule" which is being sought. If a more balanced relationship between the local and provincial levels of government and politics is not attained, then the units of local government will be tempted to continue to look for support and guidance to the central authority, that is to say, to the ministers in the Government in London. Secondly, one must face the probability that in England the dominance of national over local politics will persist, thus constituting as it always has done, a major obstacle both to any parallel decentralisation on a local and provincial basis in England as well as to a genuine devolution of political authority to the national minorities themselves. For it is hard to discern what kind of constitutional structure might accommodate both the present degree of centralisation in England, and patterns of devolved government elsewhere providing for a substantial dispersion of powers and political rights.

These aspects of the argument about the future shape of the United Kingdom tend to be neglected. No doubt it speaks volumes for the English view of the significance of local self-government that this is so. The danger is that devolution, like local government reform too, will be treated as an exercise in administrative re-shaping and that the political dimensions of the matter, both at the local level and at the level of the national communities, will not be understood.

In pursuing the theme of devolution a lot of stress has been placed on the desirability of trying to understand it in the only categories in which a solution can be found, namely those of constitutional relationships. For this reason it would be helpful to turn next to another theme which is in a very precise sense "constitutional". This is the definition and protection of rights" is no longer as strange-sounding as it might have been only twenty renewed attention in Britain, so much so that the concept of a "bill of rights"is no longer as strange-sounding as it might have been only twenty years ago. This will also provide an opportunity for reflecting on a much broader subject, the place of law in the British conception of the political order. Law and politics must always be intertwined, at any rate in any society which seeks to place constraints on the exercise of power. It is one of the oddities of the British approach to this question – or should one say, of the English approach, for here again Scottish traditions are somewhat different, just as are Scottish lawyers from English – that the prevailing prejudice is in favour of keeping the two spheres apart, tolerating their interaction as rarely as proves necessary. The consequences of this belief have been serious. As suggested before, it has left this country with an improverished vocabulary with which to analyse the problems it faces and out of which to construct new procedures and relationships for the future. However, this is already to anticipate the next stage in these reflections.

CHAPTER 8

Law and the Polity

There is a growing feeling in Britain that the role of law in the social and political life of the country requires to be reassessed. But to consider this basic issue it is first necessary to raise some questions about rights in Britain. Whether one calls such rights "basic", "human", "natural" or anything else of a similarly awe-inspiring nature, is not of major importance for what follows. My assumption is that it would not be disputed in a liberal society that human beings are entitled to treatment which respects their dignity as individuals and allows them the opportunity of self-determination in the shaping of their lives. If that is accepted, then we are committed to the language of rights and to the maintenance of a framework of law in which such rights can be exercised.

Let me start, however, from some broader political reflections, for law is in important respects an eminently political phenomenon. In the Western tradition of political thought there are two insights or points of departure which have often served to create a gulf between thinkers, even though there have been a few who could span the divide. One of these insights has been into the manner in which individuals emerge from their history and are shaped by the relationships, procedures and other shared experiences of the society or community to which they belong. We might take Burke as expressing very clearly this view of the way in which we should begin to reflect on the character of political experience and the foundations of government. Such an approach is bound to induce scepticism towards any relationships or proposals for establishing relationships of a political kind which do not take account of the history of the society in question and of its previous political experience, for it is here that the source of such sentiments and loyalties as might sustain a political association is to be found. At the other extreme is the insight that it is possible, more or less plausibly, to ground a statement of political relationships as ideally they might become on certain postulates, that is to say to proceed by a deductive argument from whatever may be the presuppositions (and these have been various and contrasting, of course) which are selected. Bentham provides one model of this approach, Hobbes another and a very different one, Kant yet another.

What I am underlining here is the unoriginal point that there is one stream of political thought which prefers to start from the variegated pattern of particular experiences, arguing from there to general conclusions (if any), whilst there is another which prefers to assume certain general principles or conditions, and then to construct an argument leading to particulars on that foundation. It is a contrast of this kind which lies behind the questions now being raised about the status of rights in Britain, and is reflected in the discussion of whether it is prudent to continue to rely solely on the methods with which we have generally in the past dealt with these questions. Similarly it has a bearing on the ideas we have had about the rule of law in political life and government, and about the terms on which political institutions have been expected to operate. Though there are risks attaching to over-simplification, it can hardly be denied that we have in Britain taken a historical view of rights, regarding them as understandings about relationships which emerge gradually from social experience, and safeguarded — in so far as it is proper to use that term — by such confidence as that experience engenders. In arguing on these lines I am not asserting that there has been no interest in England in such general assumptions as might underlie particular rights or claims to rights; equally I do not want to imply that rights have not been specifically declared or enacted on some occasions in the past.[1] But the predominant opinion and practice has been in favour of the historical view of rights according to which they are most secure if founded on custom and the accretion of precedent. Abstract statements of rights have been treated sceptically, regarded as a good starting-point for an argument, but not as the best security against wrongful arrest.

The notion that rights in this country are rooted in custom was mirrored in the growth of the common law, and it was through the common law that custom became embodied in legal theory and practice.

---

[1] An obvious example is the Bill of Rights enacted at the end of 1689 after the expulsion of James II. Its terms were cited as recently as December 1975 by the Master of the Rolls, Lord Denning, in giving judgement against the Home Office in the case of *Congreve* v *Home Office*.

And, as is well known, all this had a profound effect on British constitutional development, distinguishing it sharply from most of its neighbours. It was the vitality of the common law which did more than anything else to frustrate the emergence of an absolutist state, and then ensured that so long as the scope of public powers remained narrow there was no need for more serious discussion of the effectiveness of the protection given to individual rights: the courts and the judges were confident that they could do all that was necessary to this end by drawing on the resources of the common law traditions which they embodied.

But there was another idea at work here which was also very important. It was generally assumed that individuals in society might do anything which was not expressly forbidden by law, though this by no means excluded the possibility that they might justifiably be constrained in many ways by custom and convention. The presumption that there were no inherent public prohibitions, justifiable in relation to some public interest which might be declared by a public authority, became gradually part of the texture of the common law. Instead such prohibitions as there were emerged from the understandings by which society was held together and were "discovered" or expressed by the common law itself. In time, of course, it came to be accepted that new prohibitions might be declared and enacted by Parliament. But the influence of this historical view of rights combined with a negative view of the scope of any public authority superimposed on society has been deep, pervasive and continuing. It explains why the concept of the "State" has played such a modest part in English political philosophy (with the one exception of Hobbes, and even he was by no means free from the influence of the ideas under discussion); it explains why the belief has persisted that there is strictly no such thing as "public law", but merely law applicable to certain authorities as if they were private persons, this law in turn being subject to the abiding principles of the common law, itself the formalisation by judges of principles sanctioned by the experience of the society; and it suggests reasons why explicit constitutional principles have been regarded with suspicion and, further, why the courts of this country have shown so little concern with broader questions of *Recht*[2] as compared with what can be

---

[2] There is, of course, no satisfactory terminology in English with which to distinguish betwen *Recht* and *Gesetz*, *droit* and *loi*, *diritto* and *legge*: 'law' has to serve both for law as in "rule of law" and specific legal enactments.

argued from precedent, from individual cases and from the exact words of the statutes.

All this has meant that there has been a quality of specificity marking both the definition of rights in Britain and their protection or vindication. If human rights are held to exist as fundamentals of our condition, then we have preferred not to say so formally and have been more interested in such matters as the precise limitations affecting what an individual may do and the particular powers which this or that authority may exercise. For the rest the assumption is that the individual has the right to act as he pleases, unhindered except by specific prohibitions, and that as long as the courts are able to maintain this happy condition by drawing on the resources of the common law, there is no need to worry about the absence of a formal statement of rights.

This approach to the protection of rights, no matter how much robust common sense it has expressed in the past, is now obsolete. The fundamental reason why this is so is that it takes no account of the density and completeness of public regulation in our world. Indeed, the traditional doctrine does not really contain any conception of public regulation, public authority and a public realm at all. This is not to deny that the common law view of rights rests on a strong perception of social solidarity and on the importance of mutually reinforcing obligations between members of the society. But it has fundamentally no place for that kind of public authority which has become inescapable in our world, and no concept of the citizen. It follows that the old tradition cannot of itself find effective means of doing what any adequate system of public law must attempt to do nowadays, that is to say, to interpret the limits of governmental powers in the interest of citizens and for the protection of their rights.

The point which is being made here can be illustrated in numerous ways. There are many occasions on which the individual finds that he simply has no means of challenging the actions of a public body at all. This may be because the discretion conferred is openly stated to be unlimited, or it may be because the traditional legal order has no principles with which it would be possible to re-define or interpret the powers claimed by the public authority. Again, it may turn out to be possible to challenge an action in a particular situation, only to find that the judicial decision establishes no rule valid for the future: the individual plaintiff may get through the procedural thicket, but the decision is taken on narrow and technical grounds which fail to establish a principle for the future. Another trend is for public authorities in an increasingly bold way to proceed by assertion, threat, bluff. They address their demands to citizens in terms which suggest that they have legally valid powers, and then they hope that a natural disposition to comply will combine with the likelihood that there is indeed no remedy on most occasions, to ensure that they can get what they want. Then again, we in Britain have to an unusual degree withdrawn vast areas of public service provision from any control by the courts and the application of principles of justice. I need cite only the huge sector of social services, including the provision of a great range of financial benefits, the wide and complex sector of physical planning or land use control, and those aspects of employment regulation where claims to benefit and compensation arise. These are but a few examples (though of great importance) of the extension of governmental action which has taken place with but marginal provision for the intervention of the ordinary courts of the land and of the doctrines which they have fondly thought still underpin our legal system. Indeed administrative discretion is extensive and the need for the arbitration of disputes is met by the growth of a twilight jurisdiction, exercised by a complex and sometimes bizarre pattern of informal bodies, usually called tribunals. Whatever qualities such bodies have, they are rarely those of courts and it can hardly be said that it is a body of law that their activity builds up.

It is not an unfair conclusion that in Britain we have allowed the powers and duties of public authorities to be expanded with very little regard to the desirability *in the interests of citizens* of subjecting these authorities to certain general principles conducive to the protection of human rights. Perhaps the Franks Committee of 1956–7[3] was the last official body to say anything of a fairly general nature on this matter, and even it was concerned almost exclusively with quasi-judicial procedural principles such as the right to a fair hearing and the right to have reasons stated for decisions taken by a public authority. There was no attempt to formulate principles adequate to the problems inherent in trying to

[3] The Committee on Tribunals, set up to examine the exercise of quasi-judicial powers by ministers and the increasing number of special tribunals empowered to rule on claims advanced by individuals both against public authorities and private associations. Its findings constituted a skilful holding operation.

safeguard individual rights in the face of the expanding activities of the contemporary public service state, principles which might bring a reversal of that situation to which Lord Justice Scarman refers when he remarks of administrative tribunals: "The justice of the decision as distinct from the legality of their proceedings is beyond review by the courts".[4] Justice and legality have not been seen as being in need of harmonisation. Thus there could not be much progress towards grappling with a problem which in essence has to do with the preservation of the rule of law in a radically different context from that in which the concept was shaped in Britain.

The obverse of the duty of public authorities to observe certain principles in their treatment of individuals and in the exercise of their powers is, of course, the right which citizens have to require and enforce fair treatment and a reasonable use of public powers. Too often there is uncertainty, confusion and restriction in the procedural methods open to plaintiffs in Britain, to say nothing of cost and delay. There is nothing comparable with the relatively easy access to special courts of administrative jurisdiction which several countries have. But on the other side the resources of the public authority in the shape of circumlocution, ambiguity and escape clauses are very formidable, and it is not uncommon for the citizen to find that he has no reliable procedural instrument by which either to get what are for him the relevant questions before a court, or to ensure that his particular demands are judged in relation to general principles favourable to something like equal treatment.

People tolerate this state of affairs for perhaps two reasons. The first is that they cannot imagine any other: they have no insight into what might be the resources of the law for the determination of what is reasonable in the regulation of relationships between public authorities and themselves. The second is that the oppressiveness of public authorities avoids the cruder manifestations of such behaviour. Indeed, many agencies behave with politeness and consideration, studiously counteracting any impression of arbitrary decisions. For this reason there is rarely much sign of strong dissatisfaction with the actions of public bodies, and the belief is maintained that there are after all ties of confidence and trust between "l'administration" and "les administrés". Unfortunately this means that the descent into arbitrariness and the capricious exercise of powers can

---

[4]Sir Lesie Scarman, *English Law – The New Dimension*, Stevens, 1974, p. 40.

sometimes proceed gently and quietly, with nobody ever being able to assert confidently that a stage has been reached at which a halt must be called.

One could multiply almost indefinitely examples to illustrate the defects outlined. What would characterise them all is the absence of any doctrine or body of principles purporting to set standards of behaviour and to prescribe procedures which the public authority must observe. *Mutatis mutandis* the citizen does not know where to go for the ground rules by which his rights are to be upheld. If he is tiresome enough to pursue this question, then like as not he will be told even in this day and age that his final protection lies with ministers responsible in some mysterious way to Parliament. Many of those raised in the common law tradition will protest that this view underestimates the resources of the law. But the evidence is hardly in their favour. Despite some signs of "judicial activism" the courts have been able to strike relatively few outstanding blows for liberty and rights in recent years.[5] They have worked away at the margins, watching rather helplessly as the powers of the administrative state advance. Nor are these merely the doubts of a sceptical and perhaps ill-informed student of government and politics: they have been vividly and forcibly expressed recently by one of the most distinguished and thoughtful men on the judicial bench.[6] This alone is a sign that something may be seriously wrong in this sphere.

The upshot of this discussion so far is that a negative answer has to be returned to the question whether it is desirable or even practicable any longer to rely exclusively on the common law tradition for the protection

[5] In a number of recent cases, especially during the sixties, the courts have asserted a judicial discretion to define the limits of certain rules thought to be of a constitutional nature, and in so doing rejected an implied executive discretion to interpret them. Examples are *Ridge* v. *Baldwin* (1964: right to a fair hearing); *Burmah Oil Co. Ltd.* v. *Lord Advocate* (1965: scope of the prerogative in war); *Conway* v. *Rimmer* (1968: determination of scope of Crown privilege in respect of documents); *Padfield* v. *Minister of Agriculture* (1968: abuse of administrative power or *détournement de pouvoir*); *Anisminic Ltd.* v. *Foreign Compensation Commission* (1969: extent of the right of review of administrative acts by the courts). Whilst fully recognising the importance of such cases as a sign of a judicial determination to maintain the powers of review claimed by the courts, it nevertheless seems to me that they do not amount to such a reinforcement of judicial arbitration as seems to be required to correct the imbalance which exists between individuals and the State as a consequence of the expansion of public powers.

[6] Scarman, *op. cit.*

of the bulk of our civil rights. This is not to suggest that the common law, its procedures, remedies and assumptions, is all ripe for the ash-bin, nor that we are bound to make a choice between something quite new and retention *in toto* of our traditional habits. The long experience of the United States is enough to show that it is nonsensical to imagine that any such choice is faced: it is possible to relate the common law traditions fruitfully to the application of very broadly defined statements of principle concerning the rights of man and the obligations of government. Nor is it denied that there are some rights such as free speech and protection against wrongful arrest or imprisonment which on the whole are still effectively protected by the inherited procedures and precedents of our courts.[7] The error lies once again in the exaggeration of certain assumptions and habits, in the belief that to depart significantly from earlier approaches to the definition and protection of rights would be like pulling down the pillars of the temple. It would not be so at all: it would rather be expressive of a readiness to take up the challenge presented by the expansion of public powers and to find ways of attaining a new understanding of "the rule of law" in contemporary conditions. Now, admittedly we may not want to do this. But if that is so, then at least it should be recognised that this would represent a political decision in favour of the encouragement of arbitrary government, whereas a determination to grapple with this problem of defining rights and protecting them more effectively would reaffirm commitment to what, after all, is still at the heart of the Western political tradition.

The conclusion to be drawn from these considerations is that some formal statement of rights is needed, that a new bill of rights should be enacted. This is a proposal which is now gaining some support, and certainly it is discussed far more seriously than only a short time ago. My concern is, however, chiefly with some of the implications of the proposal rather than with its merits, important though these appear to be. For if we do not take a clear view of some of the postulates on which a bill of rights must rest and of some of the consequences of having such a document, then either no progress can be made in this direction or if it is,

---

[7]In the case of wrongful imprisonment there are, of course, also statutory provisions, notably the Habeas Corpus Act of 1679. Even that, however, is not entrenched in any way.

expectations will then be deceived because the scheme produced will rest on intellectual confusion. After looking at some of these aspects of the problem, another more starkly political question arises. This is whether it is reasonable to believe that any progress can be made towards defining and protecting rights, if there is not at the same time an effort to stabilise and fix the terms on which public authorities themselves act and interact. In short, the question I shall come to concerns the interdependence of rights and powers as far as the constitutionalisation of the rules affecting both is concerned. It may be that no serious weight can be conferred on a bill of rights unless at the same time progress is made towards a constitution for the institutions of the State.

A bill of rights is, of course, a statement of political values, expressing particular views of human beings and their relations in society and prescribing ways in which people should be treated and should treat each other. It may be somewhat meticulous like the European Convention of Human Rights; it may be bold, simple and ambiguous like the bill of rights enshrined in the American Constitution. But the exact content of such a statement is not the issue here. What matters is that it provides terms of reference in the light of which all concerned can, if they so wish, try to determine what is due to them. In short, an understanding of rights is a condition of justice. In practice, of course, there is little point in positing rights unless they are made enforceable on public authorities and others who might abuse them, that is to say, are declared to be positive conditions which are to be observed in the ordinary law of the land. This is one of the first and most serious implications of this kind of proposal: there would have to be a court entitled to apply and interpret the rights, whether an entirely new creation or one of the existing higher courts, and citizens would have to be enabled to invoke the rights in their own disputes with a public authority or with any association acting in a manner analogous to a public body.

Now this apparently obvious deduction from the idea of a bill of rights brings into the open a considerable number of difficulties, most of them expressive of changes of practice and thinking which would become necessary if such a step were to be taken in Britain. There is the straightforward point that we do not have a judiciary which in the main (and there are shining exceptions) is hospitable to the possibility of having to interpret more general statements of rights. English judicial interpretation has been narrow and often arid, and the judges are endowed usually with an education and experience which hardly suits them for such an unfamiliar task. On the other hand, they are men of a cultivated ability and innate shrewdness at least equal to what is found at the top of other distinguished judicial systems. So perhaps there is no reason to doubt that if thrown into the sea of rights interpretation, most judges would be able to swim and some might even enjoy the experience. There is, however, a broader problem than that of the qualities of the judiciary, and this is that the bill of rights proposal does assume that judges will exercise a political role far more visible and important than has been expected of them in the past, or indeed would have been tolerated. Rights cannot be interpreted in their application to particular situations and relationships without political questions being raised and answered, and indeed it is clear that the whole task of interpretation depends upon a readiness to introduce concepts far more abstract and more subtle in their logic than have been familiar in the British tradition of judicial thinking.[8] Thus the possibility of defining rights goes far beyond the challenge implied in it to the capacities of judges and to the character of our legal education. It is before all else a question addressed to the people of this country: are they prepared to accept a different view of the role of law in their government and to accept more often as authoritative the decisions of a court of law?

The omens for such a willingness and such an understanding of the implication of having a bill of rights are not good. Powerful political interests are lined up against any development which might limit the discretions which they enjoy and which would diminish the authority they claim to have. Despite its special difficulties the experience of the attempt to introduce a measure of new law into the regulation of industrial relations is particularly relevant.[9] This was finally defeated by a campaign of opposition which, whatever the narrow and selfish trade union interests it expressed, also brought out into the open the continuing strength of the belief that many facets of social relationships cannot and should not be

[8] A small number of British judges has already explicitly recognised this point: see below the remarks of Lord Denning.
[9] As attempted by the Industrial Relations Act 1971, repealed in 1974–5. Despite the campaign against this measure, subsequent enactments such as the Protection of Employment Bill indicate that it is accepted that more law in some form or other must be applied to certain aspects of employment and the relationships it gives rise to as well as to the position of the organisations active in this field.

regulated by appeal to an authority quite detached from that pattern of relationships itself. It was immaterial to point out that such an authority in the shape of a court can usually arrive at fairer, more objective and more consistent conclusions in the resolution of conflicts, or to lay emphasis on the protection which only a court may be able to give to the man or woman who is alone and in a minority. There remains a strongly held and obstinate belief that the judgements of a court represent some external, imposed authority and that it is better to put up with uncertainty and injustice, indeed with sheer arbitrariness, rather than accept such an authoritative interposition of general principles constraining what can be done in the course of unimpeded social relationships. Closely linked with this suspicion of the very idea of widening the scope of interpretation by judges is the dislike of the finality attaching to legal judgements. Political decisions always have a discretionary, provisional quality: they can be amended easily and are often stretched with impunity. In contrast a court's decision cannot be argued with: if the opportunities for appeal have been exhausted, then the decision has to be applied without further ado unless we are to bring the whole legal order into disrepute. The fear of final and binding decisions is strong in Britain, and has become stronger as the arrogance of special interests has grown. Each is fearful of the curbs which might come from subjection to principles intended to protect the individual as citizen. Moreover, this problem has an additional dimension here deriving from the attachment of our courts to precedent, a practice which appears to underline this quality of finality and rigidity attaching to judicial decisions. In reality this could easily be overcome (as indeed the House of Lords has tentatively shown already in its judicial role). Nevertheless, we are a long way from any popular awareness of the existence of a *via media* between the sheer caprice and mutability of political judgement on the one hand, and the rigidity of precedent-bound courts on the other. Yet experience elsewhere demonstrates the existence of such a *via media*: the question again comes back to the capacity for change and for understanding questions in a new light.

For Parliament and the doctrines associated with it there are at least two major consequences of a viable and effective bill of rights. One is entrenchment, the other is reconciliation to the idea of judicial review of acts of Parliament and consequently of their possible invalidation. Clearly acceptance of such consequences would finish off the parliamentary sovereignty doctrine for good and all.

It may be that logically one can conceive of statements of rights which are both useful in practice and neither entrenched nor used as criteria against which to test the validity of laws. Experience does, however, indicate that the effective application of such statements of rights has nearly always been combined with something like the consequences and conditions I have just referred to. Where it has not, then usually the rights have been a fraud or, in rare instances, the statements of rights were scarcely needed. Such indeed was thought until quite recently to be the happy position of Britain: a formal declaration of rights was not needed. But this is now in doubt. If we were to have resort to a bill of rights, then this would be basically because it had come to be believed that neither Parliament nor the common law was a sufficient safeguard of those rights: by definition we should be deciding to supplement the common law and place curbs on Parliament. There appears to be no escape from this conclusion, though it has to be recognised that many judges and politicians find it hard to swallow, even those who are sympathetic to the notion of declaring rights. The magnetism of the old institutions and of the memories of what the common law has achieved remains strong. But it should not be allowed to obscure the logic of this particular proposal.

Interestingly enough there are small signs that the courts already see analogous consequences stemming from adhesion to the European Community. Not long ago one of the most distinguished and reflective of English judges gave a judgement in which he acknowledged at length the special and different qualities of European law which compelled the judges to fill in the "gaps and lacunae"; at the same time he stressed the finality and superiority in certain circumstances of both the relevant article of the Treaty of Rome and of the European Court as the organ of interpretation. Here in outline was acceptance of a new situation, of a finality other than Parliament and of the conferment on judges of a new dimension of discretion in the arbitrament of causes. If this is possible in respect of European law and all that follows from accession to the European Community, it is hard to see why comparable steps as conclusions drawn from having a bill of rights should be so utterly impossible.[10]

[10]*H. P. Bulmer Ltd. and Showerings Ltd.* v *J. Bollinger S. A. and Champagne Lanson Père et Fils* (Appeal Court, Times Law Report, 22 May 1974: Lord Denning).

One last remark which I will make on the implications of a bill of rights is that we should have to acquire an unfamiliar vocabulary, or at any rate tolerate an enrichment of the concepts with which the courts resolve the questions coming before them. There is no reason to underestimate the significance and difficulty of this change: the slightest acquaintance with English constitutional law and with the arguments used in many of the decisions affecting the claims to rights and the exercise of public powers is enough to confirm that English legal theory is in these matters at least very thin gruel indeed. The gap could be filled only gradually out of the on-going interpretative activity of the courts, but a necessary condition would be a change in legal education of a dramatic kind. It would be necessary to set about thinking of how to educate into existence a new breed of public lawyer, sensitive to what was called previously a new science of justice. This could be founded only on a recognition that in present conditions a distinction has to be drawn between private persons and public bodies, a distinction which the common law tradition refused to make – and that in reverse hardly any sharp lines can be drawn between legal, moral and political concepts. For it is in virtue of this latter conclusion that judges, and indeed academic students of law, can claim some authority in this difficult task of determining how rights intended for the protection of citizens are to be interpreted and re-interpreted in a social context in which the claims made for a public interest are subject to constant change.

Perhaps enough has been said to sustain two of the three main points with which this essay deals. The first was that we in Britain have retained a narrow view of civil rights which is defective and inadequate now that there is virtually no limit in substantive terms to the activities which may be regulated and controlled by public or governmental action. The second was that we have drawn sharp lines between the spheres of law and politics, with the result that law was essentially concerned with remedies and their application, but excluded from considering most of the issues affecting the general character of rights, their bearings on citizenship, and the limits they might impose on the actions of those in political office. In consequence we have moved into an increasingly complex condition of social and economic regulation without having full use of the resources of law and legal interpretation to help resolve some of the difficulties and conflicts which inevitably arise. *A fortiori* the burden which has thereby been imposed on our political institutions has increased, and in many instances they have proved incapable of bearing it successfully. Let me come now to the third matter on which it seems useful to make some remarks. This is really the question whether it is possible to get very far towards "constitutionalising" individual rights, perhaps by the passing of a bill of rights, without going further and engaging in the attempt to give constitutional definition to the rights and powers of the institutions by which the society is governed. Is there some kind of necessary connection between what appear to be the two main parts of any modern constitution, the statement of rights and the definition of powers?

Before trying, in however fragmentary a way, to give an answer to that question, it is worth considering what might well be the effect of having a bill of rights in this country if it were not conjoined with some constitutional definition of the powers of the principal institutions in the State. There would be no obligation on Parliament (which means equally the Government) to respect such rights in its statutes, for even if the enabling legislation expressed an intention of maintaining respect for them, that could presumably not bind a future Parliament. One could be reasonably sure that very soon problems would occur for which the most convenient solutions appeared to be ones which circumvented the new rights. Under political and party pressures governments would find it expedient to cut corners in this way. Then, again, were the courts to take it into their heads to quash or invalidate sections of statutes which disregarded the rights granted, they would immediately face the prospect of an irate government pushing through amending legislation, as indeed has happened several times before when the courts have decided that a public authority was acting *ultra vires*. Admittedly, in such circumstances of dispute about rights the courts could stand and fight, refusing to accept measures in conflict with the bill of rights and compelling the Government and Parliament either to submit to that judgement or to proceed to modification or repeal of the rights themselves. Perhaps no society can win its way through to a new definition of rights without a conflict of this kind. But if that is so, then it would be better to face the conflict at the outset over whether Parliament should itself be limited rather than engage in protecting rights in which the cards would be stacked against the very organs which would have the task of taking the lead in declaring such protection. In other words, we need to settle the *question préalable* before embarking on what at best could be only half of a constitutional experiment.

This is really to give an answer to the question raised about the connection between an interdependence of the two natural parts of a constitution. To declare rights is to accept an obligation to enforce and protect them: he who wills the end must, if he is serious at all, will the means. But to accept that there are rights to which all citizens have an equal claim and on all relevant occasions must logically entail the conclusion that government itself ought to be subject to them and committed to their maintenance. This is quite incompatible with the basic postulate of the British Constitution, which can be formulated in terms something like: "There are no limits to the discretion of an entity, Parliament." (To put it like this does, I trust, bring out the barrenness of the sovereignty of Parliament as a foundation for constitutional reasoning. Nothing useful can be deduced from it: one is landed in a closed circle — or an Austinian desert — in which the only reality is the command of the political will of the moment.) The question at issue is, of course, an old one, and it was last posed seriously in the England of the seventeenth century. Ultimately it was decided in favour of Parliament, though we would be guilty of projecting the present into the past if we imagine that even at the time of the vindication of limited monarchy and of parliamentary rights in 1689, the claims made on behalf of Parliament were already identical with those made two hundred years later. For it is too often assumed that Parliament has always been as it is now conceived, and we remain indifferent to or ignorant of the strength once possessed by contrasting and competing traditions. In fact, even whilst the question of supremacy was in dispute an alternative answer was discerned as is shown in those remarkable words of Cromwell: "In every Government there must be a Somewhat Fundamental, Somewhat like a Magna Charter, which should be standing, be unalterable. . . . That Parliaments should not make themselves perpetual is a Fundamental. Of what assurance is a law to prevent so great an evil, if it lie in the same legislature to un-law it again?"[11] What we are really concerned with today is the discovery or rediscovery of fundamentals. And all fundamentals are inherently to do

---

[11] Quoted by Scarman, *op. cit.*, p. 17, referring to Lauterpacht, *International Law and Human Rights*, London, 1950, p. 128.

with procedures, adumbrations of the conditions according to which people hope and intend to regulate their interactions one with another and between themselves and the public authorities they establish. It is because the political order has virtually ceased to show any understanding of these conditions that it would now hardly be possible in Britain to confer upon a code of rights the special status which it demands as a fundamental, unless a further step is taken to ensure that the political institutions too are circumscribed within another fundamental or set of fundamentals.

It is no doubt hard for most Englishmen to admit that this is really the question before which they stand: if the rule of law as a state of justice, as a *Rechtsstaat*, is to survive, then a constitution is needed. Most of those who cling on to positions of power and influence in the government of the country are extremely reluctant to contemplate the possibility: those who wield the big stick in private associations like trade unions have even less desire to see their power subjected to the limits imposed by constitutional authority; and as for what are nowadays called "ordinary people", they have been so well schooled in naive prejudices that many no longer appear to have much appreciation of their dignity and rights as citizens. They are instead more likely to see themselves as subjects or victims than as the proud possessors of rights. But even if there is a widespread reluctance yet to face up to the choice which needs to be made, perhaps there are some who are alive to the manifest advantages which could be gained from accepting the constitutional implications of a bill of rights for the political institutions of the country. We would change the context of ideas within which the problems of the limits of government action might be considered; we would be able to look afresh at the relationships between Government and Parliament and within Parliament between the two Houses; there would be scope for developing more generally applicable categories in the structuring of public authorities and in the definition of their obligations; we might acquire some foundation of principles on which to deal with the demands for autonomy, whether from provinces, regions or local communities; and in growing into the European Community there might then be some prospect of Britain having something to set on the credit side of the politico-legal account to make good the borrowings which will undoubtedly have to be made from the Continent.

But above all there would not only be advantages accruing simply to the practitioners, to those whose job it is in political and administrative life to solve particular problems. At a pinch they can manage with a very small conceptual stock, though not, I believe, one as meagre as that with which they now seek to survive. Far more important, however, would be the consequences of a serious attempt to define rights and to proceed further to a formalisation of institutional relationships for the general body of political, legal and moral discussion in this country. At present, the analysis of British government proceeds in something like a void. Those who seek to describe and explain its characteristics and operations find themselves floundering in a world of dry, shapeless and sometimes frivolous empiricism. This is perhaps most marked in works of political and administrative analysis and report, but things are hardly any better in the constitutional law textbooks or in the discussion of how particular social claims and needs can be fitted into a structure of political values. There is a widespread sense of the lack of any foundation for principled argument about the public realm and public affairs. But if the society were to recapture a sense of institutions as the expression of values, as the translation of procedural norms into stable relationships which can then be directed to the achievement of substantive purposes, there would be a foundation for the revival of a constitutional understanding and of a tradition of constitutional argument. And this would make a great difference. It would become possible to talk and to argue in serious terms about any political theme from referendum to abortion.[12] People would recognise that there were value questions at stake and they would have something by way of a body of principles with which to structure their arguments. A constitution is indeed a corset for those who seek power: that is its rationale. But constitutional principles are not corsets for the political discourse of a free society: they are the necessary condition for

---

[12] It is clear that the 1975 referendum on EEC membership evoked practically no constitutional discussion of a significant kind: the conceptual context was simply not present to permit this. A neat example of the same problem is provided by the contrast between paragraphs 19 and 122 of the White Paper, *Our Changing Democracy: Devolution to Scotland and Wales*, Cmnd. 6348. The former asserts that the Government must guarantee the basic rights of the citizen throughout the United Kingdom, the latter that a Scottish Assembly should decide policy on (*inter alia*) abortion. Even though "basic rights" is no doubt being used informally, it is remarkable that a question involving the right to life can be dealt with so lightly and with so much possibility of contradiction.

having any discourse at all about how purposes are to be fulfilled in that society.

The questions affecting the manner in which we determine the rights and powers of public bodies and the bearing of all this on constitutional matters are difficult. They require us to think in terms of principles, but equally it is wise not to forget that many of the hardest problems arise in applying principles to cases and in the design of appropriate institutions. As far as that part of the present subject goes which is concerned chiefly with law and jurisprudence, some risks have been taken anyway in treading on ground generally reserved to the legal specialist. But even in that part which is nearer to politics as conventionally understood, and administration, much has been missed out which has a bearing on the interaction between legal and political ideas, and between judicial and administrative practice. In particular next to nothing has been said of the actual machinery for the control of powers and the protection of rights which exists in Britain. Nor have I examined the manner in which the remedies open to the citizen actually operate or considered in detail their achievements and shortcomings. The growth of what we are now forced to call administrative law and of the many devices which have been evolved for taking some account of the interests of those caught up in disputes with public authorities has been neglected. Nothing very specific has been said about the role of the judiciary proper nor about the extent to which it is reasonable to talk about a certain strengthening of judicial controls ("judicial activism") in recent years.[13] Nor have I mentioned such specialised topics as the Parliamentary Commissioner for Administration (the so-called ombudsman), public inquiries or administrative tribunals. But then this is not a treatise on administration and the legal instruments which can be taken up and used in that field. I mention these matters in passing now for the sake of indicating that some kind of case might be made out to the effect that the poverty of the law and legal traditions of the country is not quite as patent as has been suggested. The growth of the administrative state in the service of an omnipotent Parliament has not taken place without some response on the part of those who realise that

[13] My own view on this claim is, as indicated earlier, somewhat negative. It does not seem to me that the contrary arguments advanced, for example by Professor H. W. R. Wade, are wholly convincing.

this process has grave implications for individuals, for associations, and for a particular view of the rule of law. My contention is, however, that this response has been slow and inadequate, too pragmatic, too shaky in its grasp of principles, and too uncertain of what the direction of advance should be. If there were time and space, this claim could, I think, be supported without difficulty from official reports, learned articles and judicial decisions of the past quarter of a century.

This failure is to some extent attributable to the narrowness of the idea of the rule of law which has prevailed in this country. This in turn reflects the narrowness of the term "law" and the British inability to see it as having the enlarged sense of *Recht* or *droit*. So the "rule of law" has meant essentially equal subjection to such law as exists (and only to law), an equitable administration of justice by one set of courts only, and more doubtfully the assumption that the law should satisfy certain criteria of precision and fairness. None of these assumptions is adequately met today, and in addition, as already pointed out, there is at the back of this classic view of the rule of law in England an assumption about the equality of public and private persons which has now become dangerously unrealistic. But since the dominant approach to the rule of law has been empirical and procedural, it should not in theory be difficult to change the methods and procedures so that a new correspondence is established between the ideal and the reality. In other words, it is not denied that the positivism of the traditional English mode of thinking about the rule of law contained an important hold on realities which it would be well to preserve. The crucial addition which needs to be made is to bring back into the conception of the rule of law something of the dimension of a Commonwealth under the guidance of law. This could be achieved only if these matters were to be considered more politically, and if an effort were made to see the uses of law as one aspect of the problem of establishing and maintaining political authority. But here I come back to the point at which I have arrived several times before. The challenge is to construct a different relationship between law and politics, and in so doing to give law in a revitalised sense a new and wider part in the regulation of the affairs of the society.

It is not an easy task, for at the start we must work in stony ground. Yet all the signs are that it is of great importance to make a start. The destroyers are already at work, some of them heedless bigots, for whom law in the literal and simple sense is no longer an impediment, others frightened men who have lost touch with the realities of the world and so dare not stand up for the protection which all need to be able to claim from the law. It is the actions and inactions of such people which have in the past few years made many doubt whether the "rule of law" is any longer upheld. The exceptions have become too numerous and too serious to permit an optimistic answer to be given. It seems rather that until stronger barriers in the shape of institutions firm in their principles, and opposition grounded in a body of arguments and commitment to certain constitutional values, are built up again, then there can be no firm prospect of arresting this drift away from what even the unsophisticated understand by the "rule of law". It is to turn this tide that the categories of the *Rechtsstaat* − the state under the law − need to be brought in to supplement and revivify a flagging notion of the "rule of law".

Those who reflect on politics should recognise that an understanding of the subject must be rooted in historical knowledge: the *res gestae* of particular men and women. Of course we need to theorise about institutions and the postulates on which they rest if we want to understand the choices that we might, if we are so minded, put to ourselves.[14] But in order to understand a predicament and the reasons why our choices are so constricted by *la force des choses*, we have to consider how the actors have acted. It is to this difficult and contentious subject that I must now turn. Put simply. the next theme will take us away from the rules to the character of the rulers. In the language of political science the focus must shift to parties and political élites.

[14] Something like this point is expressed in Maitland's view of constitutional history as a history, not of parties, but of institutions, not of struggles, but of results (*Constitutional History of England* p. 537). I owe this insight to a footnote in *On Human Conduct* by Michael Oakeshott.

CHAPTER 9

Parties and Political Élites

It has been contended here that Britain has experienced a decline of political understanding and some of the consequences of this have been examined. An attempt has been made to delineate a condition in which the achievement of substantive purposes is now endangered, or even frustrated, because there is no longer any assurance about what are the rules and procedures of political life. In other words, it is questionable whether the political association we call Britain any longer has a constitution which permits it to generate sufficient authority to resolve effectively the problems which must be faced.

In the past history of this and other countries similar conditions of political *anomie* have been pretty common, and have often been brought to an end by the harsh force of circumstances – war, starvation, revolt or usurpation. Such events forced some kind of reconstruction of the political ground rules, though sometimes only after interregna of confusion and violence, or even of exhaustion. In the contemporary world there are still many states precariously exposed to the force of circumstances, particularly some of those which lie on the margins of stability dividing the great powers one from another or in areas of great material poverty. But for others there is a certain insulation from the realities of life, though, of course, no one can forecast how durable this condition will turn out to be. At any rate it would be wise not to assume that such insulation can last indefinitely. Britain seems to fit eminently into this category: the decline can proceed almost gently because the country is protected in various ways – by its allies, by its trading partners, by international financial institutions and so on. In differing degrees these external forces have an interest in propping Britain up, in showing forbearance towards a power which has come down in the world and whose precipitate collapse might be expected to disturb or damage their interests too. So we live in a state of protection, and this is one of the reasons why there is as yet very little perception of agency in the reaction to this decline within Britain. There is still a feeling of comfortable inevitability, softened by a lingering belief that we are a special case, endowed by history with some kind of saving grace and entitled to count on the benevolence of the world outside. There is, therefore, no widespread disposition to recognise what might be the inner causes of this failure, nor to think of the problem in terms of identifying the active agents in this process.

If one goes back to the major writers on politics of the past, one finds that most of them recognise the possibility of decline: political communities or states are mutable and they may fall or wither away. In considering what might be the major causes of such a declining fortune, many of these older writers clearly recognised three broad categories of circumstances which might initiate or accelerate decline. Put simply the survival and health of a polity or state was held to depend on the wisdom of its laws or what we might call the strength of its institutions, the quality of its rulers and the sentiments of its people. Naturally any or all of these conditions could be cancelled out by adverse objective circumstances, which were in any case more likely in the pre-modern era to appear to be uncontrollable. But assuming that a state had a modicum of luck in its relationships to its natural environment, then it was held that its success and survival depended extensively on the factors just mentioned. Indeed, it is striking that the importance of the sentiments, values, beliefs, behaviour patterns, etc., of the people only received full recognition and was only explained in some detail by relatively modern writers, Montesquieu and de Tocqueville for example, and in a rather different way, Hegel. Some attention has already been paid to the state of British institutions – the quality of the laws of the Constitution, and I will say something later about "the sentiments of the people". This part of the discussion will be chiefly about the quality of the rulers. It is this element in the traditional components of political health which now needs to be looked at in the contemporary British context.

Before getting close to the subject it is worth noting again how reluctant most observers are to recognise it as a matter of importance. Perhaps this is in part attributable to the tendency in modern sociological and political writing to play down the significance of "agency" altogether, and to prefer explanations in the categories of social and economic forces or pressures. One consequence of this prejudicial error is that human decisions can always be explained away as either inevitable or excusable, and from this standpoint human agents are to be regarded as the not very important victims of circumstances. Of course, there is much hypocrisy in the application of this theory: its advocates tend to abandon it whenever they wish to shout "J'accuse" in the faces of those who pursue ends and policies of which they disapprove. However, there is a simpler explanation of the reluctance to consider the quality of our rules. It is that to do so can be embarrassing: to refrain from questioning the qualities of those engaged in the direction of public affairs (except when they indulge in financial corruption or sexual peccadilloes) is one of the conventions of political commentary, reinforced by the rather incestuous relationships which exist in Britain between those who seek and obtain political office and those who are in different ways concerned with understanding and commenting upon our political life. May be this is a temptation which exists nearly everywhere, and it is possible that it has become stronger under the influence of popular participation in political affairs. When the rulers are determined to pretend that they are just like "ordinary people", it is hardly surprising that there is a certain reticence in talking about their failings. For to do so too openly is to come dangerously near to suggesting that there are limits to the wisdom and virtue of "ordinary people" themselves. And that, after all, might lead to very disturbing conclusions.

So far the old-fashioned word "rulers" has been used. Of course, it might be argued that it is misleading to talk of "rulers" as one might do in relation to pre-democratic times. The "rulers" now constitute a somewhat diffuse and ill-defined group of people, those who, by reason of the offices they hold and the organisations they direct, take most of the more important decisions intended to regulate the affairs of the society. If one takes this in a fairly broad sense rather as did Mosca in his search for "the ruling class", then one is talking about a group or class embracing several sectors of activity outside politics narrowly defined; some civil and military officials have to be included, some industrialists and bankers, some trade unionists and so on. But as this is not an attempt to write an essay on the sociology of the ruling élite *au sens large* in Britain, these complications will be ignored, and attention will be confined to the elected political élite – the aspirants to office, as they might be called. And since Britain is so centralised, this means that very few people belong to such a group who are not already in national politics or trying to get there.

Furthermore, there is a justification for this narrow view of the ruling élite. The political traditions of this country have concentrated authority in elected (and earlier, hereditary) representatives to a degree unusual elsewhere. Despite the forces which may render this élite ineffective or even impotent, there is still a widespread popular belief that if anyone is entitled to exercise authority, then it should be members of this élite, legitimated by election to national representative institutions.

The political élite in Britain, as in many other states, emerges from a pattern of activity within political parties. The rulers and the aspirant rulers are all identifiable with parties, all depend in some degree on party approval and support, and nearly all have had their most decisive experience within parties. So any consideration of the qualities of the political élite must start from some account of the parties as the associations which provide the patterns of values, behaviour and objectives within which this élite takes shape. It is rather like considering the parties as the compost in which rulers have to be grown, and then asking whether they constitute really good compost or not.

Let me start with the Conservative Party. To a remarkable extent it remains a social institution, its component parts scattered throughout the country, an instrument for projecting an élite into national politics, sustaining and renewing it. Equally it is a structure of communication which helps to maintain certain preferences, sympathies and styles of behaviour which are themselves the foundation (or were until recently) of Conservative politics. What is striking is the relatively limited interest which the party shows in political ideas and programmes. Naturally, the higher one goes in the hierarchy of party organisation, the less this is so. But at the working level, where most of the party members are active, it is not uncommon to encounter a feeling that even to raise political questions is out of place: the party is merely an organisation which serves certain social purposes and at the same time maintains in office a variety of leaders, local and national, the latter being, of course, far more important than the former. Though the party has often in its history been led by clever people, even intellectuals, its dominant tradition has been hostile to ideas, to intellectual argument, to theorising. Though usually rated a source of strength, this has in recent times meant that the party has become dangerously isolated from the intellectual community, despite the fact that many of these secular priests sympathise with the party and have hearts which beat on the right. The party has thus become the prisoner of its own prejudices and of the contempt for intellect and ideas which it has affected.

This mistrust of rationalism in politics was traditionally ascribed to the dominant part played in the party by the social stratum most likely to be suspicious of theorising, what used to be called the landed gentry and those who imitated them in some measure. (It is remarkable how many echoes of the styles of life and thought associated with the landed gentry do survive in Britain — the industrialist going to his weekend retreat in a Sussex or Cotswold village, the successful politician dabbling in farming.) Nevertheless, *de facto* this social element is no longer of decisive importance: the Conservative Party stands chiefly for suburban, middle to lower middle-class England, and the only substantial economic interest with which it is associated and on behalf of which it regularly pleads (and even then in a rather loose and confused way) is that of the private enterprise business community. The maintenance of a mistrust of political argument and analysis in deference to a social condition long vanished, and to a conception of aristocratic leadership which became irrelevant long ago, is undoubtedly one of the reasons why the party faces a support crisis: it lacks the capacity to generate any vision of what it stands for and to make this comprehensible to its present and potential supporters.

This failure has two aspects. There is the actual composition of the Conservative élite, still too heavily marked by those characteristics of social exclusiveness which the English have contrived to sustain in a peculiarly self-destructive way. This means that the public representation of the party risks appearing archaic and finds it hard to express effectively the sentiments of many of those who support it. And, secondly, there is this affected disinterest in "ideology" and in coherent thinking which makes it extremely difficult for the party now to present any serious arguments of principle (let alone of experience) against many of the measures advanced and put into effect by its rivals. It has fallen into a kind of simplistic pragmatism which has made it more and more difficult to determine where and for what the party stands.

To make this criticism is not to imply that the party's difficulties would be overcome simply by acquiring a rigorous doctrinal foundation. This would be out of keeping with the style of the party. But it is to suggest that it has suffered from an inability to develop into the kind of thinking and self-critical political movement which the social and political circumstances of our time demand, and within which some understanding of the real conditions facing this country might begin to emerge. The need is not in the first place for programmes and policies understood as a catalogue of substantive benefits to be offered to the electorate, despite the attractiveness of that pathetic fallacy: it is rather for a restatement of Conservative philosophy, embracing the terms on which economic activity should go forward and the role and limits of government. Despite some stirrings after electoral defeat in 1974 the party is still groping for and failing to find a statement of social values and of economic principles which might be joined with a conception of political rules such as would offer hope of sustaining the authority of government and support for a free society.

The élite which is produced by the Conservative Party reflects in various ways the condition just outlined. But it also expresses the capricious autonomy of constituency party organisations and the haphazard impact on the party of social change. On balance the party at the top has become more mixed in its social origins and manners than it was even twenty years ago, and represents a wider range of professional activities, though some of them are very much of the "get-rich-quick" kind and others relate to advertising and the communications industry. But constituencies vary considerably and have very different ideas about what they are looking for and what will suit them. The outcome of many separate decisions and of the interplay of numerous individual ambitions is an élite which has become oddly shapeless and mixed. It has in fact changed in recent years: it no longer sees itself as an almost hereditary, bourgeois-cum-aristocratic ruling group. Yet it is not liberated from the influences of an earlier period and tends to ape the manners and style of the past. In its limitations it expresses many of the weaknesses and blind spots of the selection groups from which it issues and to which, in an obscure way, it continues to feel obliged to make some kind of response.

The political sociologist knows little about the Liberal Party, the eternal losers. When small the party received little attention because it was so unimportant. Now that it has become so much more of a threat to the large parties, the event is too recent for the analyst to have done his surveys and got the material on to the operating table. Nevertheless, one can be reasonably sure about one or two things which bear on the character of the small contribution to the political élite which the Liberal Party makes. The first is that until recently the party produced representatives who differed little in their characteristics from many of those in the Conservative Party or in the middle-class spectrum of the Labour Party. Very recently there have been a few signs of change towards a rather more populist, grass-roots kind of person, but since so few of them have got through, they have not made much of a difference. However, this does point to the other major feature of the Liberal Party, and that is that it represents far more of a protesters' vote than the support of a solid and committed body of opinion. In other words, traditional liberalism remains a narrowly based affair (as it now is in most European countries), but round that has clustered an extremely heterogeneous body of discontent and protest. Another characteristic of the new or revived Liberal Party is its concern with local and community politics. At this level its successes are hardly outstanding, but the importance of local activity has been elevated by many of the supporters of the party into a matter of principle. Not surprisingly the outcome tends to be that the party leadership is pushed along by a rather muddled populism, many of the exponents of which have no wish to get involved in national politics.

The reappearance of the Liberal Party as a significant electoral factor has, of course, so far had few distinguishable effects on the political élite. This is simply because the electoral provisions have deprived the party of anything like the level of representation to which its support now entitles it. Indeed it is relatively in a weaker position in Parliament than the Scottish National Party which at least benefits from being able to concentrate its support in one part of the country (and which, as far as the composite nature of its support goes, resembles the Liberal Party). But if the Liberal Party can be imagined to have gained a more equitable number of representatives, then one might have to assume that the majority of them would have been vaguely middle class, probably nearer the lower end of the middle-class economic spectrum than the upper. Some would have been serious and hopeful people, unfamiliar with many of the knotty obstacles to political action; others would have been starry-eyed and impatient idealists, soon disillusioned when they find that their quack remedies do not work. And a few would have been careerists or play-actors, the kind of people one finds in all the parties. What is to be doubted is that a much larger Liberal contingent would have resulted in the injection into the existing parliamentary élite of an element likely to introduce immediately a substantially different scale of values: the party does not nourish a new Puritan ethic nor does it come as the bearer of doctrines and policies notably different from those applied by its Conservative rivals, particularly under Edward Heath.[1] Despite the fact that the Liberals do not inherit that suspicion of ideas and of intellectuals of which the Conservatives have made a virtue (though this is not always true of the home-spun populism which sometimes carries the Liberal Party forward), they have singularly failed to secure that measure of intellectual backing which might enable them to claim that they stand for a tolerably coherent view of society, social and economic objectives and political relationships.

In ideas and in the search for support there are resemblances between the British Liberals and their counterparts in certain European countries.[2] For example, the Free Democrats, the Liberal Party in Western Germany, had for many years a relatively clear ideological position, particularly on the economy, on the importance of property, and on the undesirability of increasing the interventionist role of the State. The erosion of the Free Democratic Party's strength as an exponent of that approach and the search for new sources of support in the later sixties produced a somewhat unstable mixture: echoes of the traditional *laissez-faire* liberalism and its emphasis on self-help, along with a haphazard collection of policy preferences intended to meet the need of appealing to varied groups of potential supporters in different places. Not surprisingly many of these latter preferences became opportunistic and "progressive", tending to put the party on the Left of the political spectrum, regardless of whether that is where most of its leaders wanted to find themselves. All this is true of the British Liberals and can be observed in the political record of the party

---

[1] It is noteworthy in this context that the Liberal Party has been in the past two or three years firmly committed to a statutory wages policy. In this it agrees with certain elements in the Conservative Party. But the commitment itself shows how far the party has moved from the doctrinal roots of classical liberalism.

[2] In some European countries (notably the Federal Republic of Germany) there has, of course, been the major difference that Liberal groups have had a share in government as a result of the need to form coalitions.

leadership. But should one not rather say the "English Liberals"? For the party is no longer one of the Celtic fringe, as it was until a few years ago, but rather of England and even of suburbia.[3]

Now let me come to the other major party, the Labour Party. It has always contained two major elements, representative of organised industrial workers and largely middle-class social reformers. It must be acknowledged that, drawing on these sources the party has, for much of its history, brought rather more talent and energy into our political élite than any of its rivals. Because of its origins in the trade union movement and the structural links which it has maintained with the unions, the party has provided a presence of the working-class in British politics which has had a major influence on the broad direction of social and economic policy for many years. If this working-calss component of the political élite has, on the whole, furnished relatively little in the shape of governmental talent, it has nevertheless often enough provided an invaluable ballast of common sense and tolerance.

As far as the social reform element goes, as the progressive party Labour has always appealed to able, serious-minded and well-educated people who have been drawn into politics at least in part for reasons of moral duty: the kind of people who have believed that they ought to use the advantages they have enjoyed for the benefit of the less fortunate. Far from being hostile to intellectuals, the party has on the whole welcomed people with ideas and an interest in argument, and in an age in which there has been a rapid increase in the size of the "intellectual class", this has been a significant advantage for it. Such a characterisation of this group expresses something like the ideal of a social reformer in the modern liberal and social democratic idiom, a person who applies intelligence and reason to political problems, who propagates the ethic of service to his fellow men, and who believes that enough of them share his beliefs to make the whole enterprise of social progress credible. For a while the Labour Party seemed to be the effective instrument of such ideas and of such people. But that time is over. The structure and character of the contemporary Labour Party are such that the very forces which previously expressed the mission of the party, the creative contribution which it could make to progress in this country, are condemned to sterility. Those

[3] This point is supported by the distribution of electoral support for the party in the 1974 elections.

who are or were liberals and democrats, and who saw the party's task as being in the main the achievement of a continuing rhythm of social improvement and reform, now for the most part take refuge in a weary and even frightened tolerance of misguided and absurd policies. Regrettably, there are also some who reveal the disposition of the Gadarene swine, being ready to provide specious and often foolish grounds for rushing over the edge of the cliff without further delay.

The reasons why the Labour Party is now condemned to sterility, to exist in an impasse, are reasonably easy to identify. They arise from the structure of the party, the interests which support it and the doctrines to which it is committed. In the structure of the party there have always been the two main elements just referred to, the trade unions providing the money and the mass support, and the social democratic reformers. But in addition another group is to be distinguished, what I will call "the activists", the people who in the party organisation constitute the core of continuing and committed activity. Of course, the categories are rough and ready, and it is perfectly obvious that they overlap: trade unionists may be activists and so also may be the social reformers, and so on. Yet without doubt these distinct categories can be observed in the structure and everyday activity of the party. The trade unions provide the bulk of the organised working-class support, and by their continued affiliation maintain this (or at any rate tend to do so). The social democratic reformers mobilise a substantial body of middle-class support which the party has — teachers, technical employees, the lower levels of public administration, etc. As for the activists, this is a small and socially heterogeneous group. Some of them are intellectuals in a specific professional sense of that term, but many are not. They are half-educated people who have picked up a stock of clichés with which they try to justify the naive programmes to which they have committed themselves.

As was just noted, all these groups interlock and overlap, though I suspect that it has become more difficult to hold them apart in recent years. The normal situation until sometime in the early sixties was for the policy of the party and its approach to the electorate to be determined by an alliance between the trade unions and the social democratic element, the latter being the driving force in the parliamentary party. The result was an amalgam of social democratic reformist policies and commitment to parliamentary procedures which may often have been less carefully thought out than would have been desirable, but which for the most part rested on a pragmatic view of social realities. Nor did it threaten to disrupt the broad understandings on which the economic and political life of the country were thought to rest.

What has now happened is that the balance within the Labour Party has shifted radically. The trade union movement is still the dominant numerical factor, and indeed more dominant than ever before as measured by the power it wields. But during the past decade or so its leadership has moved to the Left. This has led to a dissolution of many of the close links between the social democratic reformist group and the unions, the outcome of which is that this group has become steadily more beleaguered within the party, though for historical reasons it continues to hold a substantial share of the senior positions in the parliamentary leadership. But in reality the parliamentary party has gone into decline. Meanwhile, the activists within the constituencies and inside a variety of organisations tied up with the party have become more radical in their views and more insistent on pushing forward their candidates. To make matters still worse, the death of Gaitskell in 1963 meant the loss of the one opportunity for strong principled leadership which the Labour Party had had since the departure of the 1945 generation. Under his successor there were but few signs of resistance to this redistribution of forces inside the party.

The outcome of all this could be vividly illustrated in several policy contexts. Particularly clear was the division within the party over continued membership of the European Economic Community. Fundamentally this was not an argument about the Community – though it is true that some members of the Labour Party appear to regard their continental neighbours with something akin to moral repulsion and passionately seek to avoid contamination – but about the political direction within the party. Those whose vision is essentially of a socialist society, no matter how unspecified that may be and particularly as to its political characteristics, opposed continued membership as a frustration of the dream which they believe is within striking distance of realisation. Those who are reformist social democrats, who are on the whole in favour of maintaining an extensive area of private ownership of economic resources, and who accept that without some measure of market competition relative impoverishment is inevitable, supported Britain's adherence to the commitments entered into by the preceding Conservative

Government. But it is the Left which is now in the ascendant, not so much in the sense that it controls day-to-day decisions made in government, but that it sets the framework of argument and lays claim to the moral initiative within the party. Even though an opportunist leadership finally carried the day in the country on the Common Market issue — chiefly by appealing to the people and by relying on the support of its political opponents — there is now little doubt that it enjoys at best only qualified support from many of the vital elements inside the active party organisation for many of the unpalatable policies which it is forced to pursue. At bottom this is because the issue of what the party stands for and the kind of social and political order to which it is committed, remains unresolved. And because it is unresolved and a matter of conflict between rival factions inside the party, it follows that fundamentally the party is condemned to sterility. It has become a coalition of negatives: its *lex suprema* can only be its own survival.

An argument often advanced against the thesis that the Left has gained ascendancy in the Labour Party is that after all reformist policies continue to predominate, and that a large part of the leadership remains "social democrat". Yet this is unconvincing. The question is not whether the party moves suddenly and irrevocably to some kind of socialist position, it is rather what kind of blackmailing power the Left possesses (and has possessed for over a decade) within the party as presently constituted. And here there is undoubtedly a profound change from the days when Clement Attlee had no compunction in keeping both activists of a Left-wing persuasion and trade union bosses in place. Inexorably the social democratic element has been pushed into the role of the guilty party, called upon to justify its preferences and to demonstrate its fidelity to what are asserted to be the ideals of the party, or "the movement" as the true believers love to call it. Equally relentless has been the drift in policy towards acceptance of some species of state-controlled economy managed in the interests of the trade union movement, a trend which has in the period since February 1974 been notably accelerated by the very dilemmas of economic decline. To all this the Right, the moderates, the Centre — what they are called is not very important — have proved incapable of offering anything more than token resistance: for the sake of the unity of the party they have sacrificed virtually every principle for which they once stood.

There is another dimension to the paralysis of the social democrats which is worth a few words. This is that the Left fail to make explicit the political values to which they are committed and which would prevail in the Utopia they seek to build. Of course, the Left profess to be democratic socialists, dedicated to the ideal of the socialist society achieved by persuasion and majority votes, and presumably maintained by the same civilised means. The fact that no such socialist society is known to exist neither depresses nor deters them. To the political dilemmas inherent in that degree of centralised collective choice which must be required for the economic functioning of a "socialist" society, they remain blind and insensitive, though it is hard not to believe that some recognise these problems well enough, but judge it prudent to suppress their preference for an authoritarian solution for the time being. How, if at all, consumer preferences are to be made effective in the coming Utopia, what responsibilities worker managers or board members are to assume along with the powers they claim, what criteria are to be applied to judging what interests and activities are "for the good of society", what is the nature of political representation and the rights of a "representative", what is the foundation and purpose of law, these are only a few of the questions of a highly political sort to which the Left give as good as no answers. But is the British Left any exception here? Perhaps a capacity to face the realities of politics is incompatible with the infantile Utopianism which everywhere produces the political attitudes commonly characterised as democratic "Left". Be that as it may, the consequence of the Left's refusal to face up to political questions is that the Right is always at a disadvantage: they can be accused of mistrusting the *bona fides* of their comrades on the Left and of failing to realise that all that the Left desires is to bring about a land flowing with milk, honey and goodwill at no political cost at all. Who but a person of singularly uncharitable disposition could cavil at that?

However, the most serious problem facing the Labour party is not the ideological shift to the Left nor even the tensions which exist between the major elements within the party. It is rather that the organic relationship between the party and the unions, long regarded as the very foundation of the party, has outlived its usefulness and its original justification. It now constitutes an impediment to the future development of the party and to the pursuit of some of the ideals for which it has stood. More than that, this particular relationship distorts the whole pattern of party politics in

Britain and has even begun to call into question the reality of the electorate's right to change its rulers.

There are several reasons why the intimate relationship between the Labour Party and the unions has assumed this destructive character. The increase in the power of unions, born of the realisation by many activists in them that contemporary society is peculiarly vulnerable to the disruption of industrial activity and vital services, has brought about an even more lop-sided situation in the party's internal relationships, with the parliamentary wing nominally bearing political responsibility, but all the time aware of the dangers of offending the unions and of the need to trim its policies to suit its paymasters' preferences. In order to maintain support in elections as well as in the interests of effectiveness in government, all parties need to appeal to a broad cross-section of the electorate and to maintain co-operative relations with a wide and varied range of organised groups. Yet commitment to a trade union affiliation now prevents the Labour Party from doing this seriously: against the will of many of its members it is forced to be sectarian. There is, too, the contemporary insecurity of much of the trade union leadership, now deeply conscious of the forces which can be mobilised against them on the industrial shop floor and of the appeal of extremist slogans. This also filters through to the parliamentary representatives, often making them more sensitive to such pressures than to the opinions of the electorate which they represent and on whose behalf they must act. And, finally, there is the grumbling incapacity of the British trade union movement to decide where it stands on basic economic questions. Does it accept an economic order in which market principles and private ownership have a major role, and *a fortiori* co-operate in making a success of such an economy, or does it aspire seriously to a socialist economy, accepting then such political and social controls as this would imply both over the processes of production and distribution as well as over the activities of the unions themselves? To judge from the rhetoric of conferences and the language of public political argument, it would appear that the majority view in the unions does now incline to the socialist answer. Yet in the day-to-day handling of specific issues no such clear commitment emerges: most union representatives look first for cash on the table and have little to say about how and by what form of economic organisation the cash is provided.

It is understandable that the Labour Party parliamentary leadership should have been weakened by the continued strain of coexisting and striking bargains with powerful forces which have their *raison d'être* not in the pursuit of a popular majority entitling them to assume the responsibilities of government, but in the continuing effort to satisfy highly specific sectional interests. Yet there is a substantial element of bluff in the behaviour of the trade union movement which the social democrats have either failed to recognise, or no longer dare to exploit. Most of the present-day trade union leaders of a Leftist persuasion are committed to the usual slogans about the socialist or socialised society. But there is something else to which they are all even more passionately committed, and that is the maintenance of "free collective bargaining". In other words, what is most precious to them is their right within the economy to pursue without having to acknowledge any specific responsibilities for the health of that economy, the self-interest of their members. It is an unflattering commentary on the calibre of so many trade union leaders that they find it hard to appreciate the illogicality of this commitment to a free collective bargaining principle which is plainly incompatible with the socialist Utopia which they also advocate. Of course, this is not true of all of them, yet how few and quiet are the voices pointing out this living contradiction. As far as the Labour Party goes, the effect of this schizophrenia within the trade union movement is that the party too is forced into policies which, whether of the Right or the Left, are condemned to unworkability even before they have been put into effect. In its pursuit of some kind of "mixed economy" (whatever that ambiguous expression might mean), the Right are denied the co-operation of the unions and such appreciation of economic necessities as is essential to success: and the Left are now able to embark on experiments in state guidance and control which are equally doomed to failure because the unions can see their role in them only in "capitalist" terms and have no intention of foregoing their claim to squeeze the orange until the pips squeak.[4]

---

[4]It is notable that the various extensions of state control and ownership which have taken place in British industry in the 1970s (some of them under a Conservative government) have not been accompanied by serious evidence of a trade union desire to make them work in economic terms, i.e. profitably. This negative reaction generally appears more strongly at the level of the plant union organisation than at the national level.

What all this adds up to – and there is much more that could be said on the present condition of the Labour Party – is that one of the major parties of this country is condemned to internal conflicts – part ideological, part arising from the peculiar structure of interests within it – which, so long as they last, must cast a blight on whatever policies it pursues. On the ideological plane these conflicts can be resolved in only one of two ways: either the efforts of the Left are crowned with success and the party commits itself to a programme of radical social, economic and political change, indistinguishable one might add from that pursued in many countries of eastern Europe, or the liberal and social democratic forces in the party reassert themselves, even at the cost of dividing the party into two distinct groups, one dogmatic and socialist, the other within the mainstream of the traditions which shaped it in earlier years. As far as the conflicts engendered by the structural disabilities of the Labour Party go, these can be mitigated or removed only by escape from a dependence on the unions which has become burdensome, in other words by the dissolution of those organic ties between the party and organised labour which are virtually without parallel in the Western world. Any of these outcomes would, of course, change the face of British politics and open the way to both a realignment of forces and a clarification of choices such as has not been within our grasp for a very long time. In terms of foregone opportunities the price which the British people pay for the survival of the Labour Party in its present form is astonishingly high – a macabre tribute both to sentiments of loyalty and devotion as well as to those of apathy and indifference.

If more attention has been paid to the Labour Party than to its principal rival, this is because the dilemmas it faces are more acute and their impact on politics more immediate than those affecting the Conservative Party. Essentially, the latter is living on borrowed time, waiting for something to turn up both in the form of doctrine and of a style of leadership. Meanwhile, for different and contrasting reasons, both parties are in virtue of their internal condition, unable to put in the service of representative institutions a ruling élite which, in so far as this can ever be hoped for, might measure up to the demands now being imposed on it. Nor are the smaller parties exempt from such weaknesses, for they, too, are subject to the circumstances and procedures shaping party activity and competition in the country at large.

So far this critique of parties as the principal means by which government through representative institutions becomes possible has been developed chiefly with reference to party attitudes and internal relationships. But there are more general factors affecting all the parties in some degree or other which underline their weaknesses as instruments for projecting able and dedicated people into politics. The parties are weak in active subscribing members: the generous figures often quoted for the Conservative Party reveal little, for they are not a reliable guide to the level of involvement in the party.[5] The same goes for the Labour Party, and in particular for the huge cohorts of trade union affiliated members, most of whom play no part in the life of the party at all. The result of a tenuous and fluctuating membership situation is that the parties are surprisingly poor, a condition made worse by the widespread illusion in England that politics can be had on the cheap. And in an inflationary world neither trade union funds for the Labour Party nor the dwindling support of industry for the Conservatives can keep the politicians and their apparatus comfortably afloat for much longer. At any rate by German or Scandinavian standards our parties are badly organised, ill-equipped and poorly staffed. One fairly obvious result of this is that the amount of information and propaganda which they can direct at the electorate is small: it is hardly an exaggeration to say that during the past fifteen years or so political activity and campaigning in Britain has become steadily less visible. What the citizen sees and hears immediately around him has dwindled: there remains only the television, that blind eye given over to a repetitive and empty trivialisation of events based on the principle that whatever Tweedledum says today, Tweedledee must be encouraged to deny tomorrow.

The truth of the matter is that parties do not bite deep down into the political and social life of this country. This may seem a surprising assertion, given the long history of parties in Britain as well as the evidence

---

[5] The Conservative Party's last formal publication of membership figures was in 1953 when 2·8 million were claimed. Estimates made in 1970 suggested that the Conservatives might have had 1·6 million members, the Labour Party 350,000 (i.e. individual members), and the Liberals 50,000. These figures too give no guide to the level of regular activity or regularity in payment of dues. See D. E. Butler and M. Pinto-Duschinsky, *The British General Election of 1970*, pp. 265, 279.

of such intimate ties between party and social interests as those between the Labour Party and the unions or, a century ago, between the Liberal Party and nonconformity. And it may also appear to conflict with the evidence we have of homogeneity and consistency in voting patterns suggesting the broad span of stable party loyalties. But the point here goes beyond actions at the ballot box. The issue is rather the qualitative nature of parties in the society. British parties have not achieved (nor generally even sought) a deep ideological penetration in society, nor have they seen themselves as major agencies for the allocation of specific benefits to their supporters, actual or potential. They command little in the form of patronage and jobs. They offer to hardly any of their members secure and satisfying career prospects, though in national politics the man with a safe parliamentary seat has some hope that in middle age he might with luck spend about half of his time in office. At the local level the position is not much different: there are few prizes to be won, though there have been here and there rare examples of a local boss who, for a mixture of motives, acquires a complete dominance in his area. Yet there is nothing in this country resembling machine politics as encountered in the United States with the party as a monopolist dispenser of social benefits; nothing like the German parties' influence over the bureaucracy in city, Land or federal government; nothing like the pervasiveness of party interests and influence to be found in Italy or Austria, Israel or Holland. Instead parties in Britain resemble fragments of a thin pie-crust, floating on the social stew. They rarely penetrate deeply into social relationships, they do not themselves embody sharply defined or substantial interests in the society, and they are no longer even pre-eminent for the expression of opinion on many political questions. Why is this so? It is chiefly because they have become victims of the idea of party simply as an agency for the competitive production of rulers. It is this idea, propagated by many as a singular sign of political maturity, which has steadily loosened the bonds between party and society, turning parties into essentially careerist organisations: clusters of local activists and notabilities (supplemented by the unions in the case of the Labour Party) whose mission is to get their nominees into national politics. The outcome is the dissolution of any serious link between territory (by which I mean place, community, locality, province) and the capacity to exercise power. We have acquired a professional political élite, by which I imply nothing about its competence or professional skills, but merely indicate that it is dedicated to the profession of politics as it is understood in this country. It lives for and from politics, and for precious little else.

So far most of these remarks have been about parties and their impact on our rulers, the élite. But, of course, the quality and behaviour of those who rise in political life through the parties is influenced in a serious way by the institutions and procedural values according to which their activity is shaped, just as these institutions in turn affect party. Indeed, as will already be apparent, the discussion has begun to shift over to looking at institutional demands affecting the parties, and this line of exploration must now be followed a little further.

Reference has just been made to the British version of the professionalisation of politics as an activity. Important in this connection is the security of tenure which many members of the political élite enjoy and their tendency to stay in the game for a long time. The rate of natural renewal or turnover in the British Parliament is low and rejuvenation a slow process. (And, of course, it is not always young members who bring rejuvenation.) There are probably no reliable estimates of the numbers who leave politics voluntarily, but they are certainly low, and particularly when compared with the relatively high level of voluntary turnover found in some countries. As has been remarked before when considering the House of Commons, there is something rather surprising about this, given the risks, the strains and the practical disadvantages of politics as a profession. However, the purpose here is not to explain the relatively stable composition of the élite over time. What is of some practical concern is the fact that it is stability of membership and long tenure which inevitably mean that the experience of many members of the parliamentary élite is extremely narrow. This is a trait which has been strengthened, too, by the tendency for the age of new entrants to fall: elect a man of twenty-eight in a safe seat and there is the prospect that forty years on he may still be there, his experience of life dominated by the rituals of Parliament and the folklore of the party he happens to belong to. Such is hardly any longer the school of the nation from which effective rulers can be drawn. (Nor is there much force in the argument that Britain has depended on a parliamentary élite for a couple of centuries or more. Before 1914 social conditions were vastly different and the substantially aristocratic élite of the nineteenth century had many opportunities outside the confines of its public service to acquire experience different from that which it gained in Parliament and party.)

It might, of course, be countered that the parliamentary experience is an enriching one, and that in any case Members of Parliament pick up much else in the course of their work outside Parliament which is valuable for those actively concerned in various ways with the conduct of government. As far as the extra-mural professional experience of politicians goes, there is evidence suggesting that this has narrowed during the past two decades or so. The proportion of Members of Parliament with substantial outside professional commitments has declined, and so has the number of those who have close and continuing contact with persons and organisations involved in the handling of practical problems. *Pari passu* there has been an increase in the ranks of those who are in the first place talkers, communicators, persuaders, agitators, link-men – people who may have a useful task to perform but who also can exert a debilitating influence if too numerous and too vocal. Meanwhile, as the responsibilities of government have widened, so those in the political élite who are not at a particular time holders of executive office, have been steadily pushed to the peripheries of the arguments and consultations which must go on in the determination of policies and the preparation of schemes for executive action. The organised interests in our society connect overwhelmingly with government, with the permanent administration and those who happen to be the ministers of the day. They turn to Members of Parliament either as a last resort or by way of mere genuflexion, or sometimes when what is being advocated has a cranky and unusual tone which makes a sympathetic hearing from the executive side unlikely.

The gradual narrowing of the political élite's experience outside of Parliament is compounded by the unsatisfactory nature of what is gained inside the institution. Useful involvement in the examination and amendment of legislation is marginal; select committee work has a spasmodic and desultory quality about it, despite the increase in scale in recent years; much of the activity in plenary session is part of an elaborate charade, a way of using up time through the performance of various parts, but with no recognisable results at the end of it; and there is that exaggeration of the role of Members of Parliament as welfare officers for their constituents which limits the horizons of so many of them, and makes them progressively less able to think in the broader terms which are required in the appreciation of so many of the issues which come up for consideration and approval.

Another interesting facet of the manner in which the British Parliament affects the careers and aspirations of the political élite is that it offers no prospect of achieving anything other than ministerial office. In Parliament there are no positions other than those of executive authority which have any real significance at all (barring one or two purely intra-party offices such as that of the chairman of the back-bench committee of all Conservative Members of Parliament). In other words, there is no ambition other than office which can be satisfied within it. The most serious effects of this may not lie in the strengthening of party oligarchies which it encourages. Perhaps they are far more to be found in the impulse to stereotype behaviour which stems from the frustration of a parliamentary career leading either to office or to nothing, and in the exclusion from governmental responsibilities of virtually all those outside the parliamentary group. That the existing aspirants have a vested interest in their monopoly is hardly surprising. That this monopoly now works to the public good is more than doubtful.

There is, however, not merely the impact of particular parliamentary conventions to be considered. We must also remember that the élite which is projected into national politics proceeds in a most unusual way from what are sometimes called the grassroots, as indeed I began to indicate when discussing the Conservative Party. Constituencies in Britain enjoy a remarkable degree of freedom in the selection of candidates, that is to say the party organisations in them. Provided the individuals concerned are on the central party lists, the local party groups are likely to have a very free hand. Yet this does not mean that as a rule candidates are chosen on account of their position in a locality or their ability to represent its interests. Indeed, as the ties of party discipline have become stronger, so the concern with representing local interests and territorial influence has declined. (Not that it was ever very strong: there is a sense in which England has always been ruled by a pre-existing and centrally based élite in search of localities which its members can then claim "to represent".) Candidatures are now often offered more or less by competition, and aspirants present themselves who have little or no connection with the area which they say they would like the honour to represent. In fact, so far has this process of competitive selection gone, that one can best picture it as a game of chance in which the aspirants to membership of the ruling élite compete for cards of differing values. Those who are lucky (or who have had a few previous shots at the game) draw a good card with high points — this is called a "safe" seat. Others get dummies and have to hope for better luck next time. What is remarkable is the dissociation which exists in so many cases (not in all, it is true), between the aspiring representatives and the localities which they hope to represent. This underlines the earlier argument that the political élite in Britain does, to an increasing extent, constitute a free-floating body, cut adrift from real interests in the society. Out of the self-selecting aspirants the constituencies can generally choose somebody who suits their particular preferences — which means in fact the preferences of what may be a tiny knot of people. This is the freedom which they have, and it must be said that in all parties they use it often in surprising ways. Each party contributes something different in terms of attitudes, manners and political ideals. But equally there are common characteristics which cut across party divisions because all are playing by the same rules. The outcome of many random decisions is an élite which, in an increasingly fluid and shapeless social context, is idiosyncratic, heterogenous, unpredictable and often somewhat shallow in its abilities. Its members are chosen not for their skill in building up a local connection or power base, not for what they might already have achieved in some sector of public action or service, not for their specialised skills and knowledge gained in a private profession which may be needed in party and legislature, not even (or only rarely) for the promise they show of being capable of filling high office, but rather because they suit the varied and particular preferences of little groups of people who run the local party organisations and embody party ties and beliefs in the country. It is not without some irony that the price which so many of the "successfuls" then have to pay for their success in the constituency competitions is that they must, when elected, at any rate keep up the appearance of putting the complaints and grievances of their constituents at the top of their list of priorities.

It may be regarded by some as a gesture of unkindness to underline so heavily the limitations and weaknesses of those who finally enter the ranks of the political élite. But if I have not acknowledged sufficiently the positive qualities and virtues which many of them undoubtedly possess, it is in part because this side of the coin has been exhibited too often, and with a note of sycophantic respect by some writers. Of course, there are people in the parliamentary élite who have high abilities, dedication, honesty of purpose and consistency of intent, just as there are those who take seriously the notion of trying to "represent" their constituencies and particular interests with which they happen to be associated. But the argument here is that if we look at the general quality of the political élite today and survey its members *en gros*, then we have to conclude that it reveals serious weaknesses. Too few of its members measure up to the needs of the time and to the gravity of our condition. There is a superficiality, a brittleness and a certain lack of seriousness about the political élite which erodes its claims to authority. And above all it suffers from vanity. Again, it was Weber who discerned so sharply and portrayed so scathingly the effects of vanity in politics.[6] It is a quality which destroys responsibility and an awareness of the politician's obligation to accept the consequences of what he does. It is a condition in which men cease to respect facts, disguising realities and subordinating their actions to the desire to cut a certain figure on the stage of public life. It is a vice which persuades men that even their own impotence and shrinking away from duty is but a tribute to their worldly wisdom. It is a disorder which signifies that those who suffer from it are no longer to be taken seriously: they suffer from a kind of blindness which prevents them from seeing whither they are bound.

Without seeking to find the yardstick of a mythical golden age, it is still possible to get some measure of the changes which have taken place in the quality of political leadership by looking at earlier periods of British history. That alone will illuminate the difference between the present style of politics and an engagement which has been in different ways and at different times a more serious business. To read the words of politicians nowadays as well as those of many others with differing responsibilities in public life, is to subject oneself all too often to a retreat into mere words, into verbiage. Harsh and unpleasant circumstances and conditions are sugared over and evaded; there is a propensity to take refuge in whatever happens to be popular prejudice, the latest collection of pseudo-scientific jargon generated often enough by those whose professional livelihood depends precisely on their skill in so doing; there is the flight into party

[6]Max Weber, *Politik als Beruf, passim.*

dogma; there is the mere repetition of empty phrases, sterile formulae, flimsy pretexts and sometimes plain nonsense. To read many of the debates on major questions in the House of Commons (let alone discussion in the press and elsewhere) is today all too often a depressing experience which demonstrates this deterioration. Quite apart from the attachment to party shibboleths there is the virtual disappearance of any language in which the serious political questions of our time can be analysed and discussed. It is thus that the appeal to principle, to the argument that this or that should not be done in that way because the rule or procedure implied is harmful to the political relationships in the society, becomes impossible. When men no longer understand the language of a principled argument in politics, they are as good as deaf: politics becomes the mere assertion of will.

Yet it is hard for a political élite to set itself above the general standards of its milieu, and particularly in a democratic political system. The trivialisation and, indeed, the corruption of mind of which I have written has taken place far beyond the bounds of such groups as have been discussed here. The instruments of communication in Britain have, and more particularly in the field of political and social commentary, engaged in a steady and competitive depreciation of standards. For those who manage and provide such services all that matters is the cheap drama of gladiatorial contests, and unfortunately there are those whose vanity persuades them to play along with this preference. The result is the cult of instantaneous and preferably excited comment, a passion to manufacture a clash of party opinions where none need exist or over questions which represent a misunderstanding of what is at stake. These tendencies affect television more seriously than the other media of communication, but now can be seen at work nearly as often in what is called "the quality press"; here, too, there is no longer, as a general rule, reporting of that level of seriousness and thoroughness which is still to be found in half a dozen or so of the world's leading newspapers. There is too much obtrusive comment from busy opinion-formers, and unfortunately still a remarkable degree of insular disinterest in what happens in the world outside. Nor is the academic and teaching world exempt from its share of responsibility for contributing to this condition. Too many people have allowed their beliefs about how they would like the world to be to overrule their capacity to understand the world as it is. This is, of course, at the very origin of the pursuit of illusions. It rapidly produces a state of mind in which people lose the ability to pursue critical reflection, and in so doing to subject the terms in which they understand the world to that continuing reappraisal which alone offers hope of wisdom.

However, these broader social aspects of the deterioration of the political vocabulary cannot now be pursued further. It is a negative balance sheet which emerges from the present argument and it is, therefore, only reasonable to ask whether anything might be done to counteract the deterioration of the political élite which has been asserted to exist. Let us leave on one side a discussion of the broader aspects of that question, including the possibility that a society can be changed and its leadership too only through the harsh discipline of circumstances. Looking at the matter more narrowly, there might in principle be changes which could be made in political procedures and institutional relationships which would be likely to have some beneficial effects on the character of the élite. In so far as the problem is susceptible of institutional treatment, it is best understood as one of widening the élite, bringing into it (and not necessarily on a lifetime basis) people with a greater diversity of experience and thus of reducing the formative influence on it of the present conventions of party and parliamentary life. It seems to be possible, though not certain, that electoral reform would make a contribution in these directions. Depending to some extent on the kind of reform introduced, it would provide an impulse to bring about major changes in the character and structure of the parties, and similarly in the conditions of activity within them. This in turn would modify, even if only gradually, the way in which aspirants are selected and what people take to be the relevant criteria of choice. Another consequence of this kind of change would be its tendency to create conditions in which the traditional roles of Parliament would have to be re-assessed, thus offering the prospect of the disappearance or attenuation of some of the very factors of parliamentary experience which now have such harmful effects.

Another change or set of changes which could be contemplated (though hard to define precisely and put into effect)[7] is to alter formally the

[7] An interesting comment on the exclusions from active political life is provided by the House of Commons Disqualification statutes. Looking at the steadily lengthening lists of those excluded by category or office from membership of the Commons – which means *de facto* from any active party engagement – one wonders who eventually will be left free to compete for election.

conditions governing the passage from various sectors of public employment and service to political life, in other words to render movement easier and the penalties for going into politics less rigorous. Similarly, another approach to this possibility is somehow or other to tolerate the assumption by people in official positions of some degree of public and political responsibility: thus the political élite would be widened by incorporation into it of people whom, according to the present conventions, we have to exclude. (The difference can be seen easily if we glance across the Channel at France: to define the political élite in terms of those who seek national elected office only would be hopelessly unrealistic.)

It is possible, though hardly certain, that a serious degree of decentralisation or devolution would also have a beneficial impact on the quality of élites. Here I am thinking primarily of those who would be taking up responsibilities away from the national level of government and legislation and who, therefore, would not for some time make any contribution to changes at the centre. Indeed, here a rather curious paradox becomes apparent. If we were to assume, rather unrealistically, that genuine measures of decentralisation in favour of provincial and more locally based authorities were to take place, we would then have to expect that such a challenge might evoke a response strengthening the quality of sub-national direction and leadership, and that this would happen at least to some extent at the expense of the national élite. In other words, there would begin to be some point in holding sub-national office. As a result it might be suggested that such a development would make the problem at the centre worse, increasing the risk that the national élite would become yet more dissociated from real interests in the society. Yet this might be a risk which it would be worth taking. The fundamental need is to cultivate and release far more energy and initiative in the society: there is plenty of reason to believe that centralisation is inimical and harmful to this purpose. A genuine decentralisation – the precondition of making sub-national political activity worth while to people of talent and ambition – implies that the damage which the centre can cause would have been diminished by the very reduction in its powers. To a certain extent, therefore, the country could afford for a while at least to worry less about the capabilities of those at the national level of political leadership. But more important is the probability that in time a reinforcement of political resources away from the centre, backed up, too, by a strengthening of other influential groups in administration and in the economy, would feed back into the national arena. The national élite would face tougher competition, would be forced more often to demonstrate the validity of its proposals and would need to recognise more often its own limitations. Such an experience would encourage a re-invigoration of élites and a new seriousness with regard to the tasks and duties of those who aspire to govern at the centre.

It must, however, be remembered that every political class is enclosed within the moral condition of the society it claims to guide. This is why it is necessary to turn next to consider some features of this moral context, the environment of feelings and attitudes within which political institutions and political leaders must work. Some references have already been made in the preceding discussions to these matters. In order to avoid too much repetition I shall, therefore, concentrate on a particular aspect of this moral condition or context, that which bears most directly on the survival in Britain of a liberal constitutional order. That is to say, consideration will be given to what some of the older political philosophers would have called "the sentiments of liberty", those moral attitudes and beliefs which are conducive to the maintenance of a free society with limited government. The question really is: We talk of freedom in its political sense, but does a large body of opinion really want to preserve it? And it may be held that that question is but another way of asking what is meant by freedom and what are the terms on which it is attainable.

CHAPTER 10

The Sentiments of the People towards Government

In attempting to delineate the condition of the political order of a society and its expression in constitutional arrangements, it is hardly realistic to leave out of account the moral attitudes of the people, or at least some consideration of those beliefs and habits which appear to have a direct bearing on political life. Yet this leads one into highly elusive and contentious matter, the judgement of which is difficult and very much dependent on the moral stance of the observer. Most of us recognise that the moral environment of politics is of importance, and that particular forms of government express what people want and what they are prepared to tolerate (let alone what in some circumstances they cannot escape from). Nevertheless, there is no satisfactory way of providing an objective measurement of how moral values affect political behaviour, nor of the specific causal relationships which may exist between such values and particular political decisions or events. It is a question of trying continuously to discern how changes in the moral perceptions of individuals impose limitations on what is thought to be possible in the shaping of political relationships, and for this reason on what can actually be done through particular modes of political co-operation. Yet despite the absence of simple and incontestable answers to the perplexing questions which are presented by the interactions between moral values and political arrangements, only the frivolous and the shallow-minded will deny an interdependence here. And I take it as a reasonable assumption that a liberal and democratic political order is unlikely to survive if individuals no longer care much for their own liberties, and if they apparently accept that the satisfaction of particular social interests should regularly take precedence over the maintenance of those principles which are intended to determine the character of the political association itself.

Notwithstanding the difficulties, I shall try to make a few remarks about the moral attitudes affecting political life in Britain, and more particularly the role of government. But they will be selective, underlining for the most part only those attitudes and values which seem to be linked in rather obvious ways with political consequences and the government of the society. This means that much is neglected which the keen observer might well decide is of great importance in determining the subtle and ever-changing links between private life and the public realm.

Let me begin with some recapitulation of what has gone before. The chief outward manifestations of decline in Britain have been economic. There has been a long and persistent failure to manage efficiently the affairs of the domestic economy, with the result that resources have declined relative to the expectations of benefits which have been nourished throughout the society. The response so far has not been a serious attempt to agree upon at least some of the reasons for this failure and to devise remedial measures, but instead a desperate effort to achieve the impossible — credit ourselves with benefits in the form of consumption and public services which have not been earned. This in turn has stimulated a competitive struggle amongst sectional interests which the political authority has been able to moderate, if at all, only at the price of accepting the bulk of the demands put forward, no matter how harmful their effects might be. Inevitably in such circumstances public policy has lost all claim to coherence.

The statistical expression of economic mismanagement is to be found in the British rate of inflation,[1] in the devaluation of the currency, in the accumulation of indebtedness, in the vast deficits in public spending, in the weak and fragile position of foreign trade earnings and so on. But what cannot be found in the statistics are the corrosive effects of the social values which have carried forward this attempt to flee from the recognition of necessities. These values have for a long time expressed a belief that individuals are entitled to consume whatever they demand, regardless of what they contribute to the creation of resources. We have experienced a disjunction between the individual's entitlement to benefits of all kinds and his obligations to help make the provision of these benefits

---

[1] It is, of course, well known that inflation rose to unprecedently high levels in 1974–5. But it should not be forgotten that the tendency to tolerate inflation rather than face up to economic requirements is long standing, certainly reaching back far more than a decade.

possible. Not surprisingly, as the effects of this situation have become more and more self-contradictory and the prospects of satisfying all the individual claims have diminished, so there has been an upsurge of envy and mistrust in society. This condition in turn is fired and inflamed by the very conflicts which it generates. Nor do the statistical tables betray any evidence of the consequent wear and tear on our political values: they say nothing of the fact that a society which proves so incapable of grasping the nature of its economic situation and of the conditions of its being able to satisfy the expectations of its members at a level compatible with its own survival, must be suffering from the decay of political authority. In short, it no longer has the means of sustaining an authority capable of acting in the interests of the whole.

This, broadly, is why it is difficult to escape the conclusion that the character of the political order for the future is now in question. That this is so may not yet be wholly explicit. Ritual obeisance is still made to time-honoured practices, and there is the lingering belief that somehow or other the British constitution is *semper eadem*, capable of weathering any storm (a foolish belief after all, and especially when expressed by those who assert that it is the very flexibility of our constitution which has sustained a capacity to make changes in it). But if there are no political means of controlling events, then events impose their own logic. Either the political order descends into a condition of disorder, of war of all against all, or there emerges a will to reconstruct the rules of the political association, to re-establish political authority. Whether Britain goes the one way or the other, there can be no doubt about the challenge to the customary understanding of political procedures and relationships: they are failing and their very failure presents questions to which answers must be given.

To the multitude of economic and social problems which present themselves there are no doubt many different solutions which might be offered, even within the limits set by the recognition of objective constraints. But in respect of the renewal of the political order the range of choice is much narrower, though it is reasonable to hope that what is at stake might still be more easily understood by the majority of people than are the technicalities involved in so many of the economic problems which cry out for attention. (Yet even in discussion of the latter a radical simplification might more often be achieved than has been usual in recent British experience.) The political choice is essentially between principles which will sustain authority in virtue of the opportunities for self-determination which they offer to individuals, and such as will not do this. But self-determination is not to be understood primarily in social and economic categories, in terms of placing individuals in society in a situation in which they have such access to economic benefits as will enable them to satisfy their varied social needs. Indeed, in this limited sense the concept of self-determination risks being destructive of an awareness of political rights. The vital element in self-determination is rather the capacity of individuals to shape the conditions of their political association, to see themselves as citizens who have a continuing concern with the terms on which they are associated with each other and on which authority is exercised. Particular consequences then follow in this matter of political choice. For principles which will support self-determination in this sense and at the same time achieve what must always be achieved if there is to be a state at all — that is to say, sustain an authority encompassing all — have to satisfy certain conditions: they must postulate the rights of the individual in such a way as is conducive to his political self-determination; they must uphold a framework of law which safeguards these rights; and they must define the conditions under which a continuing agreement in these principles can be harnessed to the creation of an authority responsible for the tasks of government. Only on some such foundation is a constitution of liberty to be envisaged.[2] Nor is there any hope of rest or perfect fulfilment in the maintenance of such a constitution of liberty: it is a never-ending struggle against those appetites which, as so many have argued for so long, render the idea of self-determination in its political sense a foolish fancy.

This brings me back to the moral environment of political action and institutions in Britain. Fundamentally it is necessary to ask whether there is any longer a taste for this continuing struggle to restrain our appetites for the sake of freedom and political self-determination. Do those sentiments favourable to the repair and maintenance of what has just been called "a constitution of liberty" still retain sufficient vitality to offer grounds for hoping that we can engage successfully in the necessary task of political reconstruction? Of course, the conventional view has been, and perhaps still is, that there is no need for anxiety on this score: the British have a strongly individualist tradition and it is thought by many to render

[2] The phrase "constitution of liberty" is, of course, the title of a well-known work by F. A. v. Hayek.

them virtually immune to the erosion of their civil and political rights. Moreover, it might well be argued that the very weakness now of those in positions of political authority is a kind of perverted tribute to the inherited suspicion of authority and a demonstration of the vitality of the traditions out of which it springs. Yet this seems to be a superficial view. It plays down the vast increase in the powers of government which has taken place over many years, and with very little dispute about the principle involved, despite such reactions of frustration and opposition as there have been and such limits to the effectiveness of public action as in fact exist; it overlooks the evidence of a mounting disregard for consistency and "due process" in the public treatment of individual rights as well as in the regulation of both the rights and duties of corporate bodies and associations; and it ignores the extent to which a climate of indifference and weariness has established itself in which it is increasingly difficult to arouse any interest in the questions of principle posed by the extension of public and private powers.

I shall not spend much time in describing in any more detail the extension of public powers, more particularly those of the central government. But there is one characteristic of this process which deserves to be underlined yet again. This relates to the manner in which such powers have been extended. To a substantial degree what has happened is that powers have been conferred in a way which encourages, and indeed is intended to encourage, a more or less discretionary intervention on the part of political and administrative authorities in spheres of activity which were formerly outside the range of government, and for this reason alone thought to be the responsibility of private agents. In other words, the extension of power has offered opportunities on a rapidly increasing scale for the assertion of political will and discretion according to the passing judgement on those who happen to hold office at any one time,[3] rather

---

[3] An example of this on the grand scale is provided by those sections of the devolution proposals published in November 1975 (Cmnd. 6348) which envisage a delegation of law-making powers to a Scottish Assembly, but subject to the condition that "the Government" checks the *vires* of Assembly measures and considers whether they are acceptable on "general policy grounds" (paras. 57–9). Such an approach, with its claim to total discretionary authority, is incompatible with serious constitutional argument and arrangements. The proposals referred to here were modified subsequently by Cmnd. 6585, Devolution to Scotland and Wales, Supplementary Statement, para 13. But the discretion of the central Government is to be reduced, not removed.

than taking the form of a determination of such conditions as are to apply generally to private individuals and associations or to the public agencies themselves in carrying out whatever their activities may happen to be. This development has been assisted, indeed hurried forward, by weaknesses in British public law and the absence of an adequate body of concepts for the structuring of public powers. Without doubt, too, it has been facilitated by those traditions in politics and administration which stress the values of persuasion, consultation (even though this may often be a one-sided business), and informal compromise. All these qualities have their uses and virtues, but when exaggerated they easily become a veil for political licence and for a situation in which those in government prefer to proceed by "say-so", investing themselves with powers so loosely defined that there is no obstacle in them to this tendency.

There has been great deference shown in this country to a large and arrogant interpretation of public powers, particularly if they are wielded by the central authority in government. This could be illustrated in many ways. Indeed, hardly a week passes now during which one could not extract from the pages of leading newspapers half a dozen examples of this. Private businesses have allowed themselves over recent years to be sucked into terms of financial dependence on public authority which they do not want and have sometimes been too foolish and weak to avoid. To an ever-increasing extent it has been accepted that the satisfaction of private needs — whether these be in the form of housing, pensions, welfare benefits, education, the maintenance of employment or the development of the physical environment — can be assured only by arrangements which diminish the responsibilities of individuals, groups, associations and subsidiary public agencies, and which instead assume that an all-caring central authority will provide. Throughout the society there is an unwillingness to accept responsibility and to live with the consequences of so doing. There is a timorous reluctance to challenge constructively the claims which those in authority put forward, regardless of the fact that many of these claims are patently incapable of fulfilment or serve no useful purpose. One consequence of this passivity is that there are more and more signs of a certain arbitrariness and contempt for principle in the decisions of public authorities. It is as if they realised that a people unwilling to assume responsibility slowly becomes indifferent to actual abuses of power which deprive individuals of rights which they can properly claim.

The condition just outlined is expressed most vividly in the accumulation of powers in the hands of central government. There special factors apply. It is perhaps an ultimate perversion of the notion of parliamentary sovereignty which in the minds of many sustains the belief that *prima facie* the central political authority *must* have the right to act: who else can save us? But the tolerance of an extension of public powers extends far wider. For example, there are few Western countries in which local authorities have more extensive powers to control the use of land and to provide housing. Yet there is ample evidence of the way in which planning controls have frustrated development to a remarkable degree, and as for publicly financed housing, a situation has been produced which is economically absurd, socially unjust and politically divisive. The root cause of this lies in a willingness to entertain naive expectations of what the public authority itself can achieve, and in a failure to understand that better results could have been secured by reducing rather than increasing the powers of the public authorities, by compelling a greater reliance on private and co-operative initiatives, and on the ability of all of us to judge where our interests lie and how best they might be harmonised with those of others.

The complacent acceptance of wider public powers also stems in part from a failure to discern that private advantage does very often mean public benefit. When contemplating the strength of an individualist tradition which emphatically asserted that the pursuit of private advantages did constitute public benefit, there is a peculiar irony in this failure which it is hard to explain. Perhaps the explanation – or a large part of it – lies in the absence of a sufficiently wide diffusion of property in Britain and in the social divisions to which this condition has contributed.[4] Not enough people have felt that they have a tangible stake in the society, and for this reason they have become steadily less aware of the extent to which the well-being of the whole does depend upon their own efforts to maintain and increase their particular stake. Instead there has developed over many years a prejudice against private action and private property which sees both as inherently harmful and capable of benefiting only a minority. This in turn has served to strengthen the

[4]It might be countered that the high proportion of owner-occupation as a form of housing tenure (over 50 per cent of all households) suggests a wide diffusion of property. But owner-occupation seems to me for many reasons to be an inadequate yardstick by which to judge diffusion of property ownership in a society.

position of social organisations, notably those engaged in the pursuit of cash benefits for their members, which see themselves often enough as the residuary legatees of the individualist tradition. Because we have been negligent in encouraging a wider diffusion of property and of the responsibilities and opportunities which accompany that, it has become more difficult to resist the claims of such social organisations to act on behalf of the individual and to subject him to their interpretation of his interests. The individual thus becomes a victim of both public and private power. He surrenders his right to judge what are his own interests and obligations to those who claim to act for him.

The decline in self-reliance and the willingness to accept responsibility which this entails has been favourable to a steady and yet haphazard extension of public powers. At the same time we have become less concerned with consistency in the terms on which public powers are conferred and with due process in their application. This springs partly from a traditional disposition to tolerate a large discretionary element in public action, that in turn justified by a belief that popular sentiments of what constitute "due process", fairness and reasonableness would guarantee protection against the abuse of power. Unfortunately popular sentiments no longer perform this trick, or only rarely so. It is true that if flagrant mistakes are made by persons in authority, and especially at those lower levels where individuals may be quickly and directly harmed, some form of inquiry will often be instituted, e.g. in the field of social care and welfare, or occasionally in respect of police action. But there are few signs of a consistently active body of public opinion sensitive to the gradual erosion of the conditions of the rule of law in many areas of social and political life where, in the nature of things, the confrontation with authority is less dramatic and more complex, or simply does not occur at all.

The significance of this developing state of affairs lies in the contribution it makes to dismantling the barriers to the arbitrary use of powers, and to creating in the minds of individuals a feeling of insecurity and resignation, a realisation that the cards are stacked against them and that it is unlikely that they can do anything effective to protect such claims as they have to fair treatment. This is a change of outlook and feelings which can take place gradually, almost by stealth, and so it has happened. The sense of having rights to protect, of being able to stand up and set limits to public authority interference, of being able to compel such authority to justify itself in consistent and reasonable terms has slowly atrophied. The notion of a Hampden asserting his rights has faded away.[5] And many have reconciled themselves to this situation. After all the processes of law are complex and uncertain, and they are expensive into the bargain. On top of all this is the likelihood that anyone who protests against the use of a public power or of a publicly sanctioned private power on the grounds that it is destructive of his rights and therefore of the conditions of liberty, will at best get little popular sympathy and at worst be regarded as no more than a Don Quixote.

The awareness of rights which an individual is entitled to have protected and which he may properly defend by all means available to him under the law, has been undermined more recently just as much outside the sphere of public action as within it. There is in particular the destruction of individual rights which has been practised within trade unions, and the erection of this claim to power by trade union organisers and members into a principle which the State is expected to uphold. Broadly speaking, the position has been reached when labour unions claim the right to force people to join them, to impose a variety of sanctions, formal and informal, on their members for non-compliance with union instructions,[6] and in the pursuance of their sectional interests to impose

---

[5] It might be held that the case of *Congreve* v. *Home Office* represents the contrary, a successful contemporary Hampden securing annulment of unlawful executive actions. In a way this is so: the Court of Appeal did assert that the Executive must confine its actions within the limits of what was allowed by statute, and by so doing attacked the tendency of government departments to proceed by pretending to possess powers which they do not have. But the particular provision at issue in this case was a narrow one and in itself not a tribute to the quality of public law. See *Congreve* v. *Home Office*, Times Law Report, 4 December 1975.

[6] The behaviour of trade unions, both internally and externally has been subject traditionally to few legal restraints other than those imposed by the common law whose intervention has been fitful and unpredictable. The 1971 Industrial Relations Act attempted to supplement and to a modest extent replace the common law framework for the conduct of trade union activity by statutory principles. The significance of its repeal in 1974 and its replacement by further legislation in 1975 lies in the fact that this vindicated and gave legal backing to the trade union view that in all matters affecting union obligations (as contrasted with union rights or claims) the intervention of legally enforceable rules or conditions should be minimised. It is not surprising that such a negation of the role of law in the regulation of social affairs leaves the individual helpless, e.g. in the face of the demand for compulsory union membership following establishment of a "closed shop". It should be noted that by confirming again the legality of this device, recent industrial relations law legitimises a new corporatist status for unions which choose to acquire it.

constraints on the free movement of individuals and on their right to go about their lawful business. The consequence is that an individual or an organisation involved in a dispute with a trade union has now virtually no assurance of being able to secure an impartial and enforceable resolution of the issues at stake: either there is no remedy (a situation clearly at variance with one of the underlying principles of the common law) or there are no means of enforcing against those who expressly deny them, rights duly established. All this refers only to effects which fall directly upon people in society. It says nothing of the wider political claims which these organisations constantly make, nor of their impact on the workings of the economy.

Yet these changes have occurred with the apathetic compliance of the majority of the British people and the active encouragement of a minority. It is, of course, irrelevant and misleading to play down the seriousness of the situation in this sector of social organisation, as some apologists do, by referring to the relatively small numbers who at any one time must suffer the destruction of their rights. The principle *de minimis non curat lex* has never been a plausible foundation for the maintenance of rights. The ominous fact is that conditions of this kind have been allowed to develop, and their continuance must threaten the survival of those values on which the idea of individuals as citizens rather than as submissive members of competing social organisations rests.

So far it is the spread of indifference towards the growth of powers, mainly public, but in part private too, which has been illustrated. But this torpor affects the exercise of the more straightforward political rights too. As is well known, the level of active political involvement is relatively low in Britain.[7] The record of voting in national elections is patchy, with participation tending to fall still further of late. When one turns to the other level of political representation, local government, one finds there a remarkable degree of indifference, bordering almost on contempt. Many

---

[7] I do not underestimate the difficulties and inherent weakness of cross-national comparisons in respect of indicators of political involvement. But in terms of voting levels, party membership figures, size of politically active leadership groups, electoral activity, expenditure on political campaigning and education, Britain scores low compared with many other liberal democracies.

seats are uncontested and polls of about 30 per cent are quite common.[8]
As a result there is a mantle of obscurity covering much of local political
life. Inside private, or at any rate formally non-public associations, similar
conditions are often to be found, with an indifferent or quiescent
membership playing into the hands of those who run the organisation, and
in the larger ones this usually means officials of one sort or another.

Apathy has sometimes been praised as a political virtue. But this is a
shallow view which makes sense only if it is held that the obverse of
apathy must be destructive agitation, or what the eighteenth century
would have called "enthusiasm". May be the indifference to constructive
political engagement which has developed in contemporary Britain tends
to make this dichotomy a reality. The more the people cease to see
themselves as citizens and come to rely on the powers of government for
the satisfaction of their wants, the more they are tempted into sterile
protest and defiance when they do not like the consequences of their own
flight from responsibility. And indeed there are more and more signs of
this, of a disposition to resort to obstructive action in the hope of warding
off unpleasant realities. Such a trend is not likely to be reversed by further
political retreat, but rather by a substantial increase in the degree of
serious political engagement throughout the society. For this would
reinforce a sense of individual responsibility as well as increase the
responsiveness of those seeking or holding political office. In this way, too,
something might be added to the authority of the office holders: those
who have behind them the support of at least half of their fellow citizens
could make a better claim to authority than those who are ready to
pretend that the support of less than 40 per cent of the voting electorate
amounts to a mandate from Heaven.

In considering the attitudes which people have towards the powers of
government, towards the exercise of their political responsibilities, and
towards their own involvement in social change and adaptation, something
has to be said about the impact in Britain of perceptions of class
antagonism and difference. It is clear that in many important respects the

[8]Since the restructuring of local authorities under the 1972 legislation (in
England and Wales) the proportion of uncontested seats (usually in rural areas) has
declined substantially. But voting levels have hardly changed at all. Moreover, the
number of elected representatives has fallen with the reduction in the number of
local authority units, and the frequency of elections has been cut too.

basis for traditional notions of class differentiation, that between the bourgeois property-owning and the wage-dependent working classes has collapsed. Economic pressures, progressive taxation and redistributive public expenditure policies have ironed out many of the relative advantages enjoyed by the middle class, whilst changes in the pattern of industrial earnings have done much to give some sections of the industrial working class a higher material standard of living than many of those who rank themselves as middle class. But as long as the whole matter is looked at in terms of incomes, occupations, family size and status, conditions of employment and so on, the picture remains extremely complex and variable: as some industrial workers go up, others go down, the middle classes can also benefit from redistribution through public expenditure, there are regional and inter-urban economic variations, etc. So I will not pursue further an inquiry into what might be the economic or material bases for class alignments. What seems to be far more striking in Britain, and particularly in England, is the manner in which people *feel* class adhesion, ascribe themselves to one of two ill-defined life-styles, and then often enough persuade themselves that their interests can be inferred from such an ascription of social status. And, of course, certain consequences then follow both for the structure of political life, and just as important, for the manner in which we go about the handling of political co-operation in the resolution of practical matters.

That many people continue to show a willingness to rank themselves as middle or working class, and in so doing to identify themselves with a whole range of distinctions in status and expectations, is attributable to many factors. There has always been something half-hearted about the commitment to public education in England, with the result that not only have social divisions within the education system been tolerated, but education has frequently been judged in social categories rather than in relation to the quality and usefulness of what was imparted. In everyday speech differences have been preserved which are given a social interpretation, and ironically this source of class ascription has probably been strengthened by the growth of a popular mass culture, stimulated so strongly by the media of communication. Segregation of a social kind has occurred on a large scale in housing, quite deliberately as a matter of misguided policy, and there are other areas of social benefit provision in which distinctions have been preserved between a measure of private responsibility and choice, and dependence on what is offered with the flavour of public welfare.

But perhaps the most important recent influence of all has been the weakening of the educated middle class. There have in Britain been few moral and cultural impulses proceeding from a self-confident middle class such as would persuade other social groups that the values of this level of society should be diffused and taken over. Now it is recognised that using the language of class in this context is unsatisfactory and misleading. What is at issue are qualities which, though historically most often associated with the bourgeois levels of society, are simply the indispensable conditions for a liberal political order: the capacity for self-expression, discrimination in judgement, respect for the abilities and differences of individuals, confidence in the uses of reasoned argument in the resolution of differences. Of course, over a long time many who would have to be described as working class according to economic or Marxist yardsticks have possessed and developed these qualities, but not with a consciousness of their being the prerogative of a particular class, rather in the realisation that such qualities established the reality of citizenship. The problem in Britain has been the failure of a diffusion process, and of effective interaction between people whose social experience is in manifold ways necessarily different the one from the other. The possibility of taking advantage of the increase in material resources in order to extend the opportunities to share in a common cultural inheritance has not been realised. Instead there has been a retreat into purely defensive attitudes at all levels of society which in turn has stimulated that unreflecting egalitarianism which fails to see that differentiation can be fruitfully joined with a perception of shared values.

The cultivation of antagonisms has obviously had serious political consequences, though all these will not be explored here. But it is necessary to underline two points. One is the fragmentation and attenuation of a lively and critical public opinion seeking to set standards for the conduct of affairs throughout the society. The weakening of the middle class, the self-effacement of many of its members, has played a part here. But so, too, has the diversion of many of the energies of industrial workers into the mere fabrication of claims to benefits, to the neglect of the contribution which many might have made (and used to make) to more constructive patterns of social and political activity. The outcome is not merely the breaking-up of public opinion into many competing group interests, but a greater degree of febrility and narrowness of vision in the public expression of views and feelings. Again, it is worth remembering that there has to be this diversity in a free society, but there also has to be a means of pulling coherence out of the diversity, and to this end a broader and more stable public consensus on standards of judgement and procedure is essential. The other point relates to the manner in which the arrested diffusion of shared values has encouraged an "all-or-nothing" attitude towards the taking of many different kinds of decisions. Antagonisms obviously breed suspicions, and this condition in turn stands in the way of any appreciation of the possibility that change can benefit all involved, perhaps not all at the same time, but certainly over a longer period. Instead, there is a powerful and widely held belief that most decisions must involve an absolute loss for some of those affected and must therefore be resisted. Again, what is missing here is the sense of shared values and a shared engagement. People talk past each other because they often enough no longer understand what are the basic conditions of being joined in the same political association.

Several objections might be advanced against what has been said so far. One set of arguments would concentrate on the civic virtues which can still be said to exist in Britain — tolerance, a willingness to compromise, some sense of solidarity and so on. I will come back to these matters in a moment. Another set of arguments would point to the difficulty which is presented by the need to reconcile what has been said about a growing passivity in the face of the inflation of public powers with the evidence of the growing inability of the public authority to secure compliance with its wishes. In other words, how does one explain the weakness of government?

This apparent contradiction is to be explained by recognising that certain individualist myths have survived, but at the same time those who are subject to them no longer wish to accept the consequences of living according to such myths. For this latter reason they have been willing to encourage an expansion of public powers and responsibilities, but wish to continue to lay claim to the autonomy which the individualist tradition postulates as desirable. A strong dislike of the public authority as somehow external and alien, subversive of the independence and freedom which all should enjoy flourishes, yet we are fearful of living according to this very principle of freedom. This paradox can be seen, of course, in the behaviour of labour unions which demand state control of the economy and in the next breath complete autonomy in wage negotiations. It pervades the attitude of private business which has failed to see the positive aspects of the framework of order which the State alone might provide, and yet is ready to beg for state financial support when in difficulties. It can be seen in the peculiar anarchy of an educational system in which meticulous public control of resources is made respectable by a readiness to allow the educational profession to use them more or less as its members see fit. It is expressed over and over again in a rejection of the general regulation of particular activities on the grounds that this would infringe individual autonomy, but in the acceptance of the piecemeal provision of services and benefits by the public authority as a substitute. What this often amounts to is that the general and unconditional is perceived as a threat to individual and group rights, the particular and the conditional may be accepted and justified by the benefits it confers on those to whom it is addressed.

Thus it seems that we do indeed live with a contradictory and for that reason very damaging situation. Popular understandings of the individualism which lies deep in British history have maintained an attitude of obstinate suspicion towards the action of public authority. Yet the belief that fairness can be secured in the distribution of benefits only by entrusting the very production of such benefits to the public authority has made acceptable a rapid growth of that authority. In practical terms the results of this process have been disappointing. This in turn feeds and reinforces the suspicion of government which has always been there, sometimes merely as a grumbling noise in the background, sometimes as a more vigorous and obstructive force. Conceptually the way out of the dilemma is fairly simple: the powers of government need to be reduced in order to make the exercise of those which remain more effective, and to leave room for the expression of that still surviving individualism. Reduce powers in order to strengthen authority. Yet though the remedy may be clear, its application remains hard and perhaps improbable.

Standing in the way of such an appreciation of this underlying dilemma is the widespread reluctance in British society to think problems out in terms of principles, a fact which goes far to explain the emptiness and flabbiness of so much of the analysis of questions of all kinds – social, economic, political, constitutional, administrative, etc. — which have been the subject of various sorts of public review and investigation in recent years. There has been a retreat from the search for clearly defined and consistent arguments, mirroring the disposition in the society to prefer loose and fuzzy notions, conjoined with the appeal to short-term practicalities. At its worst this amounts to a retreat into illusion and mere words, the condition of which I have already written. From top to bottom of the society, in public and private life, there is a readiness to engage in a game of pretence in which many of the participants now hardly know whether they are deliberately deceiving themselves and others, or merely do so because it has become natural to them to talk in a language which disguises realities. Hegel detected very clearly the consequences of such a flight from reality in his early work on the German Constitution: "Thus they become accustomed either to a constant contradiction between their words and the facts or else to an attempt to make events different from what they really are and to twist their explanation of them to suit certain concepts."[9] This is precisely what has happened in Britain. We are no longer surprised if, in the discussion of political and economic matters, there is plain conflict between what our experience tells us is the case and what this or that voice asserts in defiance of all the evidence to be the case. Similarly, we are often tempted to present even gross incompetence and failure as something almost like success, and then try to persuade ourselves that it really had to be like that in order to suit the consequences of a certain view of social relationships and claims which many have been foolish enough to espouse. Such a disposition, if persisted in, must result in moral decay. For a morality which has any value at all, and certainly one which is intended to support a constitution of liberty, cannot rest on the pursuit of illusion. That would be a contradiction in terms. On the contrary, a morality capable of supporting a society in the effective resolution of its problems must rest upon a perception of *some* realities, for only out of a common recognition of certain necessities of the world can come a convincing statement of the grounds of obligation.

The realist would be inclined to give a negative answer to the question posed at the outset about the survival of a taste for political self-

[9] *Hegel's Political Writings*, translated by T. M. Knox, Introduction by Z. A. Pelczynski, OUP, 1964, p. 145.

determination. He might argue that there seem to be few objective grounds for expecting a sudden reinvigoration and renewal. Instead, many signs point to the continued erosion of such elements of a liberal order as still survive, and the transition to a form of rule, mean and bureaucratised, which would also necessarily have an authoritarian bias, yet of a cringing and complaisant kind. And it would, of course, be egalitarian, yet indulgent towards those inequalities which the stronger establish for themselves at the expense of the weaker. It is to a condition of this character that the sentiments of so large a part of the people appear to point rather than to a recovery of the principles upon which a constitution of liberty could be reformulated.

Yet notwithstanding these forebodings, there remains some justification for retaining a measure of faith in the prospect of a deliberate effort to change what seems to be the present path of British political evolution, for there is a credit side to the balance sheet. There is a fund of tolerance and willingness to compromise in British society: it needs to be harnessed to a clearer grasp of principles rather than being misused to justify the easy ways out. Despite the pressures of loyalties and commitments destructive of any sense of common interest transcending the narrowness of special interests, there remains intact a residue of social solidarity and shared experience which brings many groups of people together for co-operation in a wide range of beneficial activities. The spirit of voluntary social service is still stronger and more effective in its results than in many other countries with similar political ideals. The standards of probity and fairness in the public services are still generally high, and as a rule these services can be relied on to acknowledge both political direction and public opinion. The judiciary remains vigilant and independent, and there has been no significant encroachment on certain basic civil rights – free speech, the right of assembly, freedom from wrongful arrest, the right to exercise lawful political rights and so on.[10] Though, as has been indicated before, there are dangers in the manner in which private initiative and responsibility have been eroded, it remains true that the British have continued to show skill in associating people outside the official sphere of government with the provision of very many services which, in

---

[10] Regrettably these statements – along with several others in this passage – have to be qualified in respect of part of the United Kingdom, i.e. Northern Ireland.

contemporary conditions, require a measure of public funding and support. In this way it has often been possible to avoid that degree of bureaucratisation which usually occurs when the public authority takes over completely. The universities of this country are a notable example of this particular skill at work. But this points to a further asset, perhaps the most important of all in the face of the problems of political reconstruction. This is the strong sense of the importance of institutions which is manifested in so many ways, and the awareness of procedure which is associated with that. Of course, this perception of the value of institutions also has its dangers: it can encourage an unreflecting conservatism, it may and does at present inhibit the examination of principles and of arguments for genuine change, and it can degenerate into the mere veneration of habit, disguising the failure of institutions themselves. But these are risks inseparable from this particular insight itself. Britain has a remarkably long and successful experience of institutional adaptation at all levels of social and political activity, demonstrating how it has been possible to combine understanding of the advantages of procedural limits in the pursuit of common purposes with flexibility and informality in their application. And this has been an experience widely diffused throughout the society. The question is whether it can again be used creatively.

The pressure of the moment is always to find ways of resolving an unending flow of practical problems: it is this harsh reality which often seems to justify practical men in their preference for putting on one side the broader issues affecting the terms on which this insistent demand is met. But in contemporary Britain the ability to find durable solutions day by day to the practical issues of social co-operation has weakened and ebbed away. Fundamentally this is because there is no longer enough assurance amongst the people about the framework within which action is to be taken, both by themselves and by those who act on their behalf. The challenge has thus become one of constitutional reappraisal. This means that it is also a challenge to transcend the resignation imposed by indifference and timidity, by the flight from individual responsibility and by the easy acceptance of muddled thinking. The repair and re-shaping of an indispensable political framework is not, however, quite out of reach. Though those sentiments favourable to liberty and self-government have been dulled, there are still resources of ingenuity and inventiveness to be tapped. What has to be done is to apply them constructively to the tasks of citizenship in the widest sense. It is the belief that this is still a feasible undertaking which provides the justification for trying in the final stages of these reflections to state briefly what might be some of the basic terms of a constitutional revival, of a restatement of the conditions of the political order.

CHAPTER 11

Fundamentals in a Constitutional Reform

Drawing on the preceding arguments an attempt will now be made to consider some of the terms on which a sense of constitutional rules and conditions could be recovered. The aim is to ask how political institutions and practices might be adapted and changed so that the qualities of a liberal and democratic political order are maintained, both in order to strengthen the authority of institutions and to increase individual commitment to the polity and to the rights which citizens have in its affairs. But there is no intention of presenting comprehensive reform blueprints, nor of looking closely at the technicalities of particular possibilities. It is rather to indicate some of the directions which change might take and which seem to be called for by the underlying principles which have guided this critique. Thus it follows that some of the suggestions to be made are hardly "constitutional" in a narrow and technical sense: they would probably not find their place in a written constitution even if we had one. But they are "constitutional" in a broader sense as defining some of the more important terms which it might be desirable to import into the structuring and operation of institutions.

The fundamental requirements of an effort to restore authority to our pattern of representative government, whilst at the same time maintaining its respect for liberty under the law, can be summarised as follows.

The rights of the individual need to be restated and safeguarded, both those which are intended to protect him against the abuse of authority, and those which establish his status as a citizen and from which his political obligations stem.

The rights and duties of the national political authority — of Parliament and Government — have to be given a measure of definition and should be so circumscribed that the legitimacy of the institutions in which they are vested can be reinforced and their ability to act strengthened.

The opportunities to establish and exercise political influence and authority need to be widened and diffused more extensively in the society so that the experience of self-government and of the acceptance of responsibility becomes a reality for more people than it is now.

The public status and attendant responsibilities of political parties as the means by which in the first place opinions, preferences and programmes of action are expressed has to be recognised.

The structure of public law — much of it law conferring power on public authorities — should as far as is practicable be reformed so that it becomes less an expression of the will of particular office holders, and more a determination of general obligations laid both on all those in positions of authority as well as on private individuals and associations.

The order in which these principles and objectives have been set out does not correspond exactly to the sequence adopted in the foregoing discussion of particular aspects of the political system and its constitution. In particular the questions bearing on the character and role of law will this time follow such comments as are made on the status and functions of parties. But since it is the rules according to which the political order is structured which are of decisive importance in the context of an argument about a constitutional settlement, this inversion of a preceding order may be justified for the sake of giving additional emphasis to the role of law and its relevance to the categories of constitutional argument.

On the definition of individual rights and their constitutional protection something has already been said in an earlier chapter when the question of a bill of rights was considered. There are only a few points to be added now by way of amplification. There is much to be said for the inclusion in a statement of rights of a "due process" clause, formalising what is to some extent already achieved by a variety of procedures. The same goes for a clause guaranteeing the citizen's right to seek redress from a court of law against what is *prima facie* an unreasonable and arbitrary exercise of power by any public authority, a right which currently exists only in a fragmentary way and subject to many procedural uncertainties. As to the problem of finding terms in which to express basic rights, this could perhaps be overcome with relative ease, and indeed there are already a number of hopeful signs of a growing realisation of the urgency and importance of this task. Statements of rights and liberties which might serve as models include the Convention for the Protection of Human Rights and Fundamental Freedoms, prepared by the Council of Europe and ratified by the United Kingdom as long ago as November 1951, or the Canadian Bill of Rights enacted in 1960.[1]

The chief difficulties arise when we consider what might be some of the conditions of making effective such an affirmation of rights, for after all it is useless to have a charter which contains no more than words. These conditions would have to include greater reliance on interpretation by the courts; very probably substantial changes in the character of the courts themselves; acceptance that the authority of Parliament would have progressively to be limited by the rights guaranteed; and a recognition that many institutions which do not now regard themselves as directly involved in the public realm and, therefore, as having obligations to the public, would become subject to challenge if they, too, were to flout the charter of rights. Of course, much would depend on the exact terms in which basic rights were defined as well as on the procedures devised for their protection and enforcement. It is in fact unlikely that the people of this country would suddenly develop a litigious disposition or that they would welcome a narrow and perfectionist definition of rights which might inhibit their capacity to proceed by the informal adjustment of interests and claims. But we would certainly have to be prepared to accept the prospect that far more often than at present particular actions or provisions for action would be challenged, and that validity would then have to be tested by reference to general principles. It would be wise not to under-estimate the shift of perceptions which this would call for.

Undoubtedly the traditional interpretation of the doctrine of the sovereignty of Parliament would have to be modified, and in at least two senses. There would, first, be the need for something like entrenchment of such rights and recognition by Parliament that a claim to be entitled to alter them at will and by the procedures of simple majority vote alone should no longer be asserted. Without this condition, the guarantee of rights would come near to being a contradiction in terms. To revoke

---

[1] The individual has already a certain degree of protection under the European Convention for the Protection of Human Rights. But the procedures by which an individual may seek to vindicate his claim under the Convention are complex, slow-moving and indirect. Nor does the Convention bind signatory states explicitly in respect of their domestic law. For further details see A. H. Robertson, *Human Rights in Europe*, Manchester University Press, 1963. A bill to incorporate the European Convention directly into British law was presented by a group of Liberal Members of Parliament in July 1975.

formally the right of a Parliament to amend or repeal existing law does, I accept, present great practical and logical difficulty. In principle it might be done by invoking a constituent authority or by making a deliberate breach in continuity in order to hand over authority from an old-style unlimited Parliament to a new-style limited Parliament. But it may be that there is no need to try to break out of the logical vicious circle of the sovereignty theory as presently applied to Parliament. If Parliament passed a bill of rights with a preamble emphasising its inalienable quality, *or* if such a bill were additionally approved by referendum *or* if it were provided that amendment would require a two-thirds majority in both Houses of Parliament, it is surely likely that any of these conditions would be the subsequent consolidation of convention and practice render it impossible for Parliament arbitrarily to alter or repeal the Bill of Rights. Just as the Royal Veto has vanished as a fact (though still there in remote theory), so the inability of Parliament to set aside *certain* enactments could be established as a reality of politics.

Second, there would be a need consequentially to accept that Parliament for the future would be restricted in other ways in what it might do, and that if it set aside fundamental rights in ordinary statutes, then its actions would be open to the possibility of invalidation, or at the minimum to a declaration of their being in conflict with the rights guaranteed.[2] This would mean vesting a new and unaccustomed discretion in the judiciary. This would be exercised successfully only if the courts were supported by wider acceptance than there may be now of the idea that there are certain disputes which are better settled by people deliberately set at some distance from the ties and constraints imposed by

---

[2] Parliament's claim to be able to alter *any* law at will could probably be modified by convention, i.e. by self-restraint. For example, could Parliament now repeal the "Bill of Rights" of 1689? In theory, yes, but in practice maybe not without a revolution. The same could happen in respect of a new bill of rights. Logically the supremacy of a statement of individual rights appears to entail the possibility of the invalidation of statutes found to be in conflict with it. But there may be "half-way houses", e.g. a power in the courts to suspend offending provisions, whilst simultaneously reporting such cases to Parliament so that the latter might, if it so wished, take remedial action. My own view is that half measures would scarcely be worth the trouble: a shift in constitutional doctrine is required. On some of the problems of entrenchment and invalidation see O. Hood Phillips, *Reform of the Constitution*, London, 1970, chaps. 6 and 7.

the pursuit of particular political objectives than by the discretionary judgement of those in political or administrative office.

For a while these new responsibilities would impose serious burdens on the British courts and legal profession, for they inherit little in the shape of doctrine and principles which might give them confidence in this unaccustomed task. In addition there is a deep-seated fear of judges getting entangled in politics and in the judgement of overtly political questions which would have to be overcome. (The judge and the official as *pouvoirs neutres* is one of the persistent themes of modern British political development.) But it would be a counsel of despair to conclude that our legal institutions, suitably reinforced, could not in time meet this challenge; a nation which provided much of the doctrinal foundation for the constitutional jurisdiction of the American Supreme Court can surely not be so lacking in the qualities needed to develop a new jurisdiction for its own purposes?

The implications of what has been suggested for the conduct of all the subordinate agencies of government and administration and of autonomous social organisation, too, are also profound. They equally would be bound to respect the constitutionally guaranteed rights, the public authority as a matter of course, the private association when acting in ways which affect the rights of individual members and impinge on matters of public concern. It is perhaps in this area of presumed social autonomy that some of the most serious risks of conflict might occur, and in which the effective enforcement of rights might involve a clash between the political authority and recalcitrant interests anxious to preserve their own sovereignty. We can imagine this happening most easily in relation to the affairs of trade unions, organisations which have been peculiarly exempt from public obligations and in which it is not difficult to mobilise collective emotions of solidarity destructive of respect for individual rights. Yet even here there are those who would be glad to see themselves as citizens, able to invoke the protection of an external authority against the pressures imposed by their membership of particular associations. Many parts of the public sector might also have gradually to modify their conduct. In many sectors of public service the official might find that his claim to exercise a virtually complete discretion would, for example, come into conflict with a right of individuals to equality of treatment or with their right to be given a statement of reasons for administrative decisions.

It might be found that the considerable autonomy of professional groups in the public sector, including even teachers, would have to be qualified in virtue of rights which could be claimed against them. Or again, if the right to own and enjoy property were confirmed and its compulsory alienation made subject to fair compensation, we might find that both the powers of local authorities and the terms on which they are exercised would have to be limited in significant ways.

However, there is no need to multiply examples in order to justify the conclusion that a guarantee of basic civil and political rights would be likely to have many unexpected effects. We tend to forget that whilst rights may be intended for the protection of individuals, it is also part of their function to impose restraints. If their affirmation is to fulfil this dual purpose, then it is but a platitude that there would have to be an adequate degree of readiness in society to take the rough with the smooth as a consequence of this commitment. It would make a mockery of a bill of rights if, when the shoe pinches and a public authority or a private association finds that it must desist from practices held to be sanctified by a veneer of custom, there were to be resort to the will of ministers or of Parliament itself to procure suspension or amendment of the offending clauses. The interpretation of rights must allow for changing values and perspectives, but that is a far cry from the arbitrariness of parliamentary fiat now so familiar in Britain. Ultimately, we do indeed come back to the question whether there exists or can be created a consensus which would support certain overriding procedural values, determinations of the kind of treatment to which citizens are entitled. If there is, then it is possible to reap the benefits of having a bill of rights. If there is not, and if at the same time the traditional restraints of habit and custom have worn dangerously thin, then both the security and the liberty of the citizen are at risk.

Next, there are the institutions of the central political authority — Parliament and Government. A difficult problem here lies in the adherence to a unitary conception of legislative and executive powers expressed in the notion of the Crown in Parliament. It is a matter for some philosophical speculation whether in the final analysis the State can be understood at all in terms which do not suggest the potentiality of a unified authority: to that extent the idea of the Crown in Parliament expresses a certain wisdom. Yet there is a modern theory providing an escape from the difficulties presented by a traditional doctrine which works against recognition of the different functions of government and the achievement of a balance between them: it is the idea of popular sovereignty which constitutes the ground on which it becomes possible to separate powers, recognising the representative body and the executive power as distinct but interdependent institutions.

In practice the sovereignty of the people is accepted in Britain: it was affirmed by most of the constitutional theorists of the last century and it is the principle which was invoked in 1975 to justify appeal to the people by referendum. Unfortunately this very principle has also been used to defend another objection to giving institutional expression to a differentiation of functions in the state. It is argued by some that all popular authority resides in Parliament in virtue of Parliament's representative character, and that for this very reason no separation between Parliament as a legislative and controlling body and Government as the contemporary expression of the Crown's executive authority can be tolerated. Here one is confronted with what might be called an executive version of the theory of *gouvernement d'assemblée*, a theory which in its legislative version has always been dismissed as a peculiar French aberration. There can be little doubt that if the chief problem is to be seen as one of differentiating between the functions of Parliament and Government, and of devising such institutional relationships as might facilitate a balance of powers rather than the absorption of one by the other, then it is necessary to overcome these two rather inconsistent postulates. We should cease to be bewitched by the myth of the Crown in Parliament, accepting that there is no need of that particular myth for the purposes of unifying political authority. But equally it is a mistake to see the idea of popular sovereignty as necessitating a representative authority which must absorb all others and so frustrate the achievement of a balance between institutions.

Now clearly there are many variations in the formal provisions which might be devised in order to redefine the relations between Government and Parliament. Given the expansion of powers granted to the Executive it is important for Parliament to see its primary functions rather in the control and improvement of legislation, the means by which powers are granted, than in the *post facto* control of government and in general debate. The stable door needs to be closed more often before the horse has bolted. In the light of the modern development of Parliament this shift of emphasis would call for many and radical changes in domestic procedure, and would encounter many objections from those who see in the unceasing confrontation of debate the core of the justification for Parliament. But the aim here would not be to exclude debate, rather to ensure that it is directed more consistently at what is most relevant in the contemporary context of executive action.

Amongst the procedural changes to be considered would have to be a move in the direction of a different committee structure, one which would permit more effective scrutiny and amendment of legislative proposals (including financial) and greater specialisation amongst Members. This implies the modification of standing committee procedure as it is now understood, that is to say as essentially debate according to the pattern of the floor of the House of Commons.[3] Instead it becomes necessary to look for an assimilation of standing and select committee procedures, and for the recovery by committees of far more autonomy than they can currently claim.[4]

It has, however, to be accepted that few parliamentarians warm to the prospect of substantial changes in the procedures by which they work. And the Government of the day is always against change which might diminish its control, even though there are advantages which a government might gain from being able to share responsibility (and perhaps blame, too) with Parliament. Moreover, it is clear that procedural changes alone cannot achieve the effects envisaged here. There would need to be parallel shifts in the internal structure of the parties in Parliament as well as in the

[3]It should not be forgotten that in essentials the procedures of the House of Commons, and of that chamber to a greater degree than of the Lords, assume that all business is initiated by a Member and disposed of by means of deciding a question after debate under an independent umpire. This essentially is why it is difficult to establish within the House institutions which would contain positions of substantial influence, e.g. committee chairmen. Procedure stands in the way of this. That the traditional procedure has resulted in an imbalance in favour of the Executive, whose members now initiate most substantive business, is simply one of the contradictory consequences of principles which in addition embraced the idea of the equality of status of all Members of Parliament.

[4]Let nobody claim that British politicians cannot envisage quite different committee structures and procedures inside the legislature. They have recently given ample proof to the contrary, in the case of Northern Ireland Assembly (1973–4), and of the schemes for assemblies in Scotland and Wales.

conventional view of the qualities required of Members — changes which cannot simply be engineered into existence. But if Parliament is to be saved from sinking into yet greater weakness, there appears to be no genuine alternative to an effort to revive the legislative authority of the institution. Just as, on the one hand, Parliament needs to be seen more explicitly than before in terms of its legislative functions, which after all are those in respect of which even now it most often has the right to say "yes" or "no", so, on the other, the Government would have to be seen as vested with an executive power no longer viewed merely as an emanation of Parliament.[5] The counterpart of a strengthened control of Parliament over legislation needs to be some degree of withdrawal from the attempt to assert a detailed and capricious supervision of the particular acts of ministers on the floor of the House, accompanied in parallel by a continuing effort to improve the effectiveness of administrative scrutiny by select committee. [6]

In determining the basis of the relations between Parliament and the Government or Executive a major and contentious question arises over the terms on which governments or prime ministers take office and stay there. In theory, the Crown at present nominates a majority leader, he forms a government, and governs until he decides to dissolve Parliament or until Parliament's prescribed term runs out. But the belief still persists that he stays there until defeated in Parliament by a withdrawal of confidence — something which last happened in 1895! Though the belief no longer conforms to realities, it has a powerful effect on political behaviour. It sustains the idea of adversary politics and of the continuing confrontation between Government and Opposition. It keeps alive the idea that a government must never lose a division, that to make concessions is a sign of weakness and that the proof of "strong government" lies in the passage

---

[5] Here again there are in the British tradition two conflicting principles. One is that of the complete and primary authority of the Crown: this is what has come to justify the direction of Parliament by Ministers. The other is that of Parliament as the repository of authority in virtue of its representation of the people: this is what allows it to assert an almost unlimited accountability of Ministers to it and thus to give Ministers the appearance of being but an emanation of its own authority.

[6] If a new type of permanent standing/select committee were evolved, then presumably such committees would sometimes be dealing with legislation and probably appropriations, too, and sometimes would be engaged in examining past executive performance.

of whatever proposals are put before Parliament. The need is to find means of changing this pattern of thought and expectations.

The most effective way to achieve this would be to redefine to some extent the dependence of Government on Parliament and to circumscribe the power of dissolution, taking it out of the hands of the prime minister of the day. A simple formulation would require the Crown (on which a few remarks follow in a moment) to appoint a prime minister who in turn would be subject to removal only by a vote of no confidence passed in the House of Commons. This would have the effect of undermining the basis for the belief that a defeat on a particular measure would entail resignation. Such a provision alone might not, however, go far enough, for obviously a prime minister or his government could still decide that even a defeat without the formal status of a motion of no confidence should entail resignation. This is why there is a case for looking at the other element in the relationship between Government and Parliament, the question of the dissolution of the representative body. Dissolution has now become a tactical weapon in the hands of the prime minister, to be used chiefly for the purpose of attempting to benefit his own party. But a century or more ago this was not so. It was a means by which, if Parliament was no longer willing or able to sustain a government, the Crown sought to secure a Parliament which would do so. A reversion to something like this view of dissolution might be secured by an adaptation of some of the provisions of the Federal German Basic Law which would take the power out of the hands of the prime minister, yet without handing it back to the Crown as an unqualified discretion. What I mean is that it might be provided that only after a vote of no confidence shall a prime minister resign, that the Crown then within a fixed period has to propose a successor, and that if this proves impossible or the successor is also refused support, the Crown would then have the right to order a dissolution. Only in such circumstances would the dissolution procedure come into play and then as a genuine act of the prerogative.

Such conditions would have a double effect: they would tend to strengthen a Government in its position *vis-à-vis* Parliament, and yet they would at the same time fortify Parliament by establishing an expectation that it would normally run its full term, and moreover that an adverse vote[7]

[7]It is accepted that adverse votes on some matters would have to be turned into questions of confidence, e.g. the voting of supply.

would not itself affect the fate of a government. In other words Parliament would have the chance of asserting its preferences without always being told that the Sword of Damocles of dissolution was about to fall on its head.[8]

There are, of course, other aspects of the relationship between Government and Parliament which might call for attention, though these cannot all be considered here. Ministers would doubtless continue to be appointed by the prime minister, and it might be advisable to reaffirm their collective responsibility, if only as a protection against the possible effects of divided parties in government or of division in coalitions. But there would be advantage in limiting the number of ministers more rigorously than is currently achieved,[9] perhaps by making a simple distinction between full ministers constituting the cabinet, and deputy ministers without this status. One of the purposes of such a measure would be, by reducing the number of parliamentary office holders, to exert pressure in favour of the emergence of positions of influence within Parliament itself and independent of the Executive. But it would also have another and very different effect, that is to say, to encourage a more explicit recognition of the political functions of some of those in the permanent administration by reason of the necessity of more frequently conferring on officials and administrative agencies a public responsibility at present reserved to ministers.

There are two major questions linked with these very rough ideas for the relationship between Parliament and Government which should be touched on briefly. One concerns the structure of Parliament – should it be bicameral? The other concerns the fate of the Crown as a concept in any re-shaping of the central political institutions of this country. And there is, of course, the matter of the electoral law and its effects. But since

[8] The terms above would not exclude the possibility of a minority government as an alternative to one with a formal majority. But in those circumstances, too, the prime minister would be unable to threaten dissolution, though Parliament would know that to defeat the Government on a confidence vote would entail a high risk of subsequent dissolution. Though no argument has been presented on the point, I would also argue that even in the event of electoral reform and a multi-party situation *en permanence* these provisions could work successfully – chiefly because there is no reason to imagine that Britain is likely to end up with a fragmented multi-party system similar to that of France before 1958 or Italy.

[9] Current legislation does, of course, impose limits on the number of office holders, but they are set absurdly high.

something has already been said about that before, I leave it this time to be picked up in my remarks on political parties.

It can hardly be disputed that there is something peculiar to the British in their failure to resolve decisively the question whether they want to retain a second chamber. The one we have is indefensible in composition and the value of the parliamentary contribution which it makes is a matter of some dispute. Yet we cannot agree to get rid of it or to continue it on a more rational and justifiable basis. The thrust of British political development since the last century has been towards unicameral government, and, indeed, the House of Commons still reacts like some ageing prima donna if it is suggested that either the Lords or another kind of second chamber should have a genuine share in the powers exercised by Parliament. So logically there ought to be no objection to the simple disappearance of this curious assembly, part hereditary gentlemen, part placemen and appointees of active politicians. After all, its powers are tenuous, its impact on legislation modest,[10] and there is little evidence that even the contribution it makes to public debate would be severely missed. Moreover, it can be argued that if the House of Commons were substantially reformed and enabled to organise itself effectively for the major functions of legislation and control, then there would be less need of a second chamber, either for amendment after second thoughts or to provide another opportunity to argue against.

These arguments are, however, by no means conclusive: in contemporary conditions there does appear to be a practical case for having more opportunities than can be secured only through the presence of one chamber for the examination, criticism and improvement of legislative proposals, including those bearing on expenditure and taxes. The real problem in Britain is to determine how to construct a reformed second chamber, since at present there appears to be no workable and acceptable basis for a change. The retention of an hereditary representation can no longer be justified: that much is obvious. But

---

[10]There is no doubt that as a rule the Lords do not modify legislation substantially. But in periods when a government has no majority or a small one in the Commons (as after February 1974) the Lords may venture to use their powers, particularly when faced by widely criticised Labour proposals to which the Conservative majority in the Lords objects. But the capacity of the Lords to veto effectively is virtually nil.

equally objectionable in terms of legitimacy is representation through patronage which is what the introduction of life peers has really entailed. Only two alternatives come to mind. One would be a chamber representing provinces, regions, localities, the kind of solution which might emerge from a substantial measure of political decentralisation in Britain (and assuming that something recognisable as the United Kingdom survives). There is no point in discussing what might be the shape of such a second chamber, since this would clearly depend on the character of the decentralised political structure. But one must assume that in virtue of its legitimacy (even if elected indirectly this might be true), it would be entitled to play a more decisive role in legislation and in the approval of government policy than can the present House of Lords. The need to provide personnel for it would impose a strain on the existing political parties, but it would also offer opportunities at large for seeking a political mandate which do not exist at the moment, quite apart from the influence it could confer on the regional and local levels of political life. The other possibility would be some form of socio-economic representation, a chamber of interests. This is an idea frequently played with in the past — Churchill did so in dilettante fashion in 1930–1. Whilst such a scheme should not be entirely ruled out of court, particularly as it has certain attractions in the present situation of extensive corporate power, it is open to serious objections. It is hard to define satisfactorily which interests would have a claim to be represented in such a body; difficult to devise respectable procedures for the selection of representatives; almost impossible to provide for changes to meet the continual evolution of the pattern of associations expressive of varying social and economic interests, and therefore to avoid a scheme which simply perpetuates vested interests. Above all, there are difficulties in attributing legislative rights — law-making and law-approving powers — to a body whose membership is likely to have a very fragmented interest in respect of a great many of the matters which would be referred to it. In consequence its legitimacy would always be open to question. So whilst this is not a model to be excluded from discussion altogether, it is necessary to be alive to the limitations inherent in it.

Looking at the matter in a broader context it appears that the decision to retain or dispense with a bicameral legislature must be related to the character of the future structure of the British state. The less unitary it becomes, or the more it comes to comprise other levels of government below that of national government but above that of localities, the better might be the prospects of constructing a satisfactory second chamber. Yet at the same time it has to be remembered that the need for such a body depends very much on how a reformed House of Commons discharges its functions and on the extent to which it becomes an effective check on the Executive and a more powerful representative assembly. If it were to establish a certain autonomy and to organise itself coherently for the handling of legislation and financial proposals, then the case for a second chamber becomes weaker. In that situation it might even be better to think only in terms of something like a Council of State, a small appointed body charged with certain judicial functions and with the preliminary scrutiny of legislative proposals with a view to establishing their constitutionality and their compatibility with existing law. Nor do we even lack the nucleus of such an organ – it is there already in the Judicial Committee of the Privy Council.

Let me turn now to the Crown. This has, of course, two aspects – the Monarchy as an institution, the office of monarch and such functions as still appertain to it, and the Crown as a political and legal concept. One must begin with the second and broader notion of the Crown. After a fashion the Crown is an English substitute for State: the concept works like this when we talk of the prerogative of the Crown and when we talk about the Crown being liable (since 1947) to legal proceedings. And yet the concept of the Crown is by no means exactly correlated with that of State in many other countries: that which has Crown status in Britain is determined more haphazardly than is the State in, for example, most of the countries of continental Europe, where the State tends to be equated with every emanation of the powers of government other than those which are specifically and constitutionally excluded. This in turn tends to identify the State with the executive power, as indeed has generally been the case with the Crown. Nevertheless, even on the Continent the boundaries of the State remain blurred. For example, municipalities often exercise at one and the same time State and non-State authority.

The real difficulty attaching to the legal concept of the Crown does not, however, stem from the uncertainties affecting its boundaries: that is a problem for the State idea too. It is rather that the Crown continues to express a curious mixture of corporate existence and personal authority.

The concept of the State, at any rate when it is handled by lawyers and constitutionalists, is essentially a way of identifying that corporation defined in terms of its legal powers to which all individuals and associations are in a given territory subject. The Crown has this dimension, but in addition evokes still the idea of a sovereign and personal authority. *De facto*, of course, this authority is not exercised by the wearer of the Crown, but is vested chiefly in ministers. Now what is necessary in Britain is to get rid of the aura of majesty which still surrounds the Crown as the ground of executive authority, whilst retaining something like the Crown concept in its purely political and legal sense as a construct defining the corporate entity in which powers of certain kinds are vested (that corporate entity being in turn divisible).

It has to be admitted that it is difficult to discern how this kind of distinction and change might be made by constitutional resolution. Yet perhaps we afflict ourselves with puzzles and problems which really need not worry us. Ireland uses the concept "State" as a substitute for Crown, and so does India, and for neither was that change a traumatic experience. Thus the problem may be seen as one of finding a way of shifting the attributes of the Crown as a legal concept to the term State, so that we might then be able to free ourselves from some of the more harmful political overtones of the idea in its traditional forms. Perhaps the Crown would have to retreat from being joined in law-making, becoming only an instrument of promulgation. The Government or ministers might have to be treated as exercising the central or national executive powers in the State rather than acting as agents of the Crown, whilst other institutions would similarly exercise such powers as are vested in them. Even in respect of the courts, some of whose procedures rest upon the principle that they are the Crown's instrument for the maintenance of justice, there would appear to be no conclusive objection to such a shift of concepts: the courts would remain organs of the State, and it would be perfectly possible to define in statute the remedies and procedures thought necessary to permit them to discharge their function of upholding the law and of protecting citizens in the enjoyment of their rights.

As to the Crown *qua* office-holder or as monarchical institution, the displacement of the Crown as a legal and political concept would place no obstacle in the way of treating the office-holder as Head of State, perhaps after the manner of the Japanese Constitution as a symbol of the State and of the unity of the people. Indeed, Chapter I of the Constitution of Japan contains what reads like a very accurate account of the *actual* functions of the British monarch. Nor would the change proposed affect substantially the ceremonial functions of the monarch. As to his or her political functions all would remain subject to the advice of the Government, save the important discretion of proposing a prime ministerial candidate and of dissolving Parliament in the event of a second withdrawal of confidence from a government during the life of a single Parliament.

Before passing on to the next theme it is worth reiterating that in terms of constitutional argument and reasoning, it would not be a task of insuperable difficulty to give form and shape to the functions of Parliament and Executive so that the elements of a relationship of balance between them would again come within our grasp. For this country in its present condition the advantages to be gained from such a course of action are substantial. There would be the prospect of a genuine revival of Parliament and of parliamentary government rather than the pursuit of pseudo-reforms which achieve little beyond masking for a while the weaknesses of the institution of Parliament in the face of executive power. As for the Executive it would both be checked and strengthened, subject to stronger limitations in respect of securing the passage of measures, yet relieved of some of the time-consuming pressures to which it is now exposed.

The third statement of principle underlined the desirability of working against the all-embracing and deadening influence of political centralisation in Britain. This is a difficult topic, partly because there are many models of decentralisation which might be considered, and partly because the achievement of a wider dispersion of political authority cannot be brought about simply by institutional arrangements. In other words, if the political parties (or other major interests in the society) express a preference for the concentration of power at the centre of political life, then it will be hard to make a reality of schemes for diffusing responsibilities and the opportunities for self-government. In addition the problem of decentralisation is complicated by the uncertainties affecting the future of Northern Ireland, and by growing doubts about what it is that will satisfy Scottish and Welsh aspirations. If any or all of these parts of the United Kingdom were to achieve separation, then clearly the problem takes on a new aspect altogether.

However, the purpose here is not to draft schemes for a decentralised structure, but rather to consider a few points of principle which are important. Firstly, in respect of the biggest question affecting a diffusion of political responsibilities and rights to self-government, devolution to the non-English parts of the United Kingdom, it now appears that there can be no return to the position existing before about 1968. The Scottish demand for political recognition has gained momentum; Northern Ireland, which certainly cannot be left indefinitely in a limbo of violence and anarchy, must at some stage regain a measure of political autonomy which does justice to its previous experience of domestic self-government. The position of Wales is more ambiguous: there nationalism has a strongly cultural flavour which diminishes its force as a demand for political autonomy, though the effects of whatever happens elsewhere in the United Kingdom should not be underestimated. Though identical measures of devolution all round are likely to be impracticable, and may even be unwanted, these difficulties do not count against the desirability of formulating principled and constitutionally coherent solutions to the different expressions of the devolution demand. What is essential is to recognise that rights and powers cannot be devolved – handed over to new institutions – with one hand, and their exercise made subject to a wide discretionary control by the central government with the other. A devolution scheme of whatever kind can succeed only if there is some measure of trust between the contracting parties to it. But this can exist only if the superior authority accepts wholeheartedly the limits it has imposed on itself and if the scheme itself is embodied in terms which reflect a determination to attribute to the proposed relationships a constitutionally binding quality. Given the strains to which the internal unity of the United Kingdom is now exposed, it is only on such a basis that an understanding of shared political values and the maintenance of a common allegiance can be maintained. It is such an approach, amounting to something like a re-negotiation of the "Union", which offers the best prospect of holding together the component parts of the British State in unity.

But the widening of the opportunities for self-government and for the exercise of the rights of citizenship has to be seen in relation to other levels of government, especially those which operate nearer to local communities. There are now in Britain fewer local authorities than in any other country of comparable size, population and political character. Despite what was conceived as a reform there remains a level of indifference towards local political life which has few parallels elsewhere. It is doubtful whether local community councils without any powers other than those of representing points of view and interest to the higher tiers of authority will successfully overcome some of the serious problems associated with large, unwieldy and remote territorial units. Perhaps at some stage it may become desirable actually to contemplate reversing the trend of recent years in respect of the structure of local government, looking for an increase in the number of local units of self-government rather than their compression in the interests, so it is believed, of administrative efficiency. It is not without irony that the practical case for provincial governmental authorities would have remained far stronger in England and in Scotland and Wales had the restructuring of local government not resulted in such large units that it is now hard to discern what functions a provincial level could take over, quite apart from the political conflicts which would in many cases now accompany the creation of such authorities.

Yet, perhaps more significant than the overall territorial structure of local and municipal government is the burden of central control over them. If they are to mean something as structures of decentralisation, they need to be freed from much of the discretionary influence to which they are now subject on the part of the central executive power. To some extent this is a question of habit and usage, of informal relationships which have solidified over the years. Thus change cannot take place by the stroke of a pen, nor is it strictly a matter of constitutional regulation. It would take time and effort to begin moving in a different direction. But central control is also to some extent a consequence of the manner in which powers are conferred and of the growing financial dependence of subordinate authorities on funds paid over in the form of grants from the centre. Powers could be conferred in ways which would radically diminish the capacity of the centre to intervene, whether to satisfy the civil servant's notion of what is tidy and convenient, or the misplaced zeal of Members of Parliament who fail to realise that there should be limits even to their capacity to prevail upon ministers to interfere where there is really no justification for so doing. The financial problem is hard to solve, though a change of outlook might be assisted if the notion of grants, with its suggestion of munificence on the part of the Exchequer, were replaced by that of the sharing of common revenues. But certainly that will not overcome the problems arising from the tensions between the responsibilities of the centre for general economic management, and the desirability of allowing to other levels of government adequate resources and sufficient discretion in their use. There has to be a more modest and restricted view of what the central government can achieve by *its* management of resources, together with a reaffirmation in a binding way of the rights to self-government of whatever levels of political authority exist below the national.

When thinking about the diffusion and decentralisation of powers we rarely touch on the internal constitution of subordinate authorities. Perhaps this is because of the habit of thinking about these levels of government exclusively in terms of functions and size — treating them as bits of machinery for the performance of tasks and not as parts of the national political structure with their own vitality and their own constitutional problems. In particular we neglect the internal constitution of local government where the basic principles have not changed since 1835.[11] It is an outstanding feature of the English approach to the structuring of government that more trust has been placed in committees than in any other organisational device. This operates in municipal government to such an extent that the executive authority is fused with the deliberative: government is in principle through the whole council, even though in practice it may be diffused through several committees of the parent body. The outcome of this arrangement (which has so far been copied in such schemes as have been prepared for the devolution of powers in Wales) is that as far as the citizen is concerned there really is no executive power which is visible and easily identified. Local or municipal government is lost in the anonymity of the council and its committees. A broader effect is that there is little chance of local political service being seen as a significant full-time commitment, and instead it has remained on the whole the province of unpaid amateurs. Such people may be able to make a useful contribution to deliberative functions, but are now rarely in

---

[11] The Municipal Corporations Act, 1835, introduced as a regular system for urban government the council principle, though there were, of course, earlier precedents for this.

a position to have a decisive impact on the tasks of executive direction. In that sphere they must rely on the permanent officials whose responsibilities and powers, as in national government, remain veiled and obscure. Though the point could hardly be demonstrated rigorously, there is reason to believe that the neglect throughout this century of any effort to look critically at a constitutional restructuring of the subordinate levels of representative government, with the aim of encouraging the emergence of an identifiable and politically responsible executive, goes a long way towards explaining the atrophy of local political life. Here, too, is a point at which significant changes might well be worth consideration, changes which would go beyond the provision of more generous out-of-pocket expenses for the traditional part-timer.

There is, finally, in the context of diffusing powers what might be called the functional as opposed to the territorial modes of decentralisation. And this can be brought into some connection with the question of the political role of officials. As in so many other states it has been impossible in Britain to avoid a proliferation of agencies with specialised functions dependent in varying ways on the central departments of State. Their powers differ greatly, there is virtually no consistency in the terms on which they are set up and operate, and the conditions of accountability are often obscure and unsatisfactory. In some instances it would be better if such bodies and their functions were handed over (or back) to local or even to provincial authorities, in others if they were properly incorporated into the structure of central government. Yet often this is impracticable for very good reasons. In such circumstances there is much to be said for emphasising their autonomy more strongly, and for accepting that as far as policy determination goes they are expected to act independently within the terms of their legal powers. In this way more public accountability can be achieved than is possible if they operate under the shadow of ministers and their officials, claiming to be independent, yet in reality responding to the political pressures of ministers who supervise them[12] This, too, would represent a measure of

---

[12] A certain amount of progress has been made in these directions in the period since 1970, generally under the slogan of "hiving-off", i.e. taking activities out of the central ministerial organisation. In some cases the policy functions have been vested in bodies representing the major interests affected, e.g. as in the Manpower Services Commission or the Health and Safety Commission. This may represent a hopeful trend in the dispersion of responsibility, though it is too soon to be sure.

dispersion of political responsibility and would be a step towards a more realistic appreciation of the political and policy-making role of appointed officials in the modern state which, as suggested before, needs to be developed in Britain. Eventually it might become possible to take a far less restrictive view of what is the scope for legitimate political action and comment by those in public service. Yet it remains doubtful how far new concepts and practices can take root here without some acknowledgement that the problem is also how, in a world very different from what it was forty or more years ago, to interpret the political rights of officials and where to draw the lines between politics and public service. Here one is drawn back to a different set of principles — those concerned with rights and the terms in which citizenship is defined.

I come now to political parties. They remain the indispensable means by which people are enabled to choose representatives, to display their preferences for men and policies, and to bring into existence a political will directed to the tasks of government. All this has to be accepted as part of the political function of parties and the expression of their commitment to the public realm. For this reason it is no longer practicable or even defensible to regard them as purely private associations, exempt from certain obligations stemming from the role which they have. One conclusion which this suggests is that it would not be unreasonable to lay upon parties an obligation to ensure that their internal organisation as well as the part which they play in the electoral process conform in a reasonable way with democratic procedures. The aim would certainly not be to impose a straitjacket on them, but rather to encourage the maintenance of minimal standards of regularity, openness and equality of voting rights in the conduct of their internal affairs as well as with regard to their participation in the nomination and support of candidates for election. In return there is a case for recognising that the days of the old parties of notables are past, and that the contemporary functions of parties impose on them financial burdens which cannot be met adequately out of private resources. A measure of public financial support becomes justifiable, though it needs to be given on terms which do not remove entirely the incentive and obligation of parties to gather in resources of their own. Public financial support should not become a means simply of consolidating the position of the *beati possidentes*.

The most crucial condition of all affecting parties is, of course, the electoral régime under which they operate. Equally this affects the whole character of parliamentary institutions and the manner in which they relate to the Executive, and is, therefore, crucial to other issues touched on previously. The British relative majority system is one which is rooted in the conditions of a pre-party era: individuals offered themselves for election and those who in each locality collected the most voices were chosen. In the contemporary world this idea of the representative process retains vitality, if at all, only in the United States: certainly the conditions of American politics and party organisation still reflect this situation to a far greater degree than do those of British politics. The rise of disciplined parties representing distinctive points of view and interests, and committed by their vocation to the pursuit of governmental power, has removed the fundamental justification for the relative majority system, namely that it was the fairest way of enabling voters to choose particular men. It can now be defended, if at all, only on the grounds that it appears to encourage the choice of a government by the electorate, and the integration of large and diffuse parties around a centrist position in the spectrum of political argument. But these are at best contingent reasons, and, as I have argued before, they no longer hold good in this country. Circumstances may produce a dispersion of opinion and support great enough to frustrate the supposed act of choice associated with the relative majority procedure. Additionally, the debilitating effects of two-party competition for office, elevated to the status of a principle, have now frustrated the achievement of stable and strong government in the manner thought to be a virtue of the system. All this supports the conclusion that both practical necessities and grounds of principle call for recognition of the claim that parties ought to gain representation roughly proportional to the support they actually receive. The precise details of the electoral system which is then selected to satisfy this principle of justice are of secondary importance: what matters is assent in the principle which is at stake.

The consequences of implementation of a scheme for fair and proportional representation would be profound. The basis for one-party government would almost certainly be removed, though a proportional system of representation does not of itself prevent the electorate from giving a majority to a single party. It simply reduces the prospect of such an outcome. Despite the difficulties of adaptation to the practices of coalition, it has to be remembered that the basis for single-party majority government has already been seriously eroded. This can be read off from the present distribution of party loyalties in the country as well as from the condition of both the major competitors in the old two-party system. It is for these reasons that a reform of the electoral laws is a crucial test of the ability to recognise changes in the making and to make constructive use of new situations and relationships. To take this opportunity would express a determination to work within the discipline imposed by principles which themselves seek to take account of the world as it is.

As to the effects of a change of this order on the possibilities of restoring an effective role in Parliament, it would be foolish to expect that it would suddenly render practicable a complete transformation of the present pattern of relationships between government and legislature. The matter is too subtle and complex, too deeply embedded in the history of the habits and conventions of the parliamentary institutions itself for that to be possible. But what can be said is that a different constellation of political interests in Parliament would more than any other factor open the way to changes which are presently quite impossible, whilst the appearance of a government resting upon the basis of agreement between competing party interests and aspirations would itself create a new situation in the interaction between Executive and Parliament.

The last of my five heads of principle and proposal referred again to the question of public law. In many respects this is the most difficult area in which to make changes or to specify precisely proposals for particular reforms. Nevertheless, it is a vital condition of the political reconstruction which is being envisaged here. The significance of law (which can be contrasted in interesting ways with legislation, as has been pointed out recently by v. Hayek in one of his books)[13] is seriously underestimated and misunderstood in Britain. A pervasive and unreflecting positivism is dominant (and has been for long enough) which sees law as little more than a vast bundle of powers, incoherent and expedient, the multifarious expressions of the transient will of the legislators. The decay of an understanding of constitutional norms as the very conditions of political freedom has been accompanied by a corresponding carelessness about the

---

[13]F. A. v. Hayek, *Law, Legislation and Liberty*, vol. I, *Rules and Order*, Routledge, 1973.

quality of the statute book at large. We no longer try to frame specific powers within the terms of relevant general principles: instead we seem for the most part to legislate on no better principle than that which moved Henry VIII to require Parliament to pass a law for the boiling to death of the Bishop of Rochester's cook. Sufficient unto the day is the power thereof.

Much of the difficulty stems from the absence of a body of jurisprudence relevant to contemporary needs and the effects of this on legal thinking and practice. This in turn reflects the dominance over many years of political presuppositions which have assumed that authority is most safely grounded in informal accommodations, that political activity is concerned only with the fulfilment of particular satisfactions, and that the abuse of powers can best be checked by an appeal to public opinion. There may be circumstances in which these presuppositions have a certain passing validity, and perhaps this was the case for a while in the history of this country.[14]   But it is naive to continue to believe that they alone remain a sure foundation for the reconciliation of freedom with order. And it is precisely for this reason that the character and status of law becomes so crucial. Maybe it is only in countries which have experienced the shock of a rapid and brutal subversion of law that these conditions can be fully understood. In Britain the distintegration of the idea of law as a body of general rules has been a slower and more deceptive process, hidden even by the arcane language in which the powers of authorities and the obligations of citizens are expressed.[15] But the evidence of recent years points in the same direction as it has done in societies where law has on different occasions been more openly challenged: towards the declining authority of law and a diminution in its binding quality. And these very conditions are advanced by a muffled awareness in the society that in the specific measures now enacted in the guise of law, there is rarely that

[14]Yet it is necessary to guard against mis-reading the past. Perhaps Montesquieu was not as wide of the mark as has often been thought when he saw the English Constitution of his day as one of institutional checks and balances. He also believed that one should not confound the power of the people with the liberty of the people.

[15]It might be held that English law has never developed a full sense of law as a structure of norms in which the particular elements are related deductively to general principles. But many of the achievements of the common law contradict this view, though it undoubtedly fits more adequately the character of public law, i.e. the powers vested in public bodies.

effort to ground them in principles of consistency and equal treatment such as alone can sustain the obligation of free men to obey them.

The prospect of beginning to reverse this particular state of affairs depends extensively on whether the need for a far-reaching new constitutional settlement is recognised. It would depend, too, on how such a settlement, if envisaged at all, were undertaken and accomplished. But clearly if there were to be a genuine attempt to formulate certain constitutional principles and to draw from them consequences for the shaping of institutions, then the way would be open to a revival of constitutional law and interpretation. That alone could have a beneficial influence on ordinary enactments. A substantial extension of the rights of the courts to interpret powers in the light of their consistency with particular constitutional principles or with conditions of reasonableness would be entailed, and this, too, would gradually impose a new discipline on those engaged in the framing of laws. Yet in addition it may be necessary to contemplate a wholly new approach to the actual writing of law, to the language in which powers and obligations are expressed. Such proposals are usually dismissed as Utopian — and perhaps they must remain so until a society is forced by circumstances to understand that such changes are within the reach of human intelligence. I will say nothing about the conventional reasons why it is held that law in England must continue to be written in the appalling terms in which it is now expressed. None of them affects the contention that a serious attempt to express many (though not necessarily all) of the powers now conferred in a simpler and more direct language would of itself offer a means of disentangling the general from the particular, perhaps revealing in many instances how inadequate and unconvincing are such general principles as still underpin much of our law. Moreover, this is a field to which the political philosopher and the moralist could contribute much of value. The form of law is too serious a matter to be left entirely to those who are sometimes little more than technicians.[16]

These remarks about law, and more especially that part of it which can be called public law, must bring to a conclusion this discussion of what

---

[16]Several aspects of the problems relating to the form of law are raised in the report, *The Preparation of Legislation*, Chairman, Sir D. Renton, Cmnd. 6053. But it does not break much new ground and shows many of the weaknesses of the technician's approach.

might be some of the elements in a new framework for the relationships between institutions within the State, and between the State and its citizens. Without doubt much of importance has been left out. There have been no more than passing references to the powers, rights and duties of officials at different levels of government; no attention has been paid to "openness" in government and a right to information; no attempt has been made to deal directly with the case for extending consultative rights, so giving organised interests and perhaps less formal groups a stronger position in the conduct of government and public affairs; no reference has been made to the constitutional significance, if any, of the Commonwealth links and the place of the Crown in them. Above all, the argument has deliberately not explored the implications for constitutional reform of the accession of Britain to the treaties establishing the European Communities. Yet whilst membership in the Community undoubtedly does have a bearing on the political evolution of this country, it is hard to believe that in the near future it can decisively influence — for good or ill — our domestic institutions.[17] Much that has been proposed does, however, point towards a more sympathetic acknowledgement of the virtues of the dominant continental European tradition in the structuring of powers, that which sees law as an eminently creative instrument for the shaping of political and social relationships. To that extent a move in the direction recommended would at least not run against the grain of whatever process of assimilation may slowly stem from Britain's association with its neighbours.

Many will wonder whether the achievement of changes such as have been pointed to must not mean a sharp break with our past, with the tradition of informal and undesigned adaptation to new demands. They will fear that it all looks too much like a written constitution and they will be suspicious of the constraints which this might entail. The argument here does indeed point in this direction. Yet there is no compelling reason to perceive such changes so sharply as a break with the past. Rather they might be seen as a picking up of certain threads in that past which were,

---

[17]There is one qualification currently to be made. This is the prospect of achieving by 1978 or soon after direct election of members of the European Assembly. This *could* have substantial consequences for domestic institutions, but equally *need* not. And there are grounds for believing that several member states will prefer to minimise the effects of such a change.

perhaps for good reasons at the time, let fall. It would be a return to the idea of a "somewhat fundamental". Thus we mistake our history if we assume that such a work of constitutional reconstruction would represent a total break with the past. The stress on pragmatism, on accommodation, on informality, and on "muddling through" is far more characteristic of the past hundred years than of earlier periods in British history. Our history, like that of many of our neighbours, is marked, too, by the influence of great system builders, some who worked with theories, others in the translation of their visions into practical arrangements. It is true that there has been in British political life an abiding sense of institutions as "arrangements which people have worked out in the course of a common experience", to quote a particularly felicitous phrase from a recent OECD report on certain aspects of the government of education in this country. But this shrewd perception of one of the conditions of success in maintaining institutions should not blind us to the need to be able to take thought for the purpose of creating institutions. There is no reason to believe that continuous success in the mere adaptation of institutions is a law of life, either here or elsewhere. Institutions may wear out. To live at a time when this happens is disturbing and may be painful. Yet it also presents a society with one of those rare and challenging opportunities to demonstrate that it understands something of the nature of political freedom.

CHAPTER 12

Towards a New Constitutional Settlement

These reflections took as their starting point the failure to understand some of the objective necessities of the situation of Britain. After 1945 the country found itself in a very different world from that which it had known before the Second World War, but it has been extremely slow to recognise the extent of the change and its implications for the conduct of domestic affairs. May be the actual loss of empire took place too smoothly in the years after 1945 and in a manner which did not compel any thorough-going reassessment of the country's position in relation to the world outside as well as of its internal needs. Only slowly, and against much resistance and inertia, was it realised that new associations would have to be forged and a new sense of external direction found. But the realisation of the consequences of this change for the domestic economy came even more hesitantly. Indeed, it would appear that the very magnitude of the earlier imperial achievement was a hindrance to a swift appreciation of the demands of a new and more modest situation. Not only did it obscure many of the economic realities facing the country and especially in international trade, and encourage a neglect of productive potential in favour of maintaining a range of financial and economic operations closely related to the previous position as a linchpin of the world economy, but it also stood in the way of any awareness of the possibility that political institutions and methods too are exposed to wear and tear, and in a different environment might be in need of some overhaul.

The inability to grasp the necessity of finding effective means of producing resources, and the failure to perceive the contradictory effects of the pursuit of social objectives formulated without regard to their consequences for the domestic economy, have undermined the traditional political structures and methods of sustaining political authority by imposing excessive demands on them. It is possible that these would in any

224

event have required substantial renewal, if only because they embodied so decisively the genius of the nineteenth century and its perception of how parliamentary government at home might be combined with the maintenance and extension of imperial power abroad. But the attempt to perpetuate the political conventions of a different age in the totally changed conditions, domestic and external, of the second half of the twentieth century, was doomed to disappointment. True, in a superficial sense the institutions and the conventions of the past have survived to a remarkable degree, nor is this even surprising. Political habits have great tenacity and are not easily sloughed off. Neither is it desirable that they should be: a society needs to be able to draw on its accumulated experience. Yet a distinction must be drawn between an instinctive and slavish preservation of particular political traditions and the institutions through which they are expressed, and a sense of institutional continuity which embraces a willingness to adapt political procedures within traditional forms so that they serve new purposes and values in a manner denied by the unreflecting perpetuation of the past. It is in this respect that Britain has shown for some time a lack of political inventiveness and insight. There has been too little appreciation of the fact that in a changed context the mere repetition of existing modes of political action and procedure is likely to produce results different from what was expected, and for this very reason gradually to undermine the authority of the political procedures themselves. It has been contended here that this has happened in Britain: the political arrangements inherited from the past have not encouraged a widely diffused grasp of the necessities of the country's situation, and in part as a consequence of this very failure, they have not proved capable of sustaining the kind of political values to which many have fondly believed these arrangements were dedicated. The State has become like an ancient façade, imposing and dignified if viewed from a distance, but on closer inspection revealing itself to be dilapidated and crumbling.

It is impossible to engage in serious political reconstruction unless this task is recognised as essentially a challenge to constitutional awareness. For political reconstruction does not mean finding better leaders, improving tactics and techniques in government, or setting up new bits of organisational machinery to do this or that, though all these possibilities may have a part to play. It means thinking critically about the terms on which particular political transactions are carried out — selecting representatives, engaging in elections, constituting governments, formulating policies, making laws, enforcing public accountability, providing for the protection of rights, advancing particular interests in the context of public policy, and so on. And to think critically about such terms is to ask questions about whether the rules are right, whether they are well adapted both to maintaining certain qualities in political transactions and to achieving particular practical ends. There is, too, a rather special characteristic of constitutional argument in this sense which should not be overlooked. It is that to engage in such argument entails a certain commitment to consistency. It means trying to make more explicit the principles on which political action is to be based, and this in itself makes it difficult to remain satisfied with that well-known shibboleth of British politics, "judging each case on its merits". Though this guideline of prudence has its uses, it is not one which can serve for long in constitutional argument. For in that context it is necessary to consider how far the principles which might be applied to particular cases are consistent one with another, and how far taken together they are likely to be conducive to certain kinds of preferred political relationships. It would be optimistic to believe that this is a type of argument which many in Britain would find comfortable at the present time. Yet this, too, points to the challenge of constitutional reconstruction: it would disturb many vested interests and entrenched habits, but it would compel much closer attention to the political consequences of what is being done.

But if the question or the challenge is presented in this way, it is also necessary to ask whether any of the conditions exist which might make a measure of political reconstruction a plausible undertaking, and then what might be the actual steps by which it could be brought about. Lying behind these more practical questions is, of course, the substantive problem to which the preceding section was devoted: on what kind of principles might change be based? My concern now is rather with practical conditions and prospects, elusive though these may be.

Already at different stages in this argument reasons have been suggested why there is a widespread reluctance to recognise the political nature of many of the contemporary weaknesses of Britain. The continuity of British institutions works against such recognition, so does the vagueness and inadequacy of such constitutional language as we still have. Another important factor has been the gradualness and ambiguity in the process of qualitative change which has taken place in the character of the political order. The powers of public authorities of all kinds have increased, the sphere of legitimate private activity has been narrowed, rights have been obscured whilst claims have been magnified, political parties have become less representative of genuine interests in the society as they have acquired more the character of competing professional aspirants to office, sectional interests have gained a powerful voice in public decisions, yet no effective institutional means have been devised for committing many of them constructively to political action: changes like this do mean that the constitutional reality is no longer that of parliamentary government as traditionally conceived, nor is there even limited government within a framework of law favourable to individual self-determination. Parliamentary government has become weaker and more disaggregated than the theory of collectively responsible cabinets suggests, the role of Parliament in relation to governments has been attenuated, and there is no longer that certainty about the rule of law and that predisposition to safeguard private liberties and responsibilities which are required within a liberal constitutional order. These changes have taken place in a piecemeal fashion over the space of a generation. They have provoked few serious clashes of principle and few overt challenges to traditional political habits. And yet they have left a gap between the realities of how the country is governed and what many still believe to be the character of their constitution.

Undoubtedly a major obstacle which stands in the way of political reappraisal is the strength of the interests which are opposed to such a venture, which see themselves as threatened by it. Inevitably those who are accustomed to work in and through the customary institutions — whether they be in Parliament, in the parties, in government, in public administration, in the legal system and so on — can find many reasons for arguing that it would be dangerous or impracticable to tamper with the principles on which these very institutions rest. And they more than any others are aware of the possibility that significant modifications of principle could and would change the terms on which they have to act. Institutional conservatism has no difficulty in concluding that this would be most undesirable.

Typically in the life of states the reluctance to recognise the political nature of a problem is overcome when circumstances demonstrate that particular political methods no longer work at all, or when the legitimacy of a régime is openly challenged. Complete economic breakdown in Britain, for example, would put the political system into the melting-pot. Similarly, if there were a widespread commitment in particular sections of the population to a completely different basis for government, let us say, to some kind of workers' council principle, then may be the existing political structures would be pushed to one side. But in fact neither kind of condition is yet present in Britain. There is economic difficulty of a serious and apparently endemic kind, but it has not yet issued in a disastrous crisis. Far from being exposed directly to outside threats, the country has generally been supported by its allies and partners, even though they may often have had little faith in the policies to which their support was given. Thus, with regard to the conditions for enforcing a political reappraisal, it is necessary for the present to discount the harsh thrust of circumstances: that might come, but it would be foolish to build on the prospect, quite apart from the dangers which it would hold. Nor can it be held with any strong justification that there are in Britain competing views of the foundations of legitimacy in government which pose an immediate threat to the established order. Admittedly there are cracks and fissures which are of some importance. Notable amongst these are the demands for self-government from the non-English minorities, for these are challenging the right of a single Parliament and Government in London to claim exclusive authority over them. And undoubtedly there are in industry challenges to the authority of those who manage and in some cases own which would have substantial political implications, though probably not of the kind which are conventionally assumed by those who try to transpose the concept of political democracy to situations where it cannot properly be applied.[1] But looking at the situation as a whole it is hard to find evidence of a radical and pervasive

[1] The call for worker participation in industry is, of course, the most important example of the contemporary demand for the extended application of concepts borrowed from the organisation of political life. There are many risks involved here: for example, more oligarchy and less "democracy"; slower and more ineffective procedures for taking decisions; more scope for shifting the consequences of particular economic mistakes on to the whole community. The British trade unions show signs of recognising some of the risks, though they remain keen to gain the powers which union rather than worker participation would offer.

disaffection as far as the foundations of representative government go. There is some evidence of disbelief, of uncertainty, of disillusionment with the effects of present political practices, but not of that ripening of a demand for totally new principles which on some occasions and in some places has produced political revolution.

All this suggests the conclusion that an understanding of the political nature of contemporary problems can emerge, if at all, only as a result of intelligent reflection, of a patient effort to think through some of the present difficulties with a determination to look for their political causes and to think about political remedies. From one point of view this is muted and unpromising conclusion, for past experience suggests that there is little inclination to do this, particularly when it runs the risk of making explicit conflicts of values which are at present veiled or suppressed. It is far easier to go on pretending that a bit of adjustment here, a bit of compromise there will do the job. Yet from another point of view the conclusion is more hopeful.

First, it rests on the belief that there is a stock of political wisdom and shrewdness in Britain which can be drawn on for the purposes of redefining our constitutional standards and principles. This does not imply an appeal to what is conventionally called "pragmatism", a state of mind which can easily express unreflecting dogmatism in the adherence to customary practices. It implies rather an appeal to older traditions of political inventiveness of which, from the seventeenth century on to the nineteenth, the British showed many signs. It tends to be forgotten nowadays that the major contributions which this country has made to the theory and practice of representative government and to the rule of law in a free society did not spring from a simple process of muddling through, but owed much to a tenacious concern with principles and to their applications in situations of conflicting interests and claims. Surely there is here a task for political education, a contribution founded on history to the revival of a sense of how public issues might be presented in terms which would illuminate their bearing on the quality of the political relationships we wish to preserve.

Second, it assumes that there is still present in the society a capacity to recognise that maintaining a condition of freedom and order is a continuing engagement. The objective constraints weighing on the pursuit of substantive ends have to be accepted. Yet it remains possible for individuals to co-operate together in the choice of political relationships conducive to their freedom, provided there are enough of them willing and able to apply intelligence and feeling to the task. The taste for this endeavour has declined in contemporary Britain, but there is no reason to believe that it cannot be revived. The erosion of political values and the pragmatic confusion which have overtaken the conduct of political argument are themselves sources of challenge. For when it is asserted — as it often is — that the country is governed without any sense of direction, then may be people are not too far from a realisation that what is missing is a restatement of the terms on which government should be conducted. There must always be argument and dissent about what has to be done — the policies which are to be pursued. But in a free society such argument can be supported only if there is a tolerably clear understanding of the political conditions under which such arguments can take place, conditions which are intended to maintain the quality of a free society. It is that which provides an underlying sense of direction, not as a goal to be achieved, but as a pattern of relationships to be strengthened and conserved. British political development owes much to this insight. The contemporary challenge is to revive it.

The conditions necessary for a redefinition of constitutional principles might then emerge: there is no certainty about this, but at any rate it is a possibility which it is reasonable to envisage. It is, however, necessary to consider briefly how such a task might actually be undertaken. Only in the aftermath of a total breakdown of the political order might it be expected that there would be some kind of once-and-for-all effort to redesign the Constitution, assuming, that is to say, that the dominant political forces then wanted to establish new principles of government rather than simply perpetuate the power they had acquired. But we have already suggested that such an outcome is unlikely, so that the idea of invoking a constituent power, charged with complete re-building, can perhaps be discounted. At the other extreme is the possibility of purely piecemeal reconstruction, the attempt to reshape the purpose, functions and structure of particular parts of the pattern of political institutions. But experience in recent years suggests that the auguries for such a thoroughly *ad hoc* process are not good. The task of critical reflection on such occasions tends to be entrusted either to practitioners within the present system who dislike genuine change, or to safe and sometimes ill-equipped advisers who are often too ready to contribute to an obfuscating consensus. Such has been the manner in which all too many commissions and committees of inquiry have operated during the past decade.

Two slightly more promising possibilities present themselves. One is that at some stage a government might be ready to entrust the review of a range of fundamental constitutional questions to a rather different kind of inquiry body than is commonly established nowadays for the examination of problems of government. It would need to be smaller than the conventional commission, more qualified in its membership, more independent of government in its deliberations, and more committed to a full-time preoccupation with the questions remitted to it. If there is any body which in some respects resembles what is being outlined here, it would be the Law Commission, though this comparison is not intended to suggest that a Constitutional Commission would have such an exclusively judicial and legal composition. The purpose of this kind of commission would not be in the first place to present a menu of proposals, reflecting what it imagined to be the lowest common denominator of agreement amongst politicians in and out of government. It would be rather to perform a work of analysis, to tease out basic problems in constitutional relationships, and to show what might be the political values implicit in different rule changes. In order to be able to perform such a task a commission of this kind would not have to be tied by narrow and constricting terms of reference: it would have to be entitled to range widely, pursuing according to its own judgement the logic of its arguments as they might affect any part of the political structure.

The value of such a body would reside partly in the work of political education which it might carry out. Gradually it might succeed in shifting the terms of reference in which the discussion of particular political habits and arrangements is conducted, for it is being assumed that the task of the commission would be a continuing one. And as opinion is modified, so the chances would be increased that the vested interests in political life would begin to recognise that there is less to fear from changes of a serious kind in the terms on which the society is governed than they have believed. A step-by-step yet coherent reform might become attainable.

The other possibility is that a comparable work of critical analysis might be carried out by unofficial means, by people working singly or in groups, who are prepared to examine afresh the principles on which institutions rest and to propose and justify amendment. It is a matter of historical fact both in Britain and elsewhere that significant shifts in thinking about political and social questions have often been prompted by such independent initiatives. Unfortunately the scope for such an impact from private efforts is perhaps more limited today. The pattern of public activity and governmental intervention is far more densely textured than it used to be; the sources of relevant information lie more completely within the public domain; and there is a greater disposition at large to believe that the improvement of the system of government must proceed in some way from inside that system. Consequently there is a tendency to dismiss the considerations of independents as unqualified, out of touch with the facts, more a matter for academic argument than for serious practical discussion. But if something like the first possibility were to prove unrealisable, the second might still be preferable to inaction and passivity. For in this way, too, something substantial could be contributed to the formation of public opinion, and to putting these questions of constitutional significance on to the agenda of political argument.

But regardless of the status and character of such bodies as might be established to elicit seriously argued proposals for constitutional change, it is also desirable that Parliament should in some way be associated with the work of analysis, if only to prepare the ground for the eventual acceptance by Parliament of changes which could well effect profoundly its own authority. Here there are great difficulties. Parliament works essentially in the present: its time perspectives are short, its interests constantly changing, and it is an expression of the on-going competition of parties. In normal conditions, therefore, Parliament is not well-suited to contribute substantially to the rethinking of constitutional relationships. Yet this may be too harsh a judgement. There are committees of Parliament – and in particular of the House of Commons – which are capable of standing back to some extent from day-to-day political preoccupations in an effort to distinguish the questions of principle which may be at issue in the matters which they are reviewing. The Public Accounts Committee, the Select Committee on the Parliamentary Commissioner for Administration, and sometimes the Procedure Committee come to mind as examples of this capacity. A possibility, therefore, is that the House of Commons – or both Houses of Parliament acting jointly – should appoint a special Select Committee charged with maintaining contact with the kind of formal

Constitutional Commission envisaged here, advising it when required to do so, and entitled to report to Parliament on the progress of the work of review and on such difficulties as might have been encountered. Again, the purpose would not in the first instance be to initiate action. It would be to influence opinion and to prepare the ground for changes. And it would be to ensure that Parliament had, apart from the government, its own source of advice on the progress of constitutional reappraisal.

The outcome of the kind of review envisaged here would far more likely be a series of measures than a single, all-embracing act of constitutional reformation. But perhaps the method envisaged would encourage a certain striving for coherence and endurance, so that at the end of a period of change the country would possess not a single written constitution, but a set of interlocking organic laws which would, perhaps in virtue of approval of some of them by referendum, be recognised as being beyond the reach of simple parliamentary amendment. Just as the past evolution of what has been described rather too often and too carelessly as an "unwritten constitution" has been marked by gradualness (though punctuated by sudden leaps), so the acceptance of the substance of a "written constitution" might emerge step by step and without that fracturing of continuity which is so much feared.

Several of the more specific conditions and principles which might be invoked and applied in a process of constitutional reconstruction have already been considered in some detail in the preceding chapter. It remains only to stress a few overrriding terms of such an effort intended to reinvigorate a liberal and democratic political order. The experience of more than a quarter of a century has now demonstrated that acceptance of the providential view of the role of government has had highly negative consequences both in terms of the benefits actually gained and of the effects on the rights and responsibilities of citizens. These damaging results have occurred in part because the providential view of government has been widely accepted with little concomitant inclination to surrender much of the earlier individualist anti-government tradition. Thus one tradition has contrived to frustrate another and more recent one. On practical grounds as well as on those of principle it is necessary to try to escape from this debilitating tension. But this can be done only by rejecting the providential notion of government and its omnicompetence, and at the same time recognising the inadequacy in contemporary conditions of an individualism which denies our common interdependence and sees the state and the political order in which it is embodied in too negative terms.

If a democratic and liberal political order is to be preserved in our times it must, therefore, rest on principles which seek to guarantee to its members freedom and equal treatment under the law and as many opportunities as possible to determine their own lives, but which also affirm without reservation the duty of government to preserve and improve the framework within which this freedom can be realised. And a liberal political order requires, too, a corresponding social and economic order, one in which the market is accepted as a method of satisfying many human preferences that is both effective and legitimate, in which responsibilities for and control of productive activity are dispersed, and in which diversity and opportunity are seen as crucial attributes of social relationships. Yet such supporting social conditions cannot be maintained solely by "natural means": it remains a continuing task for the political institutions of the society and for its constitution. If the constitution is to be of much help here, it must rest upon a richer body of concepts than that which Britain nowadays rubs along with. For constitutional concepts need not be limited to stating some of the rules according to which institutions are shaped and interact. They can and should embrace an idea of citizenship and in so doing provide guidelines for the fulfilment of social needs.

It is no easy task to rediscover — or invent afresh — a language in which constitutional rules and their political and social application can be expressed and justified. The undertaking implies a readiness to attempt to argue in normative categories which has become unfashionable. It requires an effort to specify in some detail the principles which at the level of institutional determinations would have to guide decisions. It requires some questioning of the terms of political authority for the very purpose of strengthening it. It imposes the need to think explicitly about institutions as devices by which powers are checked in their use, but in such a way that the dual purpose of a liberal political order is pursued, that is to say, the protection of liberty and the maintenance of an effective authority to govern. Above all, the very process of searching for a constitutional language must constantly encourage a readiness in the society to accept the consequences which flow from the idea of a constitution of liberty as a means of providing the indispensable framework of order within which the manifold forms of social co-operation can achieve their purposes. This does not point to the negative State, but it does point to the limited State. The distinction between society and the state remains vital to both.

The challenge of political reconstruction is not an entirely new one, even in Britain. It has been faced before in this country and in many others too. The peculiarity of Britain is that it is a long time since it was presented in such an acute and painful manner. Our memories of such a challenge are remote and confused, and for that reason alone we hesitate to meet it, hoping all the time that perhaps it will go away and we shall be able to drift along as before. But a stage has been reached when it would be wiser to take up the challenge. There is still time to do so with judgement, asking ourselves how we might solve the dilemma of preserving liberty whilst at the same time re-establishing a political authority more modest in the claims which it makes, yet more effective in virtue of the conditions on which it rests.

Index